A TABLE AT

STORIES AND RECIPES FROM NEW YORK'S MOST LEGENDARY RESTAURANT

SIRIO MACCIONI
AND PAMELA FIORI

Foreword by Alain Ducasse • Preface by Rudi Sodamin
Recipes Written by Jane Sigal • Principal Photography by Ben Fink

RIZZOLI
NEW YORK

New York · Paris · London · Milan

Special thanks to Rudi Sodamin, without whom this book would not be possible

First published in the United States of America in 2012
by Rizzoli International Publications, Inc.
300 Park Avenue South
New York, NY 10010
www.rizzoliusa.com

2012 2013 2014 2015 / 10 9 8 7 6 5 4 3 2 1

Art Director: Patricia Fabricant
Editor: Christopher Steighner
Photo Editor: Jennifer Crandall
Co-Managing Member, Le Cirque: Carlo Mantica
Chief Steward, Le Cirque New York: Fung Lam
Archival Image Scanning: Colt Givner

Printed in China

ISBN: 978-0-8478-3794-6

Library of Congress Control Number: 2012933745

"An Evening at Le Cirque" is a special event that
re-creates the experience of Le Cirque restaurants
onboard Holland America cruise line ships. For more
information, visit www.hollandamerica.com

Holland America Line
A Signature of Excellence

CONTENTS

FOREWORD

Sirio Maccioni and I share a lot: We both grew up in rural regions, he in Tuscany and I in Gascony. Sirio is a maître d'hôtel who also trained as a cook (at the Plaza Athénée in Paris, long before I was running it) and I am a cook who also briefly worked as a waiter. Even though we are from different generations, we both know what working in hospitality really means.

Sirio's career built his legend, and his flair and tenacity define his character. When he opened up Le Cirque in 1974, he had been in the United States for almost twenty years, patiently climbing up the ladder of his trade, at Delmonico's, La Forêt, and, for fifteen years, the Colony. Le Cirque, from its first location at the Mayfair Hotel, quickly became one of the top addresses in New York. And here is where the legend really starts: This is where society's celebrated people would come to gather and dine.

Yet, for a chef like me, the true story beyond the legend is even more remarkable. Sirio is a genuine restaurateur who has a very distinct vision of contemporary eating. He has proved it by gathering around him a great number of exceptional professionals. The list is impressive: Alain Sailhac, Daniel Boulud, Sylvain Portay, Sottha Khunn, Alain Allegretti, Pierre Schaedelin, and Christophe Bellanca, just to name some of the most famous of these chefs. I should also add Jacques Torres, who, for more than ten years, was an astonishing pastry chef at Le Cirque. And then there are those who work there in more modest roles and, a few years later, go on to acquire a considerable reputation: Rick Moonen, David Bouley, Terrance Brennan, Michael Lomonaco, and Bill Telepan, to name a few. Le Cirque was the springboard of their careers.

I believe one reason Sirio has been so successful in spotting talent is that he very deliberately plays the role of intermediary between European and American cuisines. Virtually all of the American professionals who have worked at Le Cirque have spent some time in Europe, particularly France, at one step or another of their career. And generally with the greatest mentors: Paul Bocuse, Joël Robuchon, or Alain Chapel. Conversely, Sirio has welcomed a host of French chefs

wishing to express their talent in the United States. I personally recommended to him some of them, including Sylvain Portay, Alain Allegretti, Pierre Schaedelin, and Olivier Reginensi—all four having worked with me at Le Louis XV, my flagship restaurant in Monaco. In other words, this Tuscan's restaurants have served as a *haut lieu* of French cuisine in the United States.

However, Sirio has never forgotten his Italian roots. From the beginning, these roots have lent a special color to his interpretation of dining *à la française*. To fully appreciate Sirio's contributions, we must remember that French cuisine in New York in the early 1970s was represented by very few restaurants. Most of them, including La Caravelle and La Grenouille, opened up in the 1960s. The most iconic one, Le Pavillon, opened in the 1940s and closed in the 1970s. French restaurants were rare and, more important, perceived as rather formal. At Le Cirque, Sirio brought a much-welcome touch of lightness to French dining. His long experience as maître d'hôtel had given him a sharp sense of customers' expectations. He had acquired the talent of making guests feel comfortable and possessed the charisma to communicate this instinct to his team. In other words, he introduced a very important notion: that dining is all about experiencing a moment of happiness.

Serving without being servile is a huge challenge. Sirio never pretends to be friends with his clients, especially the rich and famous, who are his usual patrons. He has always had a very professional approach to his mission, much more precise and strict than his relaxed behavior might belie. Two principles are key. One is to take care of each and every customer as a unique individual, to make the best effort to guess and anticipate each of their desires. He concedes that errors certainly are possible, but when one occurs he has his staff analyze what happened to find a way to avoid repeating it. The second principle is to pay a great deal of attention to the setup of the dining room—who should be seated where—as the guests in the dining room are like the audience of a show. The

better they feel, the better the show will be. The talent of a restaurant manager is to organize his customers in the most fluid and natural way.

In subsequent years Sirio slowly yet surely infused French haute cuisine with fine Italian cuisine. The menu has become an elegant encounter of French and Italian, *paupiettes* and *poussin* fondly dialoging with *osso bucco* and *risotto*. I like this exchange of culinary traditions; they do not mix yet just match. They can bridge each other because each one keeps its own anima.

What Sirio has achieved with his career in the United States is exceptional. It is based on a disarmingly straightforward vision of the eating experience: quality and simplicity. Easy to say, difficult to do. Yet this is what Sirio Maccioni has accomplished.

—Alain Ducasse

Painting by C.F. Payne.

9

PREFACE

One evening in the mid-'80s, when I was twenty-six years old and working for Cunard Line, I went to Le Cirque for dinner and happened to meet Sirio Maccioni. I showed him my first book, *The Cruise Ship Cookbook*, and he told me about how he'd worked as a waiter on a ship to earn his passage to the States. That evening of great food and sincere conversation would mark the beginning of what has become a lifelong friendship.

Over the next ten years, Sirio would come to the QE2 whenever it was in port and we would have lunch together. We would talk about food, women, chefs, critics, and travel. At the close of every meal, I would always ask, "So, Sirio, when are you going to do a Le Cirque cookbook?" Each time, Sirio would respond, "Let's do it next year." Decades later, I'm happy to report that "next year" has arrived.

Le Cirque, of course, was always on my agenda when my travels brought me back to New York; it became a port in the storm for me, Sirio always offering a patient ear and true friendship when life's inevitable squalls arose. He treated me like family, and that's saying something, because at the heart of everything he does is family. Egidiana, Sirio's wife, is its backbone. She is, quite simply, a wise person, knowing enough to give Sirio a home life that has always made the hard work of running a restaurant empire worth doing. And through Le Cirque, Sirio and Egidiana (in what can best be described as an old-fashioned Italian way) have taught their sons that integrity, loyalty, commitment, passion, perfection, and making the most of each moment, each relationship, are the cornerstones of a sincere operation.

Long hours and hard work aside, the most challenging part of being a restaurateur or chef is the fact that most restaurants have a sort of built-in expiration date: Menus can become stale, and even the most loyal customers can stray. That's never happened to Le Cirque. On the surface, Sirio's formula seems simple: People come because of the food—unquestionably good, traditional food—and the stellar service. But watching from the front row, I've come to believe that the sustained phenomenon of Le Cirque is attributable to something less tangible than the work of talented chefs, superlative service personnel, and Sirio's unmatched showmanship. Le Cirque is an exquisite labor of love motivated entirely by the notion of legacy, a man's love for his sons.

From the seeds of friendship sown at the dining table so many years ago grew "An Evening at Le Cirque," a special dinner featuring menu items from Le Cirque that is offered on every Holland America Line Cruise (currently fifteen ships sailing five hundred cruises every year). While Sirio's restaurants continue to wow patrons on land, the elegant ships of Holland America Line bring the Le Cirque magic to 350 ports around the world. We are grateful that Micky Arison and Stein Kruse, at Holland America Line, lent their vision and support to this exciting collaboration.

And now it's time for Le Cirque to enter the home kitchen. Why it took more than twenty years to get this book started, I can't explain (maybe it was those long hours and hard work that come with running a restaurant). But part of Sirio's genius is his timing: Changes both subtle and extreme—a menu tweak, a new chef, a new building, a new city—are always impeccably orchestrated. I have no doubt that the publication of this, the first Le Cirque cookbook, is perfectly situated in the Le Cirque timeline, which I imagine (and profoundly hope) extends much further into the future than he or I will.

—Rudi Sodamin

Le Cirque at sea: the dining rooms aboard fifteen of Holland America's cruise ships serve a dinner that re-creates the Le Cirque experience right down to the menu and table settings.

INTRODUCTION

In New York City, restaurants come and go in the blink of an eye. What's red hot can become lukewarm, then cool, then closed fairly quickly. The place you couldn't get into one week because the waiting list was so long might be begging for customers before you know it.

As a magazine editor for more than four decades, I've watched many a parade pass by. I'll admit it's tempting to jump on the bandwagon of every new restaurant in town. Lord knows, everybody else does. My instincts, however, usually told me to wait, let things settle in, make sure the chef won't bolt in a month, the service is in place, and that platters of food aren't flying around the room. Most of all, be as certain as possible that the place will be around for a while, especially for readers of a monthly magazine with a three-month lead time.

Restaurants with staying power are rare indeed. I can think of only a handful that are still around from my early days in New York. One of them is Le Cirque. It opened in 1974 in a small room on East 65th Street in the Mayfair House and has moved twice since. Each time, it has been a totally different iteration.

I first met Sirio Maccioni a couple of years after the first Le Cirque had been operating at full throttle. I was editing *Travel & Leisure* at the time. To go there for lunch or dinner was an event. You'd never know who'd be there but, rest assured, it was always somebody. No look-alikes here. These customers were the real thing, from high society to captains of industry. In the middle of it all was Sirio, moving from table to table with a seductive gait and a savoir faire that should have been bottled. That *le cirque* means "circus" is no coincidence. It goes back to Sirio's days working at Maxim's in Paris. On the mornings after a big night out, Parisians would say, "Last night was a circus." But every circus needs a ringmaster, and Sirio was New York's. His ability to draw a fascinating crowd and create a fabulous atmosphere was uncanny. No restaurateur was more charming, more irresistible, or more charismatic. No wonder he attracted such a devoted female following. (Although Le Cirque didn't

Sirio contemplating Sirio: The maestro gazes at artist LeRoy Neiman's drawing of him from 1994 (photo: Graziella Vigo).

exist when Stephen Sondheim wrote his devastating anthem "Ladies Who Lunch" for the musical *Company* in 1970, there's no question that a good many of Le Cirque customers were LWL.)

Describing what it was like to dine at the finest restaurant in small-town America, someone once said, "It's the kind of place where, when someone walks in, you say, 'Isn't that . . . ?' And it *never* is." At Le Cirque, it always was. Heads spun, necks craned, and eyebrows were raised with regularity as each new guest arrived, each more charismatic and more glamorous than the last.

Le Cirque was *Town & Country*'s canteen well before I became editor in chief in 1993 and was a favorite of Frank Zachary, my predecessor. At least once a week, he'd have lunch with his cronies,

Sirio at Le Cirque's first home, on East 65th Street.

exquisite food and service. Sirio made it a point to drop by and make sure that all was going smoothly. He didn't have to, but I am grateful that he made the effort because his presence added greatly to the evenings.

When Le Cirque moved to the Villard Houses in the Palace Hotel in Midtown, owned by the sultan of Brunei, you would have thought the world had ended (and indeed it seemed to for a few inconsolable regulars who felt they'd lost their neighborhood hangout). In 1996, Frank Zachary sent a letter to Sirio upon the closing of East 65th Street. He wrote: "In this pantheon of great restaurateurs, you take your rightful place, which is at the head of the list, Numero Uno. When you turned the key and locked the door of Le Cirque for the last time last week, I felt I was losing a second home and the companionship of a great host whom I also admire and treasure as a friend—and always will. Sad endings, as some wise man has said, are glad beginnings and I know that at its new location at the Palace Hotel, you'll make the new Le Cirque a restaurant fit for a sultan."

Now not only was the new Le Cirque in a different part of town, it was a different restaurant altogether—much larger and much more of a spectacle. Anyone who thought Sirio Maccioni was going to do a facsimile of East 65th Street was mistaken. Le Cirque went from one-ring to three-ring, with all the attendant hoopla.

In 2006, Le Cirque moved to its third and present site, at 1 Beacon Court, across from Bloomberg Tower. By this time, not only New York but the entire planet had witnessed changes no one could have predicted, most catastrophically the terrorist attacks on September 11, 2001. More changes were to come with the recession of 2008. Operating a restaurant in tough economic times is a challenge at which few can succeed. It was not business as usual at Le Cirque—or anywhere else, for that matter.

Fortunately, Sirio is not the one-man show he used to be, so his pressures can be shared by his three sons—Mario, Marco, and Mauro—who are an integral part of the company. Sirio opened Osteria del Circo, a trattoria on the West Side, for them with a menu based on their mother Egidiana's cooking. Today they weigh in on every major decision.

Le Cirque has become a brand, and an expanding one at that. In addition to three restaurants in New

including photographers Slim Aarons and Norman Parkinson, *T&C*'s beauty editor, Nancy Gardiner, or the magazine's food editor, James Villas. Villas wrote some of the earliest and best articles about the restaurant.

For John Mariani, a longtime and highly regarded food critic, Le Cirque's exalted place in American restaurant history is a certainty: "Sirio's commitment to the best—never a strong point in American gastronomy before Le Cirque—helped make New York the most exciting place to dine in the world, and he won the respect of the French with his hands-across-the-sea philosophy of sharing and promoting talent."

During my seventeen years at *Town & Country*, I often turned to Sirio when I wanted to host a special lunch, dinner, or cocktail party at the restaurant, for one simple reason: I knew Sirio and his staff would always come through at every level and in the most gracious way. He once sent his team to my apartment when I gave a dinner for Friends of the New York Public Library. Another time, Le Cirque catered a dinner for the 150th anniversary of Central Park at the Fifth Avenue apartment of an interior designer and his wife. Both were magical nights enriched by Le Cirque's

York, there are two more at the Bellagio Hotel in Las Vegas and a third that opened in 2010 at the Aria Resort & Casino, also in Las Vegas. There's even a Le Cirque in New Delhi. And if you take a cruise on one of the Holland America ships, you can experience "An Evening at Le Cirque."

Does this mean Le Cirque is going mass market? Hardly. It has etched an indelible mark in the fine-dining firmament and intends to remain there. The very name "Le Cirque" epitomizes luxury, glamour, sophistication, and superb service. That will not change.

In its nearly forty-year history and until now, Le Cirque has never published a cookbook. Not that its recipes have been a secret. Those for Spaghetti Primavera and Crème Brûlée, two of its most beloved dishes (and oddly not on the menu when they were first developed), have appeared many times in newspapers and magazines and on websites. These and others also appeared in Sirio's eponymous memoir. But it is one thing to try to duplicate these dishes at home and another to have them presented to you at Le Cirque. As one staff member says, "Le Cirque doesn't make its customers feel at home; it makes them feel as if they are having a night out."

Le Cirque is now a family-run business, but that alone is not unique in the restaurant world. What is unique, according to John Mariani, is that Sirio's sons are allowing Le Cirque to evolve, but doing so carefully, maintaining the family's commitment to refinement and sophistication despite the food media's infatuation with food trucks, pop-up restaurants, and molecular cuisine.

Author and TV producer Susan Fales-Hill has long loved Le Cirque and cites several reasons for returning, starting with the Maccionis themselves, who, in her words, "create a very welcoming atmosphere, coupled with a formality that is refreshing in this day of untucked tail shirts, track suits, and visible g-strings. Each location has had its own particular aesthetic and magic. The original had low ceilings and those unforgettable monkey murals. The Palace set turn-of-the-century robber-baron grandeur on its ear. Beacon Court is a triumph of contemporary elegance. In all three places, there was and is a sense of whimsy. Le Cirque never takes itself too seriously. Like life, it's a circus."

With Pamela Fiori (photo: Julie Skarratt).

As Sirio's sons become more entrenched in the day-to-day and as Sirio gradually (and reluctantly) loosens the reins, the future of Le Cirque will be in their hands. But not yet. Not as long as Sirio's pulse beats. Le Cirque, after all, is his life. When I asked Sirio what he hated most about the business, he flashed back a reply: "Empty tables!" This is not a man who gives up control easily.

My own gratitude and affection for Sirio and his family go far and deep, lovingly contained in a corner of my mind brimming with warm remembrances of joyous occasions. I've loved the opportunity to write this book because it meant spending precious time with Sirio, his superb staff, and with the magnificent Egi and their three sons. Le Cirque is not just a restaurant; it is a legend that will live on for years to come. I always sensed this, but now I know for sure. Even better, I fully appreciate why.

—Pamela Fiori

THE LEGENDS

Le Cirque—The First Generation by Robert Cenedella, 1998. Oil on canvas, 72 x 110 inches (183 x 280 cm): This painting depicts the dining room of Le Cirque at East 65th Street, with more than 100 celebrated habitués. To learn who's who, see page 65.

FROM MONTECATINI
TO MANHATTAN

As a young boy growing up in Montecatini, the historic spa town in the hills of Tuscany, Sirio Maccioni had almost everything going against him. Born poor in Mussolini's Italy in 1932, he was orphaned at an early age: He was only six when his mother, Silvia, died of what began as a common cold; his father, Eugenio, was in the Italian army when he was killed by a bomb in 1944—not in combat but in a small piazza right in his hometown. It was left to his grandparents to raise twelve-year-old Sirio and his younger sister Clara on the family's farm. Hardly an auspicious beginning for a child named after Sirius, the brightest star in the sky.

The Maccioni farm was a far cry from the nearby resort catering to international guests (such as Rose Kennedy, Gary Cooper, and members of the Agnelli family) who came to "take the cure" in its fabled fourteenth-century thermal waters. But it was close enough for Sirio to get a taste of the good life, as well as a healthy whiff of the sulfurous water for which Montetcatini was famous.

You could say hospitality ran in his blood. Before the war, Sirio's father was a concierge and his great-uncle a cook at the Croce di Malta hotel. When Sirio was only fourteen, he attended the local hotel school, which meant working as a waiter—long and hard—in season and learning his trade the rest of the year.

Opposite: Sirio Maccioni, c. 1952, in Paris where he worked at the Hôtel Plaza-Athénée and at Maxim's, learning the tricks of his trade.
Above: Art by Tim Flynn.

From left: Sirio's grandmother, Annunziata, in 1976; Sirio at age two; with parents, Silvia and Eugenio, and sister, Clara, 1937. *Opposite, from left:* On a balcony in Montecatini in 1972; Sirio at leisure.

"We were so poor . . ." he writes in his eponymous memoir, published in 2004, "all I could think of was not to be poor. In the hotels, I could make money."

It is one thing to start out life as a waiter; it is another to go on to reach great heights as a restaurateur. Whatever ultimately propelled Sirio—his family's predisposition, his parents' wish that their first and only son not live a farmer's existence, or a sense of his own worth and possibility—the fact is that Sirio Maccioni is indisputably one of the world's greatest restaurateurs and, not surprisingly, Montecatini's favorite son.

"All I could think of was not to be poor. In the hotels, I could make money."

BOUND FOR GLORY

Sirio's journey from Italy to stints in France (at the Hotel Plaza Athénée and Maxim's in Paris), in Germany, and then on the ships of the Home Lines, which made transatlantic crossings between Hamburg and New York and cruises to the Caribbean, is well documented. What isn't entirely clear is at what point the lanky, good-looking Tuscan realized that his true calling as a restaurateur, along with his raw desire to rise up from poverty, would not be fulfilled in Italy or anywhere else in Europe, but in America. Almost on a whim and at the end of a cruise to Havana, he decided to stay in New York, speaking almost no English but hell bent on making a life there, if only temporarily. More than half a century later, Sirio Maccioni is still there, presiding over a small but influential collection of restaurants dedicated to quality, luxury, and a rarefied brand of hospitality that he cultivated.

His first real job was downtown at Delmonico's, a restaurant favored by Wall Street investors. Owner Oscar Tucci, a fellow Italian, took a liking to Sirio and hired him as a waiter, then as a captain. There his ascent in America began.

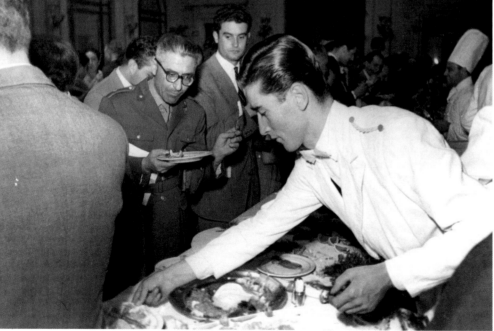

From top: At President Batista's palace in Havana, Cuba, 1955; as a student in the hotel school in Montecatini.

Opposite, from top: on the streets of New York, early 1950s; at dinner with Oscar Tucci, the owner of Delmonico's, who gave Sirio his first job, c. 1958.

Sirio left Delmonico's and headed uptown to work for Gene Cavallero, who owned the chi-chi Colony on East 61st Street and Madison Avenue. When Albert Torino, the longtime maître d'hôtel, died, Cavallero promoted Sirio. This was the chance Sirio had been longing for and for which he was perfectly suited.

The image of the courtly, tuxedo-clad maître d' certainly wasn't invented by Sirio Maccioni. That creature long preceded him in movies, in TV skits, and in the real-life restaurants of Europe and, to a lesser extent, America. But it was Sirio who elevated that image to an art form. By the time he was manning the door at the clubby Colony, he was king of the hand kissers. Nobody did it better or more smoothly.

Standing expectantly "at the door" was where Sirio felt most at home, at the ready to greet every lady and gentleman—and a few who weren't either—of American midcentury café society. Regulars at the Colony included Aristotle Onassis, Stavros Niarchos, Frank Sinatra, Billy Baldwin, Cary Grant, and the Duke and Duchess of Windsor. As he tells it, on his first day as maître d', he looked at the reservations book and saw that next to each name was a note indicating that they be seated at their "usual table." When Sirio asked Cavallero what that meant, Cavallero pointed to a single table at the bar: "You figure it out, m'boy." And, of course, he did—with artful aplomb.

At the Colony, Sirio learned to treat each customer, whether deserving or not, as a VIP—an attitude that served him well. There were times when he wanted to grit his teeth, so pressing were the demands of his clients. And then there were the women: Babe Paley, Lee Radziwill, Gloria Guinness, C. Z. Guest, Marella Agnelli—the kind of women Truman Capote dubbed "swans" for their long, elegant necks and regal bearing. As an Italian, Sirio instinctively knew how to please the ladies. He was handsome, he was charming, and he had the Continental touch that reduced even the most composed women to a puddle. Guardedly flirtatious yet always proper, Sirio led them to their tables as if he were ushering them into the bedroom. They lapped it up. Soon, they weren't just going to the Colony for lunch or dinner, they were going to see Sirio—a development that was not lost on owner Cavallero.

READY TO LAUNCH

By the late 1960s, the Colony was losing its caché. Other high-end French restaurants had arrived on the scene and established themselves. Three of them—La Caravelle, La Côte Basque, and La Grenouille—were run by protégés of the imperious Henri Soulé, owner of the legendary Pavillon on East 57th Street, once the only game in town for authentic haute cuisine (it closed in 1972). Then there was competition from an entrepreneur named Joe Baum, of the innovative Restaurant Associates. The diminutive and dynamic Baum had opened, among others, Forum of the Twelve Caesars (pompous Italian cuisine), Fonda del Sol (refined Latin), and the Four Seasons, designed by Philip Johnson and Mies van der Rohe in Mies's startlingly modern Seagram Building on Park Avenue. New Yorkers were loving to eat out and eager for the new and the next.

Much as he loved his job, even Sirio saw the handwriting on the fading walls of the Colony. In *New York* magazine's January 4, 1971, issue, in an article entitled "Colony Waxworks," critic Gael Greene practically entombed what she described as having once been "the apogee of glamour, the ultimate in elegance, style and exquisite feeding . . . an international sanctum for disadvantaged royals and fabulous pretenders, for the newly rich and the lately rich." Spade in hand, Greene went on to say, "Today lunch in The Colony dining room is like lunch at Forest Lawn, except that here the flowers are mostly plastic." Ouch.

Sirio knew it was time to move on. But where? The opportunity presented itself at the Pierre Hotel on Fifth Avenue in the form of a new restaurant-cum-nightclub called La Forêt ("the forest"). Initially, it was to be in association with Pierre Cardin, but the fashion designer pulled out. Sirio was undaunted. La Forêt would be his first brand-new venture and he was excited about it. Although still a maitre d', the job allowed him to flex his muscles more than in any of his other positions. The experience was short-lived, lasting less than two years, but it prepared Sirio for his next step—and it was a huge one.

Peter Duchin, high society's favorite orchestra leader, who himself hailed from a prominent New York family, played at La Forêt for about a month and got to

Guardedly flirtatious yet always proper, Sirio led them to their tables as if he were ushering them into the bedroom.

know Sirio and his family. "La Forêt was an attempt to do a supper club but it wasn't very successful. Sirio and I became very, very friendly—so friendly that I'd have an occasional meal with the Maccionis at home. Sirio was a wonderful, genial guy. He explained to me that his great desire was to have his own restaurant."

Duchin and his then-wife, Cheray, were close to the Zeckendorfs, the powerful Manhattan real estate dynasty. One of their holdings was the Mayfair House, a hotel on Park and 65th Street. William Zeckendorf, Jr., was eager to replace the restaurant that was there with a fine dining establishment. "I told Bill that I knew this guy who was absolutely terrific and said, 'Why don't you meet with him?'" They met, and the rest, as they say, is history. As for Duchin, the matchmaker, he says ruefully, "To this day, I kick myself for not saying, 'Sirio, five percent would do nicely.'"

Opposite: A debonair Sirio presides over La Forêt restaurant in midtown, mid-century Manhattan.

Above: The way it was—a vintage menu cover from the Colony.

WAITING IN THE THE WINGS

When Sirio made his first trip home, in 1957, he met Egidiana Palmieri, a pretty and talented singer, who lived in Montecatini. "Sirio was jobless, penniless, and staying with his sister while waiting for his papers in order to continue working at Delmonico's," Egi, as she is known, recalls. "He was very skinny and very cute. He said to me, 'I like you but I have to go back to America so I cannot ask you to wait for me.' I said, 'I will wait for you.'" Egi had more than patience. She had determination.

"We saw each other again after two years. He stood at the top of a hill with his arms crossed. I was on a bike going uphill. Finally, I threw the bike down and ran to him. After that, he came to Montecatini every summer." Fearing she might miss one of Sirio's visits, Egi stayed put in Tuscany, refusing all requests she received to perform outside the region. She even turned down a lucrative contract with RCA.

In July 1964, Sirio and Egi were married in New York. "I lived in Brooklyn with my uncle Renato Palmieri and his wife, Maria. Sirio was at the Colony as a young maître d' and making a name for himself." That's putting it mildly. Egi would go on to become the pillar supporting Sirio throughout his career and life.

This page: The courtship of Sirio Maccioni and Egidiana Palmieri in Montecatini.

Opposite: On their wedding day, July 18, 1964.

ONE-UPPING THE UPPER EAST SIDE

The year 1974 wasn't especially remarkable, at least not in terms of world events. *People* magazine launched its first issue, with Mia Farrow on the cover. Charles de Gaulle Airport opened in March. Ali knocked out Foreman in the Rumble in the Jungle in Zaire. Kate Moss and Derek Jeter came into the world. Charles Lindbergh, Duke Ellington, and Georges Pompidou left it.

What shook America to its core, however, occurred on August 8, when President Richard M. Nixon took responsibility for the Watergate scandal and announced his resignation. Meanwhile, a French restaurant called Le Cirque, on East 65th Street, opened its doors in March and was taking off in ways even its owner, Sirio Maccioni, could not have predicted or imagined. (Nixon, by the way, would become a customer.)

Here is how Bill Zeckendorf tells it: "We owned the Mayfair House, a residential hotel with a dining facility on Park Avenue that you could enter through the lobby and was two hundred feet from the kitchen. Whenever I went to dine, I was treated like a non-member entering a club. We hired Ellen McCluskey, a very social interior designer, to create a restaurant that she herself would use and bring her friends to. There was a doctor's office on East 65th Street with a lease expiring. It adjoined the kitchen. We started construction

Opposite: Sirio at the front door of 58 East 65th Street where he ruled his elegant roost from 1974 to 1997 (photo: Gerard Rondeau). *Above:* Art by Tim Flynn.

29

Clockwise from top left: Sirio with chef-partner Jean Vergnes (photo: Bill Cunningham); with William Zeckendorf, Jr.; from left, Pierre Franey, Alain Sailhac, Toni Suzette Cimino, and David Trenk (photo: Bill Cunningham).

but were missing a proprietor and a chef. Peter Duchin, a friend, brought Sirio and his chef to us. My father and I knew Sirio from the Colony, which had closed. I realized right away that this was the perfect team."

The second half of the team was Jean Vergnes, Sirio's partner. Obstinately French, Vergnes also had the talent and classical training necessary to keep Le Cirque from merely being a middling bistro. Sirio was in the front of the house, Vergnes in the back—and they wisely tried to stay out of each other's way. They didn't always succeed. On a trip with a few friends (including Craig Claiborne, Pierre Franey, and Vergnes and his wife) to a small island in Nova Scotia, they decided they'd eaten enough boar and venison for a lifetime. Sirio decided to make pasta. Lacking ingredients for a traditional tomato sauce, he reached for anything he could find—broccoli, zucchini, asparagus, green beans, frozen peas, a little of this, and a little of that. *Et voilà*: Spaghetti Primavera (*primavera* means "spring" in Ialian) was born (see recipe, page 124). The problem was that once they got back, Vergnes refused to prepare it in the kitchen on the grounds that it was not a classic French recipe, nor would he allow it to be added to the menu. But word of mouth, especially where the mouth is concerned, travels quickly, and soon patrons were requesting the dish. Deferring to Vergnes, Sirio had the ingredients cooked in the prep room and presented à table. It became one of the most popular dishes served at Le Cirque.

After three years, it became clear that Jean Vergnes and Sirio weren't the perfect match that Bill Zeckendorf had thought they were. Sirio's philosophy of lavishing the customer with perks like after-dinner drinks and complimentary desserts didn't sit well with Vergnes, who became increasingly frustrated with what he perceived as giving away food. Yet it was just such generosity that impressed a young Danny Meyer as he began building his own incredibly successful restaurant empire (Union Square Café, Gramercy Tavern, Eleven Madison, The Modern, among others). "Le Cirque taught me two important things as a restaurateur," says Meyer. "I learned the trick of using dessert wines not only as a gift to loyal customers, but also as a way to make up for mistakes made earlier in the meal. This was in 1983 and 1984. I never saw any other place serving malvasia, moscato d'Asti, and so on. And I also learned the art of bringing out a sampling of desserts."

Sirio knew the time had come for a change, one of many he was to make throughout his career. Sirio and Vergnes parted ways, amicably, and Vergnes retired. The incoming chef was Alain Sailhac, who'd received glowing reviews, including four stars from the *New York Times*, at Le Cygne on East 54th Street. Sailhac's style, like Vergnes's, was classic French, but with more latitude and flair. Although it took a while for Sirio to persuade him to come on board, Sailhac finally succumbed. Sirio, after all, was hard to resist. Sailhac started at Le Cirque in July 1978 and stayed until 1987.

Sailhac was a master chef but he was also a master at creating a team. The chefs he hired, many of them Americans—such as Geoffrey Zakarian, Terrance Brennan, Michael Lomonaco, and David Bouley— would go on to have their own successful careers, and all of them consider their time at Le Cirque an important stepping stone.

"Sirio was very demanding," says Sailhac, now at the French Culinary Institute in New York. "He wanted the best for his customers. He put white truffles on the map (they were expensive even then). He wanted the first soft-shell crabs, the first shad roe.

Preparing Spaghetti Primavera, not on the menu but definitely in demand.

King Juan Carlos of Spain (center)
at Le Cirque on East 65th Street.

in the exuberant attitude of Sirio himself. There was
so much going on at once, so much electricity in the
air, you hardly knew where to look first. It truly did
feel like a three-ring circus, with Sirio Maccioni as its
ringmaster, lion tamer, and juggler. Small wonder that
Le Cirque caught on so quickly. Who doesn't like to go
to the circus?

INSIDE THE TENT

The Zeckendorfs eventually sold the Mayfair House,
which became the Mayfair Regent, owned by a
group from Chicago and run by the Regent Hotels
Group. Like Sirio, the general manager, Dario Mariotti,
was from Italy. The Maccioni-Mariotti alliance was
an *entente cordiale*. Despite Mariotti's deference to
Sirio, he was not beyond ribbing him now and then: "I
used to call him the *Toscanaccio*, the big, bad Tuscan."
Still, he gives Sirio full credit for his dedication: "Sirio
poured ninety percent of his brain, life, and body into
the restaurant." This is a familiar refrain. Some may
disagree with Sirio's *modo di fare*, his "way of doing,"
but no one would question his total commitment to
the restaurant.

Mariotti and Maccioni were in friendly
competition, mostly having to do with who drew
the more prestigious customers. Mariotti, a well-
respected and highly experienced hotelier, attracted
a great many well-off Europeans, primarily Italians.
With Le Cirque being so close, so convenient, it was
only natural that the Mayfair guests would go there
for lunch or dinner, sometimes both on the same day.
Fashion people like the Fendis and Laura Biagiotti
came from Rome; Versace, the Missonis, and Diego
Della Valle came from Milan. Mariotti says, "They
all enjoyed the Italian atmosphere and an Italian
concierge who would spoil them as if they were at
home." French society denizens like Maud Frizon and
Yves Saint Laurent would stay at the hotel and have
both lunch and dinner at Le Cirque. The king of Spain
would go to Le Cirque with his entire entourage. The
Mayfair even added a "special of the day" from Le
Cirque to its room-service menu. Being in the Mayfair
building benefited the restaurant in less expected
ways as well: "Once when Sirio was making a special

"We would fill up Le Cirque two, maybe three times
a night. On any summer Saturday, we would serve
lobster salads for lunch to the ladies in their beautiful
hats. Le Cirque looked liked a summer garden."

The décor at East 65th Street was a little gardenlike
to begin with, with its trellised wallpaper that was
already in place before Sirio arrived. Ellen McCluskey's
design wasn't groundbreaking, but it suited the space.
The *Times* restaurant critic Bryan Miller described
"tables that are so close they make the Delta shuttle
look like a men's club lounge." Then he added, "The
elbow-to-elbow tables are part of the deliberate plan."
Perhaps that's why Alice Mason, the realtor known
for her upper-class clientele and her at-home dinners,
took such a shine to the restaurant. Mason believed
that cramming as many people as possible into a small
space and around tables that were just a little too small
was the secret to a successful party—and certainly one
way to get acquainted.

The name "Le Cirque" had little to do with how
the place looked, apart from the murals of monkeys
adorning the walls. The circus theme sprang from the
atmosphere: in the lively, important-looking crowd, in
the heightened sense of anticipation, and, of course,

Costumed monkeys at play and fanciful sconces adorn the whimsically decorated dining room (drawings: Gianni Renna, photo: Norman Parkinson).

From left: Betsy Bloomingdale; Barbara Sinatra; Barbara Taylor Bradford; Ann Bass; Barbara Walters; Duane Hampton (photos: Mary Hilliard).

pizza for Frank Sinatra, my wife, Gabriella, discovered that Le Cirque was using her special basil growing on the terrace of the Mayfair."

Everyone of prominence came to Le Cirque: Fashion VIPs (John Fairchild, Bill Blass, Carolina Herrera, Oscar de la Renta). Socialites (Duane Hampton, Blaine Trump, Pat Buckley, Nan Kempner). Moguls (Donald Trump, Ronald Perelman, Leonard Lauder, Swifty Lazar). Celebrities and performing artists (Woody Allen, Anthony Quinn, Kirk Douglas, Danny Kaye, Sophia Loren, Zubin Mehta, Andy

Warhol, Mick Jagger, Jerry Hall). The media (Liz Smith, Helen Gurley Brown, Cindy Adams, Barbara Walters, Tom Wolfe, Gay Talese). Critics and journalists (Florence Fabricant, Mimi Sheraton, James Villas). And photographers like Norman Parkinson and Slim Aarons, whose subjects appeared before their eyes with their first sip of an aperitif. The *Times*'s Bill Cunningham was there too—but never to eat and rarely inside. He posted himself, in rain or shine, in front of the entrance and captured the comings and goings.

In the early 1980s, John Mariani was compiling "The Twenty-five Greatest Restaurants in America" for *Playboy* magazine. "I dined at them all," he says, "including Le Cirque. I found it a dazzling place—bright and buzzing, with that fanciful monkey mural and the banquettes full of people who ranged from Bill Blass to Woody Allen. The food was superb—this was even before Daniel Boulud took over—very French but quite modern, with nouvelle cuisine concepts throughout. Sirio was, of course, his elegant, effusive self, deferential to some, quite talky with others."

Duane Hampton's memories are inseparable from those of her late husband, interior designer Mark Hampton: "The first offices of Mark Hampton, Inc., took up a parlor floor of a charming town house on East 65th Street. Just a few doors down was Le Cirque, where Mark took his clients to lunch and which, later, became our favorite haunt. Le Cirque was a delicious blend of grand and cozy. The staff was always all smiles and helpfulness; Sirio would come by to greet his old friends and sometimes stayed to have a real chat if he sensed that it was appropriate. But he wouldn't linger

Le Cirque

FIFTY-EIGHT EAST SIXTY-FIFTH STREET

Dinner

Hors D'Oeuvres

Salade de Homard aux Feuilles de Sucrines 20.75	Fonds d'Artichauts Gourmand 19.75
Petites St. Jacques en Salade Fleurie 10.75	Choix de Coquillages 5.75
Casserolette d'Escargots Noisettines et Croûtons 8.25	Foie Gras des Landes Princes du Jardin 19.75
Esturgeon Fumé Finlandaise 8.75	Terrine de Fruits de Mer 8.75
Huîtres Pochées Chiffonnade et Champagne 8.50	Pâté Tante Laurencie 5.75
Truite Fumé de Kimbridge Farm 8.75	Terrine de Canard au Foie Gras 8.25
Seviche de Red Snapper au Coriandre 9.75	Pieds et Tête au Carré 6.25
Pannequet Le Cirque aux Deux Sauces 8.75	Gâteau de Légumes en Gelée 5.75
Saumon Fumé de Nouvelle Ecosse 9.75	Melon Rose Jambon 6.75
Salade de Moules aux Oignons Rouges 6.25	Pâté de Lapereau au Romarin 8.25
	Caviar

Potages

Soupe à l'Oignon Gratinée 4.50	Potage du Jour 3.75
Velouté de Carottes Froid aux Cibonlettes 3.75	Consommé de Queues de Boeuf aux Paillettes 3.50
Crème de Homards 5.50	Crème de Concombres Glacé 3.75

Poissons

Panaché de Saumon et Bass au Bourgogne Aligoté 18.75

Sole de Douvre Sauté Chartreuse 20.75

Blanquette de St. Jacques Julienne 18.75

Fricassée de Lotte Baies des Singes 18.25

Suprême de Flounder Grillé Le Cirque 16.25

Belles d'Espagne au Beurre d'Anchois 20.75

Mille Feuilles de Soles aux Petites Roses 19.75

Quenelles de Brochet aux Perles Rouges 17.75

Escalopes de Daurade Grillées Dijounaise 17.75

DEMANDEZ POUR NOS SPECIALITES DU JOUR

VINS CARAFE

Blanc   Rouge

La Carafe 14.00   La Demi 7.50

Cover 2.00

Entrées

Paillarde de Capon Grillé aux Graines de Moutarde 16.75

Suprême de Volaille Fine Champagne 16.25

Poulet en Casserole Pour Deux aux Champignons Sauvages 37.00

Caveton Rôti aux Pommes, Sauce Citron 18.75

Fricassée de Coquelet Sauté au Gingembre 16.25

Poulet ou Poussin Grillé, Sauce Diable 16.25

Aiguillettes de Canard aux Granny Smith 16.75

Ris de Veau Cressonnette 18.75

Côte de Veau Alpiaté Grillé 18.95

Rognon de Veau Grillé aux Herbes 16.25

Grenadin de Veau Vieille France 18.75

Tournedos Sauté au Foie de Canard 21.75

Entrecôte Poêle au Mouton Cadet 19.75

Boeuf en Feuilles Toscane 16.95

Faux Filet Sauté au Poivre et Armagnac 20.75

Côte de Boeuf Grillé aux Herbes de Provence Pour Deux 41.00

Carré d'Agneau Pour Deux à l'Ancienne 42.00

Deux Mignons d'Agneau au Romarin 19.75

Côte de Veau Belle des Bois 21.75

(Toutes nos Entrées Sont Garnies de Légumes Frais du Jour)

Légumes Et Salades

Haricots Vert Purée 4.50	Pommes Montgolfier 6.00
Carottes Purée 4.50	Broccoli Hollandaise 4.50
Courgettes Frites 4.50	Ratatouille au Gratin 5.00
Epinard en Branche 4.50	Champignons de Couches 5.00
Champignon Sauvage en Saison	Asperges en Saison

Rugula 4.00	Epinard 4.00	Petites Laitues 4.00
Romaine 4.00	Chicorée 4.00	Boston Laitues 4.00

Endive · Mache · Radichio · Oak Leaf · Ruby en Saison

DEMANDEZ POUR NOS SOUFFLES (35 min.)

ET LA VOITURE DE DESSERT

Le Cirque

NEW YORK

FIFTY-EIGHT EAST SIXTY-FIFTH STREET

Poissons et Crustacés

Paupiette de Black Sea Bass Croustillante au Vin de Barolo 29.00
Black Sea Bass Wrapped in Crisp Potatoes with Red Wine Sauce

Aile de Raie Rôtie au Gingembre et Légumes Confits Aigre-Doux 25.00
Roasted Skate with Crisp Ginger and Sweet Sour Vegetables

Red Snapper Braisé aux Artichauts, Graine de Coriandre et Tomate Sèche 29.50
Braised Red Snapper with Artichokes, Coriander Seeds and Sun-Dried Tomatoes

Rosace de Saint Jacques et Tomate Comptée au Basilic 27.00
Sauteed Sea Scallops with Tomatoes, Fresh Pasta and Basil

Steak d'Espadon Rôti au Lard Fumé et Jus au Vinaigre de Xérès 29.00
Roasted Swordfish Steak Wrapped in Bacon with Sherry Vinegar Sauce

Homard Rôti à l'Embeurre de Chou Frisé et Cèpes à la Ciboulette 31.50
Roasted Lobster with Savoye Cabbage in Butter Sauce, Porcini Mushrooms and Chives

Darne de Saumon Piquée de Thym à la Vigneronne 28.00
Sauteed Salmon with Fresh Thyme, Vegetables and Red Wine Sauce

Steak de Thon Grillé à l'Echalote, Pommes Allumette 28.75
Grilled Tuna with Shallots, Spinach and Match-Stick Potatoes

Viandes et Volailles

Navarin d'Agneau Comme le Prépare Roger Vergé 25.75
Lamb Stew with Vegetables, Orange Zest and Rosemary

Rable de Lapin Farci d'Herbes, Chanterelles et Flageolets au Jus 28.50
Roasted Stuffed Saddle of Rabbit with Herbs, Mushrooms and Beans Casserole

Poussin de Ferme Rôti aux Truffes Sous la Peau, Galette de Pommes de Terre 29.00
Roasted Baby Chicken with Truffle Under the Skin, Crisp Potatoes and Mixed Greens

Mignonettes de Boeuf au Poivre, Cerises Séchées et Dariole d'Endive 29.75
Mignonette of Beef Tenderloin with Black Pepper, Dried Cherries and Endive Mousse

Pintade Rôtie aux Baies de Genièvre, Garniture Fermière au Foie Gras 29.00
Roasted Guinea-Fowl with Seasonal Vegetables and Foie Gras (for Two - 45 min. minimum)

Côte de Veau Poêlée aux Olives, Polenta au Thym et Hachis de Roquette 31.00
Sauteed Veal Chop with Mixed Olives, Thyme Polenta and Creamed Arugula

Escalope de Ris de Veau à la Moutarde Forte et Fondue d'Epinards 26.50
Sauteed Crisp Scalloppine of Sweetbread with Hot Mustard and Spinach

Carré d'Agneau Rôti, Gâteau de Neuf Légumes et Gratin Dauphinois 62.00
Roasted Rack of Lamb with Nine Vegetables Cake and Potato Gratin (for Two)

POUR LE VEGETARIEN: Assiette de Légumes de la Saison à la Vapeur 25.00
FOR THE VEGETARIAN: Steamed Vegetables of the Season.

Cuit Sur Le Grill

Filet de Black Sea Bass 28.75	Paillarde de Ve...
Filet de Flounder "Le Cirque" 24.50	Homard
Sole de Douvres (selon marché)	Poulet à la Mouta...
Filet de Red Snapper 28.75	Rognon de Veau et Cro...
Pavé de Saumon 27.50	Mignonettes de B...
Steak de Black Angus 31.00	

Roti à La Commande

(45 Minute Minimum)
Priced per Person

Poulet (for Two) 27.00	Chateaubriand (for...
Canard (for Two) 28.75	Côte de Boeuf (for...
Pigeon au Jus 29.75	Pintade (for Tw...
Red Snapper Entier au Fenouil (for Four) 28.75	

Légumes et Salades

Purée de Légumes du Jour 7.00	Epinards Frai...
Pomme Montgolfière 9.00	Asperges Vertes (en...
Haricots Verts Fins 8.00	Salade de Saiso...
Pommes Mousseline 6.75	Champignons de la...

DEMANDEZ NOS SOUFFLES (35 min.)
et
LA CARTE DE DESSERTS

DINNER

Le chef vous propose un menu composé... plats en harmonie avec la saison. The chef suggest a 4 course dinner with the season.

MENU DEGUSTATION:

PRIX FIXE $75.00   MINIMU...

SPECIALITES DU JOUR

SOUPE D'ASPERGE AUX CROUTONS
* * * *
CARPACCIO DE SAUMON, LOLLAROSSA ET MOUSSE D'AVOCAT 15...
Salmon carpaccio with lollarossa and avocado mo...
* * * *
FOIE GRAS POELE AUX ABRICOTS ET SALADE DE MESCLUN 25...
Sauteed fresh foie gras with abricot and young wild...
* * * *
COQUILLE St JACQUES ETUVEES AUX MOUSSERONS ET JULIENNE DE LE...
Poached Scallops with field mushrooms and assorted julienne...
* * * *
BOUILLABAISSE "LE CIRQUE" 28.75
* * * *
FLETAN POELE AUX CHANTERELLES, POINTES D'ASPERGE, POMM...
ET SAUGE FRAICHE 28.50
Sauteed halibut with chanterelles, asparagus tips, potatoes...
* * * *
MAGRET ET CUISSE DE CANARD CONFIT AUX CERISES, FONDU D'EPINA...
ET POMMES CROUSTILLANTES 29.00
Roasted duck breast and confit with cherries, spinach, wi...
and crispy potatoes
* * * *
AIGUILLETTE DE GIGOT D'AGNEAU ROTI A L'AIL DOUX, GRATIN...
POMMES FONDANTES 27.50
Roasted leg of lamb aiguillette with tomato, zucchini, egg...
sweet red peppers and melting potatoes
* * * *
BELONS AND MALPEQUES OYSTERS 14.50
* * * *
MORILLES FRAICHES DE L'OREGON 15.00
* * * *
SOUFFLE BANANE, SAUCE CHOCOLAT

Comings and goings,
tête à têtes and a bit
of bubbly. *Clockwise
from left:* Princess
Grace of Monaco
(photo: Ron Galella);
Sue Mengers,
Helen Gurley Brown,
and Barbara Walters
(photo: Bill
Cunningham);
with Walter and
Betsy Cronkite (photo:
Bill Cunningham);
C.Z. Guest and
Paul Wilmot (photo:
Mary Hilliard).

Clockwise from left:
Carolina Herrera (photo: Mary Hilliard); with Arlene Dahl and Liliane Montevecchi (photo: Bill Cunningham); arm candy by Chanel (photo: Mary Hilliard); with Bill Blass and Aileen "Suzy" Mehle (photo: Bill Cunningham).

if he saw it wasn't. He was highly sensitive to mood and nuance. And so are all of his handsome sons. Handsome never hurts!"

Malcolm Forbes went to Le Cirque so often that when he died, in 1990, Sirio was asked to be an usher at the memorial service at St. Bartholemew's. His job was to man the velvet rope (again, Sirio as gatekeeper). To Sirio's surprise, he received a note from Malcolm's eldest son, Steve. It read: "My father admired you greatly and in his Will he left you a bequest of $1,000 'as a token of gratitude for the joy [his] skills and genius have added to the lives of those who have been lucky and sensible enough to dine at [his] restaurant.'"

Christopher (Kip) Forbes, who often accompanied his dad—sometimes both of them arriving on their Harley Davidsons, decked out in helmets and leather motorcycle jackets—believes that "part of the fun of going to Le Cirque with my father, in addition to enjoying a great meal, was seeing who else among the great and the good might also be lucky enough to be dining there that day. While we never had a party there, Sirio did indeed handle one of the more unusual catering assignments of all time: preparing

box lunches for those guests going to my father's seventieth birthday party in Tangier who were flying aboard the chartered Concorde. Daniel [Boulud] even prepared little hard-boiled eggs to look like hot-air balloons." There was a tense moment, he says, when the truck transporting the lunches to Newark airport went missing and attempts to contact the driver failed. It turned out that he'd arrived early and fallen asleep. The shipment was delivered in the nick of time, but Sirio was so flustered that he missed the flight and was a no-show at the birthday party.

To someone like Danny Meyer, Le Cirque's offerings were incomparable in more fundamental ways: "When I first moved to New York, Le Cirque was the place to go to find the best combination of three critically important elements: great food, refined service, and big-party atmosphere. You could find one, maybe two of these elements in other New York restaurants, but not all three. Lutèce had great food and refined service, but it wasn't a party. Other places felt like parties, but the food or service was lacking. You simply had to go to Le Cirque if you wanted all three. Le Cirque owned that space—a haunt for people of power and celebrity and social standing. It was urbane, excellent, fun, and magical all at the same time."

"Other places felt like parties, but the food or service was lacking. You simply had to go to Le Cirque if you wanted all three."

Left: Anne Slater (photo: Mary Hilliard); *below*: Bill Cunningham and Alain Sailhac. *Following pages*: Ladies on parade, East 65th Street (photos: Gerard Rondeau).

STAR WARS

"Oh, the usual. Lunch at Le Cirque and then the abyss."

Not every critic was enamored of Le Cirque. Under Vergnes in 1977, Mimi Sheraton begrudgingly gave it one star in the *New York Times*. She thought the murals of the humanized monkeys were "corny" and she didn't much like the food, either, calling it at times "banally mediocre." Reviewing it again in 1980, when Sailhac was in place, Sheraton elevated Le Cirque to two stars. This time, she praised the food but said the staff had a "tendency to fawn over celebrities and regulars, while giving unknowns the cold shoulder." (She eventually gave it three stars in 1981.)

In his first review of Le Cirque for the *New York Times*, in 1986 (Alain Sailhac was still chef), Bryan Miller was impressed enough to give it three stars, praising the place for "its high-voltage energy." He described Sirio as "a hawk-eye perfectionist who one minute is aligning salt and pepper shakers as if the success of his establishment rested on table symmetry, while the next he is kissing the hand of a parting customer, making her feel like the Princess of Wales as she floats out the door." In his second review, a year later, Miller bestowed upon Le Cirque the long-coveted four stars, calling it "the most glamorous and electrifying setting in New York." By this time, Le Cirque was on its third chef, the on-the-rise Daniel Boulud, a thirty-two-year-old from Lyons whose food was, according to Miller, "lighter, more rustic Provencal than polished Parisian" (a reference to Alain Sailhac's approach). In 1992, on the eve of its eighteenth anniversary, Le Cirque received another four-star review from Bryan Miller, referring to it as "a mighty locomotive."

Not everyone, however, felt they could get a ticket on the train. The charge of Le Cirque's giving preferential treatment to celebrities would be repeated frequently, but never so pointedly than in Ruth Reichl's double-barreled review in 1993 when Sylvain Portay, who followed Daniel Boulud, was executive chef. Portay was a disciple of Alain Ducasse, having worked for him at Le Louis XV in Monte Carlo's Hotel de Paris. As the *Times*'s new restaurant critic, Reichl wrote in two articles about two separate visits to Le Cirque—first as an unknown, then as a "favored patron." *Quel différence.* Despite having a reservation,

Previous, from left: Kathryn Penske, Ivana Trump, Muffie Bancroft, Anne Arledge, Anna Moffo Sarnoff, Cristina Ferrare DeLorean, Marie Kimberly, and Patricia Kluge (photo: Slim Aarons).

Above: From *The New Yorker* by Robert Weber. *Opposite, from left:* Markus Farbinger, pastry chef; Sottha Khunn, sous chef; Marc Poidevin, sous chef; and Daniel Boulud, executive chef (photo: Gerard Rondeau).

"Every restaurant has to become a club for its regulars."

Reichl had to wait at the bar, where smoking was still permitted (she was not a smoker). When a table finally opened up, she sat down to a meal that she referred to as "a parade of brown food." On her next visit, she was recognized and treated like a queen (while the king of Spain, mind you, was waiting at the bar for his table). (Marco Maccioni tells it a slightly different way: "Ruth Reichl was recognized the first time, too, but the truth is we blew it. Mistakes happen.")

Restaurateurs, by nature, are overly protective of their product, so even mild criticism, whether warranted or not, is a blow to the ego—all the more when it comes from "the newspaper of record." Reichl's write-up was wounding to Sirio, not the most thick-skinned fellow to begin with. He tried to shrug it off, but, being the great worrier that he was, he was both hurt and embarrassed. To Bryan Miller, the attitude of Reichl and others like her was "misguided populism."

"Everyone should get a modicum of Le Cirque service," he says, "but what is all the whining about?

It's a business. Your best customers deserve something extra."

Danny Meyer, who knows the effect a less-than-flattering review can have, says, "Ruth Reichl's review was brilliant because it captured the restaurant perfectly. But I don't fault Sirio for that fact. Every restaurant has to become a club for its regulars." Curiously, what Reichl wrote didn't hurt business. The regulars kept coming. They came for Sirio.

LIFE WITH FATHER

In his spare time (which wasn't much) Sirio Maccioni, now a wildly successful restaurateur, was also a husband and the father of three sons—Mario, Marco, and Mauro. Sirio moved the family from East 50th Street, where he and Egi first started out, to East 62nd Street, where Hermès is now located. By the time he was well ensconced at Le Cirque, Sirio found an

Opposite, from left: Daniel Boulud, Michel Godin, Sirio, Egi, and Sottha Khunn celebrate the four-star review from the *New York Times* in 1987 (photo: Bill Cunningham). *Above left:* With *New York Times* restaurant critic Bryan Miller (photo: Mary Hilliard). *Above right:* from *Food & Wine* magazine.

Following pages: Menus and memorabilia. *Clockwise from top right:* With Paul Bocuse; with Dario Mariotti (left) and Pierre Franey; with Roger Vergé (photo: Bill Cunningham); with Craig Claiborne.

On my sixtieth birthday

Sirio — i love you.

Craig

14 September 1980

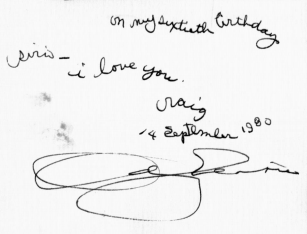

FIFTY-EIGHT EAST SIXTY-FIFTH STREET

Les Aperitifs

***

Le Chardonnay de Californie

***

Le Tignanello d'Italie

***

Le Vieux Bourgogne

***

Champagne de France

***

Les Liqueurs

Samedi 13, Septembre 1980

MENU

Petites Tapenade a

***

Saumon farcie aux
Sauce Tout-Paris

***

Sorbet aux Pommes

***

Pigeons grillé aux grai
Courgettes aux Cèpes - Haric

***

Petites Talmouse - Crême f

***

Salade de Fruits e

***

Trufettes Bened

***

Demi Tass

CRAIG CLAIBORNE

September 18, 1980

Dear Sirio:

You are one of the kindest and most
thoughtful men I have ever met. I can't tell
you how touched I was to be tendered that 60th
birthday party at Le Cirque. The food was, of
course, unforgettable, as was the occasion.

Yours ever,

La Confrérie de la Chaîne
des Rôtisseurs

LIFETIME ACHIEVEMENT AWARD

Recipients

1986
Joseph Baum

1987
Paul Kovi
Thomas Margittai

1988
Sirio Maccioni

Roger Yaseen
National President

Le Cirque

quelle belle maison et quelle cuisine formidable - Sincerement
[signature]

La Cuisine est une expression d'amitié et
nous sommes heureux d'en avoir ressenti cette chaleur
Merci Alain et les chefs. *Roger Vergé*

En toute amitié
Paul Bocuse

[signatures] *avec toute amitié*
Gourmande en vous
Pierre Franey *esperant à Paris au*
Pré Catelan

Bravo pour votre talent
[signature] Hermé's

FIFTY-EIGHT EAST SIXTY-FIFTH STREET

A l'ami Sirio
Bonne cuisine
et accueil incomparable
Tous mes compliments

Paul Bocuse
21 sept 1982
+ la meilleur de N.Y

Après le Cirque de Lola Montés
le cirque de la belle et grande Cuisine
Amitiés à Sirio [signature]

LES MAITRES CUISINIERS DE FRANCE

Délégation des Etats - Unis

Monsieur André SOLTNER, Délégué Général pour les Etats - Unis	
BANCHET, Jean	KRAUSE, Willy
BOUCHET, Claude	ORSI, Pierre
CHALMIN, Max	PASDELOUP, Claude
CHANTREAU, Maurice	RACHOU, Jean - Jacques
DIDIER, Ernest	RENE, André
FESSAGUET, Roger	SWARTVAGHER, Claude
GRANGIER, Clément	VAUDARD, L. Raymond
GOYENVALLE, Jean-Pierre	VERDON, René
HAENTZLER, Marcel	VERGNES, Jean
Monsieur Joseph CASTAYBERT, Délégué Général d'Honneur	

LES CHEFS DE L'ANNEE

1967—ANDRE SOLTNER, M.O.F.	1971—MARCEL HAENTZLER
1968—ANDRE RENE	1972—CLAUDE BOUCHET
1969—ROGER FESSAGUET	1973—PIERRE ORSI
1970—RAYMOND L. VAUDARD	1974—ANDRE SURMAIN
	1975—JOSEPH CASTAYBERT

INVITES D'HONNEUR

Monsieur le Consul de France à New York et Madame Marcel FLEURI
Monsieur le Consul d'Italie à New York et Madame Vieri TRAXLER
Monsieur le Sénateur Jacques HABERT
Monsieur le Délégué Général des Maîtres Cuisiniers de France aux U.S.A. et Madame André SOLTNER
Monsieur le Délégué Général d'Honneur aux U.S.A. et Madame Joseph CASTAYBERT
Monsieur André SURMAIN, Promoteur de la Toque d'Argent "Chef de l'Année"
Monsieur Thomas AHRENS, Professeur d'oenologie au N.Y.C. Community College
Monsieur le Président du Vatel Club et Madame Roger FESSAGUET
Monsieur le Président de l'Académie Culinaire de France, U.S. Groupe et Madame J. J. RACHOU
Monsieur le Président de la Société Culinaire Philanthropique, Henri DELTIEURE
Monsieur le Président de l'Amicale Culinaire de Washington, Jacques BLANC
Monsieur le Président de la Commanderie des Cordons Bleus de France, Groupe Américain et Madame Paul SUREAU
Mademoiselle KIKI LEVATHES, Daily News
Monsieur le Réprésentant de la Société des Cuisiniers de Paris aux U.S.A. et Madame Marc SARRAZIN
l'Hôte de la Soirée Monsieur Sirio MACCIONI et Madame
Le Maître Cuisinier Jean VERGNES et Madame

INVITES

BAILLS, Claude	JACOBS, Victor et Guest
BANCHET, Jean et Madame	LUTRINGSHAUSER, Madame
BELL, Maurice et Madame	MANASSERO, J. P. et Madame
BOUTE, Maurice, et Madame	MARBOE, Peter
BOUCHET, Claude	MARE, Claude
BRECQ, J. C. et Madame	MARTIN, Joseph et Madame
BOWLING, Frank	MELZ, Joseph, et Madame
CARGUER, W.	NANNI, Luigi et Madame
CASTAYBERT, Georges	OCCHIUZZI, Franco et Guest
CLAIBORNE, Craig	PASDELOUP, Claude
CHENUS, Roland et Madame	PIQUET, Yves
DIETRICH, J. J.	RENE, André et Madame
ESNAULT, Gaston et Madame	RICE, William
FINDRIN, Martin	RITTER, Georges
FORTIN, Michel	ROZZO, Phil et Madame
FRANEY, Pierre et Madame	SAILHAC, Alain
GINGOLD, Hermione	SAVORE, Pierre
GOYENVALLE, J. P. et Madame	SWARTWAGHER, Claude
GREAULT, Robert	TODESCHINI, J. L. et Madame
GREEN, Gail	VAUDARD, L. Raymond
HAENTZLER, Marcel et Madame	VEIRUN, Félix
HERMANN, Bernard	

Chairman du Dîner Statutaire Co-Chairman
RAYMOND L. VAUDARD CLAUDE PASDELOUP

Quatrain Culinaire

Le "MAITRE - CUISINIER", quand il déguste,
Dignité de l'art culinaire français, titre auguste.
Qui par sa servante et succulentes préparations,
De part le monde fait l'honneur de notre profession.
R.I.V.

Reception au Champagne

HEIDSIECK MONOPOLE GOLD TOP.
AVEC LES BAGATELLES APERITIVES

Froid	Chaud
Le Saumon Fumé	La Quiche aux Moules
la petite brioche de foie gras	les Huîtres au Champagne
Jambon de Bayonne avec Longuils	les crustacés en pâte du Chef

... Menu ...

1 ere Assiette
LE CONSOMME A LA DIANE
AVES LES PETITS DIABLOTINS

Riesling 1971
Cuvée Frederic Emile

2 eme Assiette
LA MOUSSE DE SOLE TOUT-PARIS
RELEVEE A LA FINE CHAMPAGNE

Chateau Duhart Milon
Rothschild 1966

3 eme Assiette
LE CARRE DE VEAU POELE DANS SON JUS
ACCOMPAGNE DE LA GARNITURE DU CHEF

LE GRANITE AU CASSIS

Chambole
Musigny 1970

4 eme Assiette
LA SALADE DE SAISON
LES FROMAGES CHOISIS AVEC RAISIN

L'Apothéose

LE SOUFFLE DES MAITRES CUISINIERS
AVEC SA FINE SAUCE A LA POIRE
ET LES DELICIEUSES MIGNARDISES

Fumeur soin patients, le café arrivera à temps
Accompagné d'Alcools et de Liqueurs
Calvados Busnel — Mandarine Napoléon
Poire Williams Cognac Otard
Mirabelle — Framboise

Le Maître Cuisinier	Hôte
JEAN VERGNES	SIRIO MACCIONI
	Co-propriétaire
Le Chef	Le Maître D'
J. L. TODESCHINI	JOE GARNI
Le Steward	Assistant Maître D'
FRANK D'ELIA	Renato PALMIERI
Sous Chef	Chef Pâtissier
MICHEL FORTIN	ALFRED BURALE

Old friends are the best friends, especially at Le Cirque. *Clockwise from right*: Taking a sip from Danny Kaye (photo: Bill Cunningham); with Yves Montand; Italian actors Alberto Sordi and Monica Vitti (photo: Mary Hilliard); guestbook inscription.

"Suddenly, someone pulled me by the
scruff of my jacket and upbraided me.
'Don't you realize, young man,
that there are ladies at this table?'
And with that he shoved me off.
It was Douglas Fairbanks, Jr."

apartment within walking distance of the restaurant. In order to see their father, the boys would come home from school, play in Central Park, and then swing by and see Babbo. "He'd come through the double doors," remembers Marco, the middle son, "but we still couldn't go inside and had to be on our best behavior." At home in the mornings, the kids had to tiptoe around the apartment so as not to wake up their father after a late night at the restaurant. (Try telling three rambunctious boys to put a lid on it.)

Egi, having given up her singing career, devoted herself to being Sirio's wife and the boys' mother. "I took the boys to school because he worked six days a week," says Egi. If we went to the restaurant, I had to make sure my handbag was full of surprises in order to entertain them. I had to go to their graduations by myself because Sirio's priority was (and still is) the restaurant.

"When I delivered my sons, Sirio wasn't there. He would take me to the hospital, then leave, saying, 'Listen, I've got to go to work. See you later.' With Marco, I was in pain and thought I was going to deliver. Sirio brought me to the hospital and off he

MERCI, Sirio!

went. Then the pain stopped and the doctor told me to go home. I called Sirio to pick me up. He said, 'I'll send you a waiter.' This young guy showed up and took me home. As soon as we got there, the pain started again and I told him, 'You've got to take me back.' And he did."

Growing up as the sons of a world-renowned restaurateur had its moments. Mario, the eldest, was perhaps the most affected by his father's absences and the first to start working at the restaurant, manning the phones. Barely in his teens, he morphed into that cliché of the crazed Hollywood producer holding the receivers to both ears and striking deals, except he was booking tables—or attempting to. "When they couldn't get a reservation, they'd ask to speak to my father." I'd put the person on hold, look helplessly at Benito Sevarin, the maître d', and get a look back that said, "You figure it out." Not unlike Sirio's first day on the job at the Colony.

Marco's memory goes back to Le Cirque's opening night in April 1974. "My mom, Mario, and I were seated in what was then termed Siberia. I got so bored that I crawled under our table and then under another table of six. I was desperate to find a way out. From the well-shaped legs, I could see that it was a table of mostly women. Suddenly, someone pulled me by the scruff of my jacket and upbraided me. 'Don't you realize, young man, that there are ladies at this table?' And with that he shoved me off. It was Douglas Fairbanks, Jr."

During Ronald Reagan's administration, Le Cirque was the First Family's favorite New York restaurant. When Reagan was governor of California, Nancy Reagan would come to lunch with her best friend, Betsy Bloomingdale, and the man *Women's Wear Daily* dubbed "the social moth," the sharp-tongued, sour-pussed Jerome Zipkin. She continued to be a patron during their White House years and afterward.

Marco remembers the day President Reagan came to lunch, in the early '80s: "There was press, Secret Service, a real scene. He'd been to Le Cirque before he was in office, and when he was running for president. It was the first time I ever followed a campaign. I will never forget seeing the president of the United States in my father's restaurant. Reagan truly embodied the image of a president." Restaurateur Geoffrey Zakarian, who was Le Cirque's sous chef at the time, remembers Reagan as "spectacularly elegant—like he was in a bubble."

"I managed to go there as often as possible and graduated to being seated at the prized banquette on the north wall of the dining room."

Opposite: With his three sons— Mario, Marco, and Mauro (photo: Sigrid Estrada). *This page, from left:* Illustration by Carol Gillott, 1995; with fashion designer Dennis Basso, 1980.

To Sirio
With our best wishes -
Nancy Reagan

FIFTY-EIGHT EAST SIXTY-FIFTH STREET

Galestro Antinori ~ 1979

Chateau Meyney ~
Prieuré des Couleys 1959

Louis Roederer ~ Cristal
Brut Rosé 1974

Saturday, March 14ᵗʰ, 1981

Assiette de Charcuterie Le Cirque

Nouilles Fraîches Automnale

Belles d'Espagne et St. Jacques en Broch

Soufflé Glacé Citron Delices des

Sabayon au Grand Marnier

Mignardises Didier ~

Le dinner du President & Mrs. Reagan

Presidents, governors, and pontiffs alike pay their respects. *Clockwise from above:* Inscribed menu; President Richard Nixon and First Lady Pat Nixon (photo: Bill Cunningham); With Governor Hugh Carey and Evangeline Gouletas (photo: Bill Cunningham); with Pope John Paul II on his visit to New York in 1995 and Archbishop Renato Martino (photo: Arturo Mari); guestbook inscriptions; with sons and President Ronald Reagan and First Lady Nancy Reagan.

With best wishes,
Nancy Reagan   Ronald Reagan

To Cirio –
with warm regards
Richard Nixon

Edward Kennedy Spring 1992

Aug. 2/85

To Cirio –
Great! Wonderful
food & service –
J Carter
Rosalynn Carter
President Jimmy Carter's

THE CRÈME DE LA CRÈME

While Sirio's wife and sons were accustomed to taking a backseat to Le Cirque, once every year they came first: in late summer, when they would return to Montecatini and from there make pilgrimages to the temples of haute cuisine in France. That meant visiting Sirio's idols: Paul Bocuse, Michel Guérard, Alain Chapel, André Daguin, Roger Vergé, and others. These legendary chef-owners created what became known as nouvelle cuisine, a lighter version of classic French cooking. Sirio first met Vergé at the Plaza Athénée. Through him, he got to know the others, all of whom were close friends. They would come to Le Cirque and, in turn, Sirio made it a point to visit them when on holiday.

It was on one of these trips in 1982 that Sirio discovered the inspiration for what would become Le Cirque's signature dessert: crème brûlée. Marco Maccioni remembers it vividly: "I was fourteen years old. We'd just had lunch at Michel Guérard's and were heading for André Daguin's restaurant in Auch in southwest France. This was during the World Cup playoffs. On this day, Italy was playing Brazil. Dad pulled into a roadside bistro. Seeing that we were Italian, the people at the bar began to ridicule us (P.S., Italy won). My father was so taken aback by this reaction, he said, 'Screw the French,' and we left. In a rage, Dad went to the first pay phone he could find."

Realizing the next game would be played in Barcelona, Sirio cannily called the attaché of King Juan Carlos of Spain. The king used to stay at the Mayfair and would always eat at Le Cirque, so Sirio felt fairly comfortable making the call. To Sirio's surprise, the king himself got on the phone: "This is Juan Carlos. I was expecting you." He invited the entire family to come to Barcelona for the semifinals—Italy against Poland—and prepared the Royal Suite at the hotel named after his wife, Queen Sofia.

"One night," says Marco, "we went to Le Goût d'Avignon, where Alain Chapel was the consulting chef. For dessert, we had *Crema Catalana*, a cold custard with a crispy caramel coating—a creamier version of flan. Dad became fixated." When they returned to Montecatini, Le Cirque's chef, Alain Sailhac, had come to visit. "Dad said, 'Let's try this crema Catalana.' The only thing we had were oval

ramekins—not the round ones usually used for flan. They made the custard, but then Mom realized that she'd used up all the sugar for the custard and had none left for the topping. She took down a box of Domino's brown sugar from the kitchen cabinet. The texture was hard, so she grabbed a cheese grater and grated the sugar over the custard and put the dish in the top rack of the broiler. It created a sheet of brown glaze. *Ecco*, Le Cirque's crème brûlée was born—by accident."

Not quite the end of the story. "Back in New York, Le Cirque's pastry chef, Dieter Schorner, refused to create a Spanish dish in a French restaurant (shades of Jean Vergnes?). He grabbed Francisco Gutierrez, our dishwasher at the time and a Spaniard. Schorner said, 'You know how to make flan. Make a dozen of these a day and put them in my office, not in the pastry department.' Gael Greene came to the restaurant and for some reason—no one quite knows how this happened—was given a crème brûlée. She liked it. Francisco was elevated to assistant pastry chef and crème brûlée gained fame as one of the world's great desserts." (The recipe is on page 143.)

Opposite, clockwise from top left: With Kirk Douglas and family; with Andy Warhol; with Sophia Loren and Benito Sevarin (photo: Bill Cunningham).

Following page: Jacqueline Kennedy Onassis, 1986 (photo: Bill Cunningham).

A SAFE HAVEN

Sometimes it seemed as if all of Le Cirque existed in a bubble. Fashion designer Dennis Basso, known for his extravagant furs, said that the first time he went to Le Cirque was to celebrate his twenty-first birthday with his parents. "It was as if I'd died and gone to heaven. Le Cirque had been open about a year and, being a fashion student, I was reading *WWD* cover to cover along with all the social columns in the newspapers. Everyone 'fab' seemed to be dining there and I had to see it for myself. That night, I ordered the signature dish of the house, Spaghetti Primavera, followed by the most amazing desserts. But more than the food was the experience of all the social columns coming to life. Barbara Walters, Ivana Trump, the Kissingers, Diana Ross, and so many others were all in the dining room.

"From that point on, I managed to go there as often as possible and graduated to being seated at the prized banquette on the north wall of the dining room. As my business grew, Le Cirque was the only restaurant I wanted to lunch or entertain in. There was always magic in the perfumed air of the impeccably dressed women. After several years of steady visits, Sirio invited me to have a house account. I was in my late twenties and felt like I'd won the Nobel Prize."

Of all of Le Cirque's celebrity customers, none drew as much attention or had as much charisma as Jacqueline Bouvier Kennedy Onassis. She became a habitué after Aristotle Onassis's death. Her usual companion was John Loring, the creative director of Tiffany and one of the writers in her stable when she was a book editor at Doubleday. Most of the time, the two had lunch at her office or his—nothing fancy, New York deli fare. One day she told Loring she was tired of sitting on the floor eating sandwiches and terrible coleslaw. (They did it so often that she once murmured to Loring in her whispery voice, "I wish Robin Leach could film this for 'Lifestyles of the Rich and Famous.'") This was circa 1988. Jackie said, "Couldn't we just go out and have lunch like normal people?" Loring replied, "Where would that be possible?" Jackie, who'd clearly given this some thought, answered, "The only person who would know how to handle this would be Sirio. Why don't you call him and make the arrangements and I'll meet you there at 12:30."

Dîner
en l'honneur de
John Loring

~

Court Bouillon
de Homard au Safran

~

Selle de Veau Farcie
aux Pistaches
Bouquetière de Légumes
Les Endives Braisees

~

Salade Trois Couleurs

~

Soufflé aux Poires
Sauce Chocolat Amère
Mignardises Le Cirque
Café Colombien

Pinot Grigio 1985   *1 octobre 1986*
Château Prieure Lichine 19   *L'Orangerie du Cirque*

The heyday of front-door diplomacy on East 65th Street. *Top row, from left:* President Nixon and Dr. Henry Kissinger; President George H. Bush (photo: Marina Garnier); with Robert, Malcolm, and Tim Forbes; with Arianna Huffington; with Pierre Cardin, on right; with the Reagans. *Bottom row, from left:* Jacqueline Kennedy Onassis and John Loring (photo: Marina Garnier); with Barbara Walters and Beverly Sills; with Gina Lollobrigida; with Bill Blass and John Fairchild; en famille. (All photos by Bill Cunningham unless otherwise noted.)

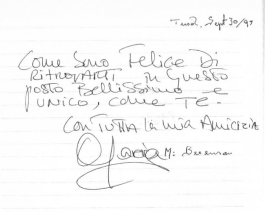

Above: Sirio serves Marisa
Berenson's pampered pooch KK
(short for King Kong). KK was
named by Truman Capote
(photo: Ellen Graham).

Tuesd. Sept 30/97

*Come Sono Felice Di
Ritrovarti In Questo
posto Bellissimo e
Unico, come Te.
Con Tutta la mia Amicizia*

Marisa M. Berenson

"I knew exactly what table we'd have to sit at,"
remembers Loring. "The same table where Nixon and
Bebe Rebozo sat . . . the one by the door where you
could get in and out quickly. I called Sirio. He said,
'Fine, I will have someone on the lookout and we'll let
her slip in.' (Sirio was an expert at this.)

"She sat during the entire lunch with her left hand
covering her face." Even so, her appearance was noted
in Liz Smith's column the next day.

Many Le Cirque lunches between Loring and Jackie
followed. "It was never about the food," says Loring.
"She'd practically eat nothing and push her food
around on the plate. As usual, the waiter would bring

an avalanche of desserts, which we would thank him for, then ask him to remove."

But one day was different. It was in 1994. "Jackie was great at pretending that everything was fine and nothing was wrong ('never complain, never explain'). The desserts started coming and I motioned for the waiter to take them away. She said to the waiter, 'If you try to touch one of these, I will stab you in the hand with my fork' and proceeded to eat everything on the plate.

"It was at that moment that I knew that *she* knew how ill she was. So why *not* eat every dessert? There was nothing to say except to continue as if nothing was wrong. I received, as usual, one of her thank-you notes: 'Everything is fine and we'll soon be having more future lunches together.'" But it was not to be. Jacqueline Onassis died shortly thereafter, on May 19, a month and a half before her sixty-fifth birthday.

Some regulars at Le Cirque were neither famous nor even vaguely recognizable. Ethel and Irving Schneider dined at Le Cirque almost every night—at the same table next to where Jackie and Loring would have lunch: table 12B, only steps from the front door. While it was the best spot for people-watching, it was the worst in terms of weather. Certain winter evenings could be so bracingly cold and windy that Mrs. Schneider would wear a heavy scarf while Mr. Schneider kept his coat on. Now that's loyalty.

One of Sirio's most unlikely customers was the rock musician and composer Frank Zappa. He used to stay at the Mayfair but decidedly didn't look like a Le Cirque regular. "We didn't allow him in because he wasn't dressed properly," remembers Sirio. "But we let his wife in with their kids. She asked if she could take a crème brûlée to her husband, who was waiting in the lobby. When I went to deliver it, Zappa said to me, 'You're the guy who wouldn't let me in.' I had no idea who he was."

Zappa came back for dinner—this time elegantly dressed. "I never wear a suit," said Zappa to Sirio, "so if the food isn't good, you pay for the suit." Sirio and Zappa became friends. "When he was dying I sent our pastry chef to Los Angeles to make him a crème brûlée before he died." Perhaps that was Sirio's version of last rites.

Above: With Frank Zappa, 1990.

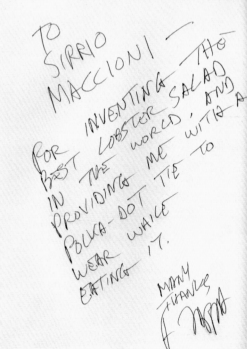

TO SIRIO MACCIONI —
FOR INVENTING THE BEST LOBSTER SALAD IN THE WORLD. AND PROVIDING ME WITH A POLKA-DOT TIE TO WEAR WHILE EATING IT.
MANY THANKS
F. ZAPPA

A SWEEPING PORTRAIT

The most indelible image of Le Cirque on East 65th Street is a six-by-ten-foot mural crafted over a period of two years by the artist Robert Cenedella. He was an unlikely candidate for the commission, his specialty being downtown bars, Midtown subway stations, and proletariat scenes. Not your typical Le Cirque clientele. But it was precisely the clientele that Cenedella was asked to portray in his composition of more than one hundred sardine-packed patrons in the legendary space.

So how did a fellow so at home in Bohemia find himself spending so much time in the tony East 60s staring at the likes of Henry Kissinger, Barbara Walters, and Donald Trump? One of his students happened to be married to the restaurant critic Bryan Miller. He introduced Cenedella to Sirio, who permitted the artist to do his preliminary drawings over lunches at Le Cirque. "I sketched about fifty meals there, always at the same corner table. . . . The staff would point out who was who, since I really didn't know."

Not everybody was happy with the results. Marvin Shanken, the publisher and founder of *Wine Spectator* and *Cigar Aficionado*, didn't like the way his hair looked and also wanted his wife seated next to him. The mural was removed to Cenedella's studio and fixed. Liz Smith couldn't fathom why in the world she was placed at the same table with Richard Nixon, but was otherwise flattered by the recognition.

In 1997, *New York* magazine ran a major piece on Le Cirque 2000 by Peter Kaminsky but failed to run a sidebar about the mural. The artist's retribution came when Philip Roth happened to be visiting Cenedella's Tribeca studio while he was redoing the mural. "Here was Philip Roth sitting in my studio. I told Roth, 'You're a better writer than this guy. . . . Wouldn't it be fantastic to put you in his place?' So I did a sketch of him on the spot and put him right over Kaminsky. I didn't say anything to anybody." It was only when Kaminsky went to Le Cirque, his family in tow, and looked for himself in the painting that he realized he wasn't in it after all.

Entitled *The First Generation*, the mural is more than a work of art, it is emblematic of an era. It was supposed to hang on the wall of the East 65th Street room it depicts, but by the time Cenedella completed it Le Cirque was on its way to new digs in the Palace Hotel. It now graces the wall of the staircase leading to the second-floor private room at Le Cirque on Beacon Court.

Le Cirque—The First Generation by Robert Cenedella, 1998. Oil on canvas, 72 x 110 inches (183 x 280 cm).

Following pages: Guestbook inscriptions.

Of the 145 people portrayed in Robert Cenedella's painting *The First Generation* (opposite and pages 16–17), nearly all were regular customers of Le Cirque at 58 East 65th Street. A few were employees— servers and kitchen staff—but most were notable people one would routinely spot at lunch or dinner. Not all are recognizable but those who are include the following individuals (see how many you can find):

Sirio Maccioni (2)
Imelda Marcos (4)
Tom Wolfe (7)
Daniel Boulud (16)
Kirk Douglas (17)
Nancy Reagan (25)
Sylvester Stallone (28)
Aristotle Onassis (29)
Mario Cuomo (34)
Dustin Hoffman (39)
Joan Collins (43)
I.M. Pei (47)
Nicole Miller (48)
Pierre Franey (54)
Bryan Miller (55)
Morley Safer (56)
Craig Claiborne (57)
Julia Child (58)
Tina Brown (61)
Bill Blass (62)
Yves Montand (63)
Margaux Hemingway (64)
King Juan Carlos of Spain (66)

Cindy Adams (68)
Woody Allen (69)
Warner LeRoy (70)
Omar Sharif (71)
Malcolm Forbes (72)
Tony Randall (78)
Ivana Trump (79)
Henry Kissinger (80)
Marvin Shanken (82)
Sophia Loren (83)
Yasmin Aga Khan (88)
Sidney Poitier (95)
Marcello Mastroianni (96)
Jacqueline Kennedy Onassis (97)
Andre Soltner (98)
Monica Vitti (99)
Bill Cunningham (100)
Anthony Quinn (101)
Adam Tihany (102)
Marco Maccioni (103)
Zubin Mehta (104)
Mario Maccioni (105)
Mauro Maccioni (110)

Roger Vergé (113a)
Fernando Botero (114)
Barbara Walters (115)
Ed Koch (116)
William Zeckendorf, Jr. (117)
Egidiana Maccioni (118)
Joan Rivers (119)
Paul Bocuse (124)
Sottha Khunn (125)
Frank Zappa (128)
Philip Roth (129)
Elle MacPherson (130)
Diana Ross (131)
Dr. Bernard Kruger (132)
Georgette Mosbacher (134)
Liz Smith (135)
Robin Leach (136)
Bill Cosby (137)
Brooke Astor (139)
Jacques Torres (140)
Richard Nixon (142)

Thank you so much for the wonderful time and the greatest food. I'll be back
Arnold Schwarzenegger

What a wonderful way to spend my Birthday!! Merci Merci!
Love, *Brooke Shields* XX 5/31/91

Merci —
Elie Wiesel

Per Sirio
Gian Carlo Menotti 1987

Are too very compliments
Jean-Paul Belmondo

Sirio Maccioni, You made this a very special evening for the Bridges family. When your name comes up, who say you're #1 in N.Y.C. Fond regards *Lloyd Bridges*

Can't wait til next time! Thanks so much! Peace *Beau Bridges*

Thanks for the lovely meal. Best wishes, *Jeff Bridges*

Connors vs Nastase 0-6: 0-6, 1-6 Ha Ha

A Most Enjoyable Evening. See you soon! *Jimmy Connors*
Amicalement *Nastase*

September 5th 1989!

A Le Cirque, Merci... Magnifique! sublime... sorry, ran out of french, it was really great. thank you, mille grazie, who says the way to a woman's heart isn't through her stomach

anniversario presto. Auguri d'buon cuore e buon festa *Nicola* N.Y. Aprile 1986 — "Ginger e Fred".
Rietta Matina

Auguri!
To Bill Wilder. I would always, Sirio, keep telling you... BILLY a splendid dinner. *Sean Connery* and you can work for me anytime! 11/16/88

Bill, anyway. Sirio tender it sorry about Tony Let's incredible! Sirio, let's start again fresh next time *Bill Murray*

Happy New Year 1998!!!

A Wonderful New Year and Birthday Party 1/1/98
Frank Langella

A SIRIO Molto Buono. magnifico Sincera mente *Burt Lancaster*

TO ALL AT LE CIRQUE IN MEMORY OF APOLLO ONE CHALLENGER and COLUMBIA MANY THANKS FOR YOUR SERVICE *Buzz Aldrin*

Best regards to Sirio — enjoyed our dinner very much — even better than your reputation *John Glenn* 2-24-99

I couldn't believe how good this was when! la-la
Oprah Winfrey Dec 10, 198?

Nice Souffle! Love Bill Joel

mes compliments aux chefs at Sirio! merci, Charlie Buckley

Sunday, May 4, 1997

Boutros Ghali

With great pleasure Milos Forman Dec. 97.

What a wonderful evening

Many thanks Sharon Stone Oct '92

Cirque fabulous spot!

Quelle joie! Au plaisir de revenir

Beautiful! Pavarotti

your restaurant is always fabulous. Cy Coleman

Un brindisi per un buon anno nuovo per Sirio e Le Cirque! Con tanti complimenti! - E grazie! 1/13/82.

L'amitié se reflète de partout dans ce merveilleux "Cirque." Sirio vous savez communiquer ce qui est si difficile à donner l'amour du beau et la sincérité - je n'ai qu'un désir revenir - 1-13-82 Roger Vergé

Mc. Paul McCartney Paul McCartney Nice food eh?

L'adresse de New York qui veut signifier la Fête = c'est Sirio. Le Cirque c'est la fête de l'Assiette - La Fête de l'ambiance unique à N.Y. BRAVO & AMITIÉS - 21 Septembre 1982

TO ALL AT LE CIRQUE: THE MOST FLAWLESS MEAL OF MY 29 YEARS... THRILLING AND NOT SOON FORGOTTEN. MY BEST TO ALL. love, Sarah Jessica Park

Muito obrigado Edson = Pelé. 1.000 goooool

Many Thanks For So many wonderful hours spent at your Table With You and your Family.

Thank You — All my thanks — What a birthday gift. Thank You

Quagiri! '77

It was good V. good 007?!!! Peace

The Smother Brothers Dick Smothers Tom Smothers Yo Yo Man

To Sirio It is always nice to be surprised to heavenly food please stay way you are

A MANSION IN MIDTOWN

For a restless soul like Sirio Maccioni, staying in one place for too long would never be satisfying. After twenty-two years, he knew the time had come to leave East 65th Street. The room— once so cozy—felt claustrophobic, the décor dated. The owners of the Mayfair wouldn't give him more space, the restaurant's contract would soon be up, and the unions were causing a stir. Daniel Boulud, whose cooking earned Le Cirque four stars, had gone off on his own. Moreover, the mood in New York was shifting, which Sirio sensed strongly. The ladies who lunched now had careers or appointments at the gym. They weren't willing to spare two hours between 12:30 and 2:30, time better spent eating at their desks or having a quick bite somewhere far simpler. The restaurant was still packed for dinner, but forcing in two or three sittings a night to make up for the decline in lunch traffic made customers feel rushed and put too much pressure on the staff, especially the kitchen.

Though the prospect of losing their "local" did not come as good news to Le Cirque's regulars, many of whom lived on the Upper East Side, Sirio had made up his mind. Not that he did so blithely; he admitted to being scared, but moved forward undaunted. Several locations were considered and rejected. Finally and with an offer he couldn't refuse, Sirio settled on the New York Palace Hotel (formerly the Helmsley Palace), owned by the sultan of Brunei, smack

Opposite: The Maccionis in the foyer of Le Cirque 2000 in the Palace Hotel, April 1997 (photo: Andrew Bordwin). *Above*: Art by Tim Flynn.

in Midtown on Madison Avenue between 50th and 51st Streets. The restaurant would not be in the hotel itself (an undistinguished pile) but in the adjacent and landmarked Villard Houses, which belonged to the hotel. And to Sirio, a Catholic by birth, it didn't hurt that the land was owned by the Archdiocese of New York and across the street from St. Patrick's Cathedral. In a sense, Sirio felt that God was his new landlord.

Based on the Palazzo Farnese in Rome, the six town houses were designed by McKim, Mead & White, for Henry Villard, a Bavarian-born railroad baron. The Villard Houses were completed in 1884 and became a symbol of the Gilded Age with their vaulted ceilings, Corinthian columns, frescoed walls, crystal chandeliers, onyx fireplaces, and mosaic tiles. As a landmark it was untouchable—literally.

Sirio hired Adam Tihany, one of America's best restaurant designers, to prepare the space. Tihany had done some necessary updating on East 65th Street (a complete overhaul would have traumatized the customers). But what could be more traumatizing than a relocation? It was a huge risk, to say the least. The new name would be Le Cirque 2000, which made more than a few traditionalists bristle. Tihany, however, saw the potential and embraced it: "Of all my projects with Sirio, Le Cirque 2000 was the most fun because it was a real breakthrough. I envisioned it as an international traveling circus. It was a real challenge because the space was a registered landmark, which means you couldn't even put a screw in the wall. Also, the public has a right to walk through the space at any time.

"I said, 'Sirio, to tell you the truth I wonder why you want to come here.'" But Tihany offered two

Adam and Marnie Tihany dine with Sirio, c. 1997 (photo: Michael Donnelly).

"Italians will design something beautifully, put in good lighting, and then place a Ferrari in the middle to create tension."

A PERFECT MATCH

Adam Tihany is one of America's foremost restaurant and hotel designers. His successes include Jean-Georges in the Trump International Hotel in New York, the Mandarin Oriental Hotel in Las Vegas, Gundel restaurant in Budapest, the Bouchon Bakery for Thomas Keller in Los Angeles . . . the list goes on and on. But the one individual he's designed more projects for than any other is Sirio Maccioni. They met in the early 1980s, and it was a moment Tihany will never forget: "I was on my way to becoming a restaurant designer and was connected with a group of Italian ex-pats who were regulars at Le Cirque. My ex-wife and I were invited to Le Cirque by an Italian count. For us, it was a big outing. The only dish I knew was Spaghetti Primavera, which wasn't on the menu, and Crème Brûlée. We ordered the Primavera at tableside. It was beautiful. My wife looked at the pasta and said, 'I didn't know there were anchovies it.'" There weren't.

"On top of the Primavera was a little cockroach. We called Sirio over. He looked at it and waved to the waiter to 'take it away and make a new one.' It didn't faze him a bit. He shrugged his shoulders and said, as if in explanation, 'New York!' He was so cool." So began a long business relationship and enduring friendship.

To date, Tihany has done seven projects with Sirio, including some refinements of the original. What is he like to work for? "He doesn't interfere at all," insists Tihany. "If he likes the idea—and it only takes a minute for him to decide—he'll say, 'Go with it.' Maybe it's because he knows I will always guard his interests . . . that whatever I do for him is like making a custom suit; it is something I will never do for anyone else.

"I love Sirio. I am like his adopted son. He is not just a good man, he is *the* man. He's my mentor. I wouldn't be who I am without Sirio."

---

options: He could simply restore the place—put in good lighting, install period furniture—and create a somewhat boring and unimaginative space. Or he could do it the Italian way. "Italians will design something beautifully, put in good lighting, and then place a Ferrari in the middle to create tension." Needless to say, Sirio chose the latter option. "We had six months to do this. Everything had to be built outside of the premises. The bar had to be removable. Drapery was put up with tension rods. Every piece of furniture was made in Italy. When I explained all of this to Sirio, he said: 'And we have to do one other thing—buy two tickets to get out of town, because we will be ruined.'"

Given the limitations of renovation, there were doubters. "One day," Tihany recalls, "a good-looking woman walked into the middle of construction. After I showed her around, she said, 'You SOB, you actually pulled it off.' It was Jennifer Raab, who was then head of the Landmarks Preservation Commission."

OVER THE BIG TOP

Le Cirque 2000 opened in May 1997. Those hoping for a larger, more lavish reincarnation of East 65th Street would be surprised. Make that shocked. The restaurant that used to be described as "elegant" and "demure" was now deemed "extravagant" and "flashy." An entirely new circus had come to town, the likes of which even jaded New Yorkers weren't prepared for.

To Tihany, it was a natural evolution of the brand. In 1996, a year before Le Cirque 2000 opened, he worked on Sirio's Osteria del Circo, a trattoria specializing in homespun Italian cooking, much of it originating in Egi's kitchen. It was also to be a launch pad for the Maccioni boys, a place for all three to build experience in the business. Tihany saw it as his chance to create his version of a circus. In his book *Tihany Design*, he explains what he had in mind: "I wanted the restaurant to reflect the lives of the

Following pages: Adam Tihany design drawings and the finished rooms of Le Cirque 2000.

GRAND HALL

Previous pages: The dining rooms of Le Cirque 2000 (photos: Michael Donnelly). *Above:* A dessert menu. *Opposite, from top:* The staff of Le Cirque 2000; with real-estate mogul Steven Roth.

younger generation—stylish, sexy, hip, with a bit of familiar daring, yet sophisticated and contemporary Italian.

"Rather than allow this undertaking to become another theme restaurant with Barnum & Bailey memorabilia, I wanted the design to suggest magical moments of a circus through dreamlike details": a ceiling that resembles a big-top, steel sculptures in motion floating through the air, and other antic elements. The Felliniesque effect is that of watching circus acts. (He would do something similar for Circo in Las Vegas.)

With Le Cirque 2000, Tihany created yet another circus, this one bordering on the outrageous. If the Maccioni-Tihany association wanted to cause a sensation, it succeeded. This time the reviews were quite different from the ones about East 65th Street. Gael Greene's for *New York* called Le Cirque 2000 "a heat-seeking missile launched from Sirio Maccioni's fevered brow."

Moira Hodgson, giving it three stars in the *New York Observer*, wondered what Edith Wharton and Henry James would have made of "the aluminum poles, Venetian glass clowns and strongmen, red-and-white striped columns of lighting, a roller coaster over the bar and a clock set to time in Montecatini." Another reviewer wrote: "It's like animation in a frame fashioned for Old Masters: Pop Art hits the Palazzo." Startling, to be sure. And an adjustment for both customers and critics. Le Cirque 2000's "new look" (not unlike Dior's in the early 1950s) took some getting used to. A year into its run, William Grimes gave it three stars in the *Times*, saying this: "Adam Tihany's circus-theme décor, much ridiculed when the new Le Cirque opened in the spring of 1997, suddenly makes perfect sense, right down to the happy clown buttons on the velvet-clad chairs." Those chairs, incidentally, had to be cut down after customers complained that the backs were too high, and blocked their view of other guests. Why go to Le Cirque if you couldn't see and be seen?

Those chairs, incidentally, had to be cut down after customers complained that the backs were too high, and blocked their view of other guests.

As for the food and to Sirio's credit, he went in the opposite direction from the décor, finally convincing Sottha Khunn, the reserved, barely English-speaking Cambodian, to assume the role of executive chef. Sottha had worked with Daniel Boulud at the Plaza Athénée. When Boulud moved to Le Cirque, he took Sottha with him. But when Boulud left, Sottha remained. Sirio had wanted Sottha to take the top job but he politely declined, content to stay on as sous chef, so Sirio hired Sylvain Portay, who was there from 1992 to 1996. By the time Portay left, Sottha was ready for the next step. Sottha's cooking was refined and sophisticated, with subtle Asian touches—a welcome counterbalance to the décor. If there were any high jinks in the kitchen, it came courtesy of Jacques Torres's elaborate desserts. Together, Sottha and Jacques became the culinary core of Le Cirque and its most tenured team. Even Ruth Reichl became a convert, calling Sottha's cooking "subtle but brilliant" and anointing Le Cirque with four stars in her 1997 *New York Times* review. Vindication at last.

The restaurant drew a bigger, broader crowd than at East 65th Street, as was intended. Instead of one dining room, there were two. That raised the issue of where to put the chosen ones. Sirio cannily figured it out: Place the VIPs in the red and yellow former dining room of the mansion and let the others spill over to the space facing Madison Avenue—the original drawing room, which was prettier and more sedate. The titans of business returned (some on their second or third wives), as did the celebrities, statesmen, and politicians, the bold-faced names in Liz Smith's and Cindy Adams's columns and on Page Six of the *New York Post*—not all of them, of course, but enough.

At the original Le Cirque, there was only one space—the Orangerie—that could be used for private parties. At Le Cirque 2000, there were three on the second floor. The kitchen was enormous and could serve five to seven hundred people a day. Suddenly, Le Cirque had become a huge operation with a staggering number of employees (170).

Opposite: Liza Minnelli, Liz Smith, and Bette Midler at Smith's birthday bash on February 2, 2003 (photo: Mary Hilliard). *Clockwise from above left:* Mary and Mike Wallace; Liz Smith and Donald Trump; with Cardinal Edward Egan (photo: Jerry Ruotolo); Cindy Adams takes reservations.

Le Cirque 2000

The Bar / HILARY KNIGHT
1997

Opposite: Drawing by Hilary Knight. *Clockwise from top left:* With Isabella Rossellini; with Diana Ross and chocolate sculpture created for her by pastry chef Jacques Torres; with Robert De Niro on his sixtieth birthday; Rod Stewart (photo: Arnaldo Magnani); Bobby Short (photo: Jerry Ruotolo).

I'm here again and will be back - I promise! Best wishes always

Hillary Rodham Clinton
12/01/01

ROBERT KENN
5/11/2000

Robert F Kennedy Jr

Business, while still comparatively good, was down in revenues. Le Cirque was expanding as a brand. Las Vegas hotelier Steve Wynn convinced Sirio to open Le Cirque and, next door, Osteria del Circo within the casino of his luxurious Bellagio Hotel. Sirio's son Mario moved there with his wife and daughter to run both. There was still cause for celebration at Le Cirque 2000. It came in the form of Sirio's eponymous memoir, written with Peter Elliot. In June 2004, a huge party for A-listers was held to commemorate its publication. Reviews, largely positive ones, followed. Sirio's place in the firmament as a legendary restaurateur was sealed.

Now Sirio had to make room for his sons. With Mario in Las Vegas, both Marco and Mauro were now integral parts of the team and involved in future expansion plans. Having their say wouldn't be easy with a father so intent on controlling every aspect of the operation. To call it an evolutionary process would be un understatement. While all three young men loved and respected Sirio, they also were aware that the future of Le Cirque would someday be in their hands, so they'd better swim, not sink.

Le Cirque 2000 lasted only seven years at the Palace Hotel. Sirio wanted to return to the old neighborhood, not be smack in the middle of Midtown. Finding another location for Le Cirque would not be easy. There wasn't much available in the East 60s, so other areas had to be considered. With every possibility, Sirio would ask a trusted customer, "What do you think? Should I or shouldn't I?" The story goes that when faced with two choices—one on Central Park South and another on East 58th Street, in the new One Beacon Court, aka the Bloomberg Building, Sirio turned to Henry Kissinger. It was akin to flipping a coin, except that the gentleman holding the coin was someone Sirio had tremendous faith in. "Fifty-eighth" was Dr. Kissinger's reply.

Opposite, clockwise from top left: With President Bill Clinton, Mario Maccioni, and First Lady Hillary Rodham Clinton; with President Gerald Ford and First Lady Betty Ford; with Robert F. Kennedy, Jr. (photo: Arnaldo Magnani); with Mayor Rudy Giuliani (photo: Patrick McMullan) *Right:* The Cosbys were the first people to dine at the chef's table, May 1997. Bill stepped into the kitchen and helped out with the dishes afterward.

Le Cirque has always been a gathering spot for luminaries from the food world.

This page, clockwise from top left: Drew Nieporent, Marisa May, and Michael McCarty; Michael Romano and Danny Meyer; with Barbara Fairchild; with Jacques Pépin, Paul Prudhomme, Julia Child, and Fred Plotkin; with Gael Greene (photo: Patrick McMullan); Mauro Maccioni and Marcus Samuelsson.

Opposite, clockwise from top left: Alice Waters and Jacques Pépin; with Mimi Sheraton; with Ruth Reichl; with Martha Stewart (photo: Gregory Pace); with Patricia Wells and Julia Child; with Alison Becker. (All photos on these pages by Jerry Ruotolo unless otherwise noted.)

THE THIRD ACT

Le Cirque's next move would be disconcerting for many regulars who believed *their* restaurant belonged in an exclusive neighborhood. The relocation from East 65th to Madison Avenue as Le Cirque 2000 was hard enough on them, but now Le Cirque was going to East 58th between Lexington and Third Avenues, across from Bloomingdale's in what is called One Beacon Court, also known as the Bloomberg Tower.

Designed by Cesar Pelli and owned by real-estate magnate Steve Roth, the 1.4-million-square-foot, fifty-four-story glass structure's main tenant is the headquarters of Bloomberg, L.P., the financial news service launched by Michael Bloomberg, who would later become New York's billionaire mayor. But the tower also contains luxury condominiums, retail stores, and, some would say improbably, Le Cirque. Housed in an extension of Bloomberg Tower and located across from it and separated by a courtyard (Beacon Court), the restaurant's space is sixteen thousand square feet with a soaring rotunda and twenty-seven-foot glass windows. Adam Tihany was again Sirio's choice as designer (with the assistance of architect Costas Kondylis). Unlike East 65th Street, which was ready when Sirio and his staff moved in, and the Villard Houses, whose landmarked interiors could not be touched by a hammer, this space was a blank slate. And for the first time, Le Cirque would not be linked to a hotel.

Opposite: Sirio unveils his third location at One Beacon Court on opening night, May 18, 2006 (photo: Patrick McMullan).
Above left: Art by Tim Flynn.

87

Of the relocation, Tihany says, "Sirio, being Sirio, needs to move from time to time. It keeps him relevant. He is a restless, creative genius who strives for perfection all the time. He knows that this city needs constant jolts. He knew he had to move before his clients knew it."

In this case, however, the leap Sirio took was a bigger one—to entirely new construction in a busy commercial neighborhood, at a time when eating-out habits had changed radically: The center of the New York dining scene had moved south, and a general sense of informality had taken over. Sirio and his fellow tenants were pinning their hopes on a beautiful skyscraper injecting some vitality and luring new business to the area. Aside from Bloomingdale's, there were middle-brow chain stores on Lexington and the D&D Building, with its showrooms for interior designers, on Third Avenue.

Taking his circus motif to the next step, Tihany says of the Beacon Court incarnation, "The new Le Cirque is the culmination of all the previous interpretations, and an American circus at that." Artist Tim Flynn created a fourteen-foot-high wire sculpture, a take on Alexander Calder's *Circus* in the Whitney Museum, and forty-six two-dimensional wire drawings with circus themes displayed along the walls of the formal dining room. To emphasize Le Cirque's legacy, Tihany had the ingenious idea to turn the family's extensive collection of portraits and paparazzi shots—more than one hundred—into wallpaper. One clever detail followed another. To give some intimacy to the double-height ceiling, Tihany fashioned what looks like either a bronze big-top or a gigantic lampshade and brought in a lighting expert. A three-story cylindrical wine tower near the bar holds 2,250 bottles. Still, Tihany concedes, "The location is a problem, because people don't hang out in Midtown."

Many of the most desirable places for dining were downtown—in SoHo, Tribeca, the Village, Chelsea, and the Meatpacking District. Midtown and even the Upper East Side were perceived as irrelevant when it came to eating out (living, too). Dress codes were diminishing. Downtown, they didn't exist at all. Hipsters had replaced café society. New York, while it slowly recovered economically from 9/11, was still affected emotionally. The prospect of ordering expensive delicacies like foie gras and caviar and rare bottles of wine seemed politically incorrect.

A STAR RETURNS

Sottha left Le Cirque in 2001 and was succeeded by Pierre Schaedelin, his former sous chef. Pierre took Le Cirque through the transition to its new location. A mere month after the new Le Cirque opened, Frank Bruni, the *Times* critic, gave his two-star assessment: The foie gras was "superb," while the risotto was "sorry." He described the Dover sole meunière as "ethereal," the lobster salad as "drab." It wasn't an entirely negative review, but Sirio was crushed. Without identifying Bruni, *Departures* magazine fired back: "a perfectly ordinary critic, who will remain nameless despite his extraordinary power, was playing way over his head when he went after the new Le Cirque and its owner, Sirio Maccioni." The magazine's bottom line was that "Le Cirque gives us hope that opulence and graciousness, haute cooking, and European savoir faire have not entirely disappeared from these mean streets."

Still, it became obvious that a new chef might shake things up. Schaedelin politely left in 2006 (he now works as a private chef for Martha Stewart). Christophe Bellanca, who'd been at L'Orangerie in L.A. until it closed that same year, was brought in as executive chef. All around, eyes, ears, and taste buds perked up. Bellanca's food was delicious, inventive, and garnering better reviews than Le Cirque had received since Sottha Khunn's cooking at the Palace Hotel. His hiring coincided with the making of a documentary about the Maccionis called *A Table in Heaven*. (The title came from a conversation Sirio had with Pope John Paul II on the occasion of his visit to New York in 1995. Le Cirque catered a dinner for him at the residence of the Holy See. Afterward, Sirio asked the pontiff to reserve a table in heaven for him.)

The documentarian Andrew Rossi followed the family around for months, and his film was previewed in Aspen and at Sundance, then aired on HBO in June 2007. If *A Table in Heaven* portrayed the Maccionis as close knit, it also showed them as competitive and at times combative. Sirio versus

Opposite: Tihany's touches at One Beacon Court.

his sons, with Mamma Egi as the mediator—it was positively Shakespearean. The movie was mainly about Beacon Court, taking the viewer behind the scenes during construction and into many of the meetings (and arguments) that ensued. Bellanca, the new kid in the kitchen, was in place the night Frank Bruni returned for his second review. To everyone's relief, it was three stars and glowing, its headline "In Defense of Decadence." Bruni praised Bellanca for providing "just the injection of energy and discipline that Le Cirque needed." Best of all, he bowed deeply to Sirio: "What he's selling isn't so much one evening of pleasure as a whole history, a whole legend, of privilege and pampering." Justice, finally.

CHANGING TIMES, CHANGING TASTES

Bruni's review and others like it refueled business, as did the novelty of the new space and a new chef. Le Cirque was packing them in once again. Both Marco and Mauro were in evidence on the floor, the staff was reinvigorated (helped by the hiring of some younger servers). Even the patrons, while by no means the downtown crowd, added spirit to the atmosphere. The main dining room, by the way, still requires jackets, at Sirio's insistence, but the bar area—called the Café—is far more casual and with a pared-down, less expensive menu, including sliders and French fries. It's catching on with a younger crowd who don't want to be hemmed in by a dress code. Some patrons not only don't mind the dress code, they like it. "So maybe it's a throwback," says Adam Tihany, "but in a city of eight million people, it is there for those who actually want an adult experience when dining out."

Film producer Martin Bregman and his wife, Cornelia, who dine at Le Cirque at least twice a week, echo Tihany's sentiment. For the Bregmans, Le Cirque is a comfort zone where they are welcomed like old friends by a polite and cordial staff. "We're fond of Sirio, the staff is nice to us, and the food is good," says Cornelia. "We've been going since it opened on East 65th Street. I remember walking in one day wearing the same outfit as Mrs. Reagan—an Oscar de la Renta brown and white checked dress with a sable collar. I left so as not to embarrass her."

Every May, Cornelia gives a birthday party for her husband. "We've been doing this at Le Cirque for years. And when Marty had his wrap parties for movies like *Serpico* with Al Pacino and *The Bone Collector* with Denzel Washington and Angelina Jolie (in her first major role), we chose Le Cirque because we knew we wouldn't have to worry about a thing, that it would all flow smoothly."

If only the U.S. economy could have flowed as smoothly as a party at Le Cirque. Things were going along pretty well at the new location and for many major concerns in New York until September 2008, when "fall" took on a whole new meaning. Beginning with the collapse of Bear Stearns and its sale to JPMorgan Chase, investment banks, brokerage houses, and securities trading firms merged or failed. The global stock markets were in a tailspin.

To Sirio, who had witnessed economic cycles all too many times in his career, this particular situation was bleaker than usual. By the recession's onset, the Maccioni enterprise encompassed the two restaurants in New York and two in Las Vegas at the Bellagio Hotel—all of them costly to run and maintain. With some restructuring and other adjustments, the company geared up to see the recession through. By the end of 2011, Le Cirque's circumstances had improved. A deal was signed with the Holland America cruise ship line to have special Le Cirque dinners served on its ships. A new Le Cirque in the Leela Palace Hotel in, of all places, New Delhi, opened, as did another restaurant at the Aria Resort & Casino in Las Vegas. The biggest news was that there would be a third Maccioni restaurant in Manhattan. Like

Tables are set with fresh linen several times a day at the restaurant.

"Le Cirque gives us hope that opulence and graciousness, haute cooking, and European savoir faire have not entirely disappeared from these mean streets."

> *"What he's selling isn't so much one evening of pleasure as a whole history, a whole legend, of privilege and pampering."*

the addition in Las Vegas, this one is named after the family's head honcho: Sirio Ristorante.

Even though the Le Cirque brand expands, Sirio and his sons realize how critical it is to keep their core customers happy and tucked in. Whitney Radio's William O'Shaughnessy is surely one of them. He has been more than a regular at Le Cirque; he is practically a fixture. At Beacon Court, he occupies the same table—to the immediate right of the entrance—whenever he dines (and it is often), so he can watch who comes and goes. Almost from the beginning, he faithfully followed Sirio from East 65th to Madison Avenue and to its present location. An unapologetic Le Cirque booster, he has little patience for what he deems unfair criticism. (He once wrote Ruth Reichl a polite but pointed "how-could-you" letter after her dual review of Le Cirque in 1993.) O'Shaughnessy has even less patience for places where the servers want to be your best friends: "At other restaurants, you encounter three Debbies, two Jennifers, one Chad, a Lance, a Tiffany, and 'Hi Guys.' At Le Cirque you are greeted by the graceful, attractive proprietor and his savvy deputies.

"There are many other highly successful eateries where all is programmed and computerized," he laments. "Some entrepreneurial business types own ten or more venues. These humorless souls talk of 'synergy' and 'return on investment.' Le Cirque, however, is all about *people* enjoying themselves, having fun . . . away from the pressures of a world spinning out of control. To others, the whole thing is a business. To Sirio, it is a profession. And he is the most sensitive, generous man in the field where glamour and style still carry the day."

Mireille Guiliano, best-selling author and former president and CEO of LVMH's Clicquot, Inc., sipped

many a flute of her favorite Champagne at Le Cirque. She puts it all in perspective: "Each Le Cirque was a sign of its time, and Beacon Court is right for the first decade of the twenty-first century. The previous two, with all their glories, would no longer work today. The clientele has changed, the mood has changed, the world has changed, and the present Le Cirque takes note of it. Sirio knows how to adapt. What remains in the third edition of Le Cirque is very fine food and service with a shorter, more focused menu and wine list, which won't ever go out of style. Its design is more contemporary and the bar larger and more relaxed. And my husband and I love the private room upstairs for its cheerfulness, airiness, and, yes, windows. It

makes a huge difference to entertain in such a natural convivial place."

Still, there are those who wish for the old days, when Le Cirque was in its heyday in a crammed space in that L-shaped room, its walls festooned with cavorting monkeys. But even Sirio will say that to return there now would be not only a disappointment but a mistake, that the interior would look shabby and feel out of date by comparison to the Le Cirque of today in its spacious, well-lighted new home. The New York of then is not the New York of now. It was a totally different time and a very different place. As Cornelia Bregman aptly remarked, "You can go forward, honey, but you can't go back."

Opposite: A coveted banquette in the main dining room.
Above: Sirio receives an approving kiss from the legendary model Carmen Dell'Orefice (photo: Tim Petersen).

RISING SONS

You might think that the wife of Sirio Maccioni would want her sons to follow in their father's footsteps. You'd be wrong. Egi Maccioni hoped her sons would be anything but restaurateurs. "I didn't like the idea of them going into the business," she says wistfully. "I wanted them to be doctors, lawyers, architects. I would see people on a Friday night on their way home, looking forward to the weekend, able to share time with their families." Sirio felt the same way but now admits to being proud that they chose what has to be one of the most consuming of professions. If you want a life, don't go into restaurants. But restaurants were what the Maccioni boys knew best, and each figured out what part of the business most suited them. Mario, the eldest, became the strategist and planner. Marco, the middle son, is most like his father in how he approaches the business—head on and with determination. Mauro, the youngest, is the family's entrepreneur, always pushing the envelope. He's also the one with the palate and the keenest interest in food.

Born in 1965, Mario Maccioni was affected the most—certainly the longest—by his father's absences. He didn't envision himself in the industry and,

"Each Le Cirque was a sign of its time."

according to his brother Marco, would do everything the opposite on purpose. He ended up going to Cornell, did various stints at Michelin-starred restaurants abroad, and finally realized that being the eldest son had its advantages. One was being sent to Las Vegas to run the two (now three) Maccioni restaurants there. In so doing, he gained his independence in a way that would not have been possible had he remained in New York. "My father and I are polar opposites. I tend to let people do what they've been hired to do and look at the big picture. I'm not a micromanager."

Marco Maccioni, two years younger than his brother Mario, caught on in ways that a clever middle child often does. Marco too graduated from Cornell. His major responsibilities at Le Cirque are operations and overseeing the wines. "I was always the one who worked closely with my dad. I took to the business right away," he says. "Consequently, I was thrown right in. I flirted with architecture—my main focus in school was art studies. I also flirted with teaching. But I knew I was destined for this business. It's what I feel most comfortable doing. Maybe I'm a waiter at heart."

Mauro is the youngest Maccioni. One of his favorite childhood memories was the result of a class assignment at Saint David's, a private elementary school for boys in New York. Each student was to find a product or experience he wasn't happy about and write a formal letter of complaint. "I decided to write about the trial dinner cooked by Daniel Boulud when he was at the Plaza Athénée." The success of the meal would determine if Sirio would offer Boulud the job as executive chef of Le Cirque. "It was Mother's Day," Mauro recollects. "When we arrived, we were given the pre-set menu. Already we were starting on a bad note. My father hates it when restaurants try to limit your choice. Without my parents knowing, I sent a complaint letter to Herve Houdré, the general manager at the time." Mauro received a letter in return: "Dear Mr. Maccioni, Please accept our apologies. We invite you back for dinner." Mauro's parents were not a little surprised. Sirio hired Daniel Boulud anyway.

Today, all three Maccioni sons thoroughly participate in the family business—for better or for worse, for richer or for poorer. They may have their squabbles, their fallouts, but they are blood brothers to the end and they know very well where their future lies: together.

HAIL SIRIO!

In a frame on a wall near the coat check at Beacon Court is a tribute to Sirio from Daniel Boulud. It is dated March 8, 2009, the night a fundraiser was held for Citymeals-on-Wheels at Daniel's eponymous restaurant on East 65th Street—site of the first Le Cirque. Contained in the frame are ten reasons why Sirio is unique:

1. Because he's not French.
2. Because he learned the restaurant business from the French.
3. Because he has John Wayne looks and Marcello Mastroianni style.
4. Because he's kissed the hand of every princess on the Upper East Side.
5. Because he has three incredible sons but still won't give up.
6. Because he invented Spaghetti Primavera—the only dish at Le Cirque the chefs were forbidden to touch.
7. Because he swears at you in Italian and kisses your ass in English.
8. Because his favorite food is Egi's gnocchi.
9. Because he is America's greatest restaurant hero.
10. Because without Sirio, I might have been a short-order cook.

BETTING ON LAS VEGAS

Building an empire was never Sirio's intention. Like so much that happened in his life, one thing pretty much led to another. His ambitions always evolved, motivated by circumstances not necessarily of his choosing. From Paris and Milan to Dubai and Tokyo, opportunities to open versions of Le Cirque are constantly popping up—some are seriously discussed, others are dismissed. At a luxury resort in the Dominican Republic, for instance, the Maccionis have opened Circo and The Beach Club by Le Cirque. Other such enterprises may follow. What has become increasingly clear to Sirio—who is, fundamentally, a family man—is that strategically expanding the company is the best way to ensure a comfortable future for his sons.

Osteria del Circo, which opened in New York in 1996, became a kind of lab where the Maccioni boys could learn how to run a restaurant. The next opportunity for family participation—and it was a big one—would be in Las Vegas, spearheaded by Steve Wynn. The prodigious entrepreneur, credited with reinventing Vegas, often dined at Le Cirque when he was in New York. When he began construction for the Bellagio, his first luxury hotel, he wanted to install a Le Cirque in the casino. This time it was more than he bargained for: Along with Le Cirque, he got Osteria del Circo. Sirio's eldest son, Mario, was dispensed to run the operations and has been there ever since.

Many of the top restaurants of Las Vegas are stunning and have unwritten permission to be over-the-top. Adam Tihany, once again Sirio's designer of choice, could have gone in that direction, but he opted for beauty instead. The challenge was to design not only for Sirio but for Wynn, a demanding hotelier. In his book *Tihany Design*, he writes: "Images of a 17th-century traveling circus came to mind. I used only the most luxurious colors and materials, from the alabaster bar to the backlit etched-glass walls and the glass mosaic tile floors." The ceiling's "multi-colored glowing raw silk billows across the restaurant to ensconce the guests in luxurious comfort."

The Las Vegas version of Le Cirque—which earned a Michelin star—is probably the most glamorous of all, certainly the most intimate and romantic. "It's where you would go," Tihany says with a twinkle in his eye, "to make a marriage

proposal." Or maybe only a proposition. This is Vegas, after all.

Osteria del Circo, on the other hand, "steers the imagination toward a circus of the future" with touches like steel sculptures by J.J. Veronis, a carpet designed with circus rings, harlequin patterns created from exotic woods, circus-ball light fixtures, and an internally lit bar. At Circo, the idea is fun, fun, fun.

What makes the operation different from the one in New York is that the restaurants fall under the Bellagio umbrella, which is in turn owned by MGM Resorts International (Steve Wynn sold the company and started another under his name). The Maccionis were content with running two popular restaurants in Las Vegas. It was MGM Resorts International that suggested a third, in City Center, their massive mixed-use complex that opened in 2009. The restaurant's concept is new, as is the name: Sirio Ristorante. Located on the second floor of the Aria Resort & Casino, Sirio Ristorante is the seventh restaurant Tihany has designed for the family. Rather than lean on the circus theme, he looked to 1950s Rome, specifically the period of *la dolce vita*, for inspiration. The menu is simpler than at either Le Cirque or Circo and so is the atmosphere.

PRINCES OF THE KITCHEN

Chefs today are like rock stars. They are their own brands, appear on television, write books, do demos, push products, lend an occasional hand to charity, and make tons of money. Their flocks of fans fawn over them at book signings and dream of eating at restaurants that brandish their names.

When the first Le Cirque opened in 1974, there was no such genuflection going on. Chefs were elevated cooks—valued, certainly, and essential to the experience of eating at the restaurant—but they weren't center stage. Not even close. Blame Sirio for the change. He was so proud of his chefs that he would trot them out to the dining room like a proud father. They'd have preferred to remain in the kitchen. But a little attention can encourage even the shyest chef. The more Sirio coaxed them out of the kitchen, the more at ease they felt in front of an audience. He was a confidence builder who knew exactly what he was doing.

As much regard as Sirio had for his chefs, he was and is aware that Le Cirque will be judged every bit as much by who is in the kitchen as by who's seated in the dining room. By the same token, any chef on the rise realizes that an experience at Le Cirque can be career enhancing. To have Le Cirque writ large on a resume is like a seal of approval and a guarantee that there's been a

Opposite: Sirio with his stellar staff, including chefs Jean Vergnes, far left; Daniel Boulud, center; and and Alain Sailhac, fourth from right (photo: Slim Aarons). *Above:* Art by Tim Flynn.

After his partner Jean Vergnes retired, Sirio knew he had to have a chef who would equal Vergnes in the kitchen. That meant finding a classically trained French chef. That chef came in the form of Alain Sailhac. He was in the kitchen at Le Cygne in New York—where he received three stars from the *Times*—when a friend suggested he meet Sirio. It didn't happen. "Maybe he thought I was asking too much money."

On holiday in Millau, his hometown in France, Sailhac heard that Sirio wanted to meet him in Montecatini. "So I drove there in my VW with my wife at the time. She said, 'See that guy walking toward us? He looks like John Wayne.' Sure enough, John Wayne was coming our way. It was, of course, Sirio. He walked like a cat . . . weaved a little." This was early July 1978. Sirio told Sailhac, "You start on July fifteen," and he did—and stayed until 1987.

"Sirio insisted that everything had to be the best, regardless of how much it cost. When you have a boss like this, you know he is a very great boss—and a generous one. We would fill up Le Cirque two, maybe three times a night with the most fantastic people.

"When the king of Spain was staying at the Mayfair, he might have ten at his table at Le Cirque for lunch. One day he asked, 'May I call you Alain?' Of course I said yes. He replied, 'Then you can call me Carlos.'"

Salvador Dali was another frequent customer. "When he entered the restaurant," says Sailhac, "he would raise his silver cane and give the benediction to everyone in the room. So one time I put a cross on a *feuilletté* of foie gras. He called me 'Master.' So I called him 'Master.'"

Sailhac was chef when Reagan was president. (Geoffrey Zakarian, Terrance Brennan, David Bouley, and Michael Lomonaco were all working for Sailhac at the time.) "We knew about the visit in advance. There were twenty members of his entourage who were to enter through the kitchen. We took the names of everyone for security reasons. Ronald Reagan was electrifying—everyone was tense because he was so powerful. It was *extraordinaire*.

"Le Cirque was unique—just the sheer humanity of the place. Recently Sirio and I were sitting next to each other in a restaurant. He looked at me fondly and said, 'Alain, you remember?' That's all he had to say. I felt very close to him in that moment."

rigorous training and exposure to the kind of customers who are extremely demanding and sometimes quirky. It's been said more than once that Le Cirque was an incubator for some of the great chefs in America. More than that, it was a proving ground.

Above: With French chefs Jacques Maximin, Paul Bocuse, and Alain Chapel. (photo: Jerry Ruotolo). *Opposite:* Daniel Boulud and Marco Maccioni fling edible missiles while Sirio uncharacteristically sits still, c. 1987 (photo: Tom Eckerle).

THE BOY WONDER

When Alain Sailhac left—he is now dean emeritus at the French Culinary Institute—his replacement was a young man raised on a farm near Lyons. Daniel Boulud would become Le Cirque's most celebrated chef. By the time he came to the States in 1980, Boulud had already worked under some of the top toques of France: Alain Senderens, Christian Delouvrier, Georges Blanc, Michel Guérard, and Roger Vergé. His first stop was in Washington, D.C., then he moved to New York, where he worked at the Polo Lounge of the Westbury Hotel on Madison Avenue. But it was during his tenure at the Plaza Athénée's Le Regence on East 64th Street that Sirio took notice.

In 1986, Le Cirque hosted a dinner party for Paul Bocuse's sixtieth birthday. Alain Sailhac did the cooking. Daniel Boulud was invited. "We were all there," Boulud remembers. "Sirio, Jaques Maximin, Paul Bocuse, Alain Chapel, Roger Vergé." At one point, Bocuse leaned over to Sirio and whispered, "You need a young chef" and gestured toward Boulud.

The week Sirio made him an offer, Boulud almost took a job working for André Soltner, the chef-owner of Lutèce. "Then I figured that since Soltner was already a chef, I'd have more freedom with Sirio. Besides that, I wanted to understand what a certain part of New York City was made of. Also, I didn't have to go far . . . just around the corner."

While Boulud wanted to respect the tradition of French cuisine established at Le Cirque by Vergnes and Sailhac, he had to do it his way. He put his spin on *pot-au-feu*, created his own version of bouillabaisse, and invented what became his signature dishes: sea scallops with black truffle slices in truffle butter (called Black Tie Scallops) and his now-famous *paupiette* of sea bass in Barolo sauce.

Boulud was excited by the opportunity to cook at Le Cirque and also by its glamorous customers. British fashion photographer Norman Parkinson would be there often. "He would clear the plate," recalls Boulud, "write an expression on it like 'Superb!' and send it back to the kitchen." Sometimes Parkinson's requests were a little, shall we say, unusual: "Once he wanted to have bangers and mash at lunch, for which I had to buy five pounds of Parks sausage meat. Another time, I made a giant shepherd's pie with a wonderful Cumberland sauce for twelve of his lady friends." Still, there were those who came for the scene and didn't

Sottha shunned the spotlight, even though he was a brilliant cook.

care about the food, content with an overdone (at their request) fillet of fish.

Boulud's natural charm and his ease with both classic and nouvelle cuisine earned him raves from the critics. Sirio could not have been more pleased— or proud. Le Cirque was humming to a fresh, new tune. Nonetheless, it was a matter of time before Boulud would want his own restaurant. "I was scared to tell Sirio and I was also scared to leave." He worried that Sirio wouldn't be happy about it. He was right. Still, Daniel left Le Cirque to open Daniel in the Surrey Hotel. It later became Café Boulud, when Daniel moved to a larger space on of all places, East 65th Street, in the former Mayfair Hotel. Daniel's private dining room, is, eerily, where Le Cirque used to be.

THE QUIET MASTER

After Daniel Boulud left, Sirio hired Sylvain Portay, who had worked for Alain Ducasse in Monaco. His term at Le Cirque was short-lived. The time was approaching for Sottha Khunn's star turn, but not quite yet. An incredibly self-effacing man from a prominent Cambodian family, many of whom were murdered by the Khmer Rouge, Sottha shunned the spotlight, even though he was a brilliant cook. His work in Paris for Alain Senderens came to the attention of Boulud when he was at New York's Plaza Athénée. Sottha came to New York in 1984 and worked under Boulud as sous chef, then followed him to Le Cirque, where they worked together for Boulud's entire tenure. Sottha opted to stay at Le Cirque when Boulud resigned. By this time, he was regarded as a member of the family—not just the Le Cirque family but the Maccionis.' They practically adopted him and included

Sottha in their at-home holiday meals and other occasions. When the job as executive chef was offered to Sottha, he first declined. It was only after Portay left that Sottha felt he was ready to step up to the task.

When Le Cirque 2000 opened at the Palace Hotel, Sottha was running the kitchen and its large staff. "It was my dream," says Sottha, "and I will never forget it. Sirio was very kind to me (he was always giving opportunities to the next generation). It was very exciting—a challenge because we wanted to show New York that we could do something new." Sottha was a master of mixing flavors, even gave a clinic in sauce making on East 65th Street. "He was so masterful," said one disciple, "that we called him Yoda."

The kitchen at Le Cirque 2000 was enormous, extremely high-tech, and a source of pride for Sirio, who would give tours, introducing Sottha as if he were his fourth son. As for Egi, Sottha often confided in her: "I talked to her like she was my mother."

Sottha left Le Cirque before it closed and went on to be a private chef for corporate honcho Sanford "Sandy" Weill and his wife, Joan, an important philanthropist. "After thirty years," explains Sottha, "I wanted a kind of different life." Today he is retired.

GENERATION NEXT

Sottha's sous chef at Le Cirque 2000 was Alsatian-born Pierre Schaedelin, who at eighteen landed a job at the Auberge de l'Ill, one of the oldest three-star Michelin restaurants in all of France. From there, he moved to Alain Ducasse's Louis XV at the Hotel du Paris in Monte Carlo—also a Michelin three-star. Next stop: Ducasse's restaurant, Monte's, in London. In 1999, Schaedelin was hired by Le Cirque, working under Sottha, then replacing him when Sottha left in 2001.

Schaedelin was reconfirmed as Le Cirque's executive chef at Beacon Court and remained there until 2006. When Schaedelin resigned, a new chef was hired. Christophe Bellanca was not from a Michelin-starred restaurant in France (although he was indeed French and worked at the two-star Pic in Valence) but from L'Orangerie, the top French restaurant in Los Angeles for almost thirty years until its closing. The stars there were its customers—actors, directors,

There's genius in the preparation.
Opposite: Sottha the sorcerer.
Clockwise from top left: Pierre Schaedelin, at right, and sous-chef David Werly (photo: Jerry Ruotolo); Craig Hopson; Christophe Bellanca; Olivier Reginensi.

"Sirio had everybody's preferences in his head."

producers, and Hollywood moguls. Bellanca, who stayed at Le Cirque for a mere two years, is best-known for being the chef in the Maccioni-family documentary, *A Table in Heaven*. There is a pivotal nail-baiting segment in it when Sirio and his staff await the Frank Bruni review in the *New York Times*. Not only does it arrive after midnight on February 6, 2008, it gives Le Cirque the three stars Sirio has been long yearning for. Despite the accolade, Bellanca left shortly thereafter. Sometimes it's *not* in the stars.

Until the end of 2011, Le Cirque's executive chef was Craig Hopson, an Australian and a radical departure from the Frenchmen who preceded him. He came recommended by his former boss at Picholine, Terrence Brennan, who himself had spent time in the Le Cirque kitchen years before. Hopson started work on December 1, 2008, around the beginning of the financial crisis. When the pre-booked parties were over, business virtually disappeared, as it did for many other restaurants. "We had to pare down and run things more like a business, so we tightened our belts and adhered to the numbers"—which was to be the modus operandi for New York restaurants in the recession.

Replacing Hopson, who left at the end of 2011, is Le Cirque's latest and ninth executive chef, Olivier Reginensi—no surprise, another Frenchman. Olivier started in January 2012, but when he came to America, nineteen years before, his first job was at Le Cirque under Sylvain Portay. Born and raised in Martigues in the south of France, Olivier cooked at several Michelin-starred restaurants including Michel Guérard's Les Prés d'Eugénie. He also worked for both Alain Ducasse and Daniel Boulud, not only as sous chef but also on their cookbooks. As Olivier sees it, there are definite Le Cirque trends he wants to foster—toward the total-experience restaurant, including tableside preparations, a menu that changes often, and a strong focus on seasonality. With his deep Mediterranean roots (his paternal grandparents were Spanish), his classic French training, and his recent experience in restaurants attracting young sophisticates (his last stint was at a new hotel in Chelsea), Olivier's aim is to create the same kind of *frisson* that ignited East 65th Street.

DISTINGUISHED ALUMNI

Not all the chefs who later went on to do great things on their own held the top position at Le Cirque. Geoffrey Zakarian, who now co-owns and manages the Lamb's Club in the Chatwal Hotel, was Le Cirque's first American sous chef. He started out as an economics major at the University of Massachusetts (he was born in Worcester). For his thesis, he went to France and, as an avocation, ate in eighteen Michelin three-star restaurants, one each week. He had one suit that he had dry-cleaned after every meal. "I'd order a half bottle of wine and from the prix-fixe menu. I was treated amazingly well—so well that nobody I knew believed it. People were always saying how rude the French were. It was only years later that I found out that I was being mistaken for someone from the Michelin Guides. It was an 'Oh, shit!' moment."

It was in France, then, that Zakarian found his calling, and it wasn't economics. When he returned to the States, he enrolled in the Culinary Institute of America. After he graduated from the CIA in 1981, he got a job at Quo Vadis, a fancy Italian restaurant on Manahattan's Upper East Side. "Schorner, a Bavarian, was the pastry chef," says Zakarian. I was an aggressive American. We clicked. When Dieter went to Le Cirque, he talked to Terrance Brennan—who was there already—about me. On my second or third day on the job, Francisco Gutierrez, Dieter's assistant, burned his hand and couldn't cook. I had to make a soufflé."

Zakarian remembers his experience at East 65th Street with tremendous fondness and gratitude. "Le Cirque was *the* place. There was a chic-ness to it, an electricity that the others didn't have." As for Sirio, "No one worked harder than him. He was always there. He tasted every sauce, every specialty. He would rarely sit down to eat. Sirio had everybody's preferences in his head. True, he was kissing ass all the time, but the way he did it was magnificent. I learned more about the restaurant business at Le Cirque than I did anywhere else."

And while the food was important, Zakarian contends that "sixty percent of Le Cirque's success was because of the front of the house." Every night the

dining room would be filled with a glittering crowd. In the kitchen were budding stars: David Bouley, Terrance Brennan, Michael Lomonaco, Rick Moonen ("he taught me how to make the sauces; he was like a general").

"We all knew who was who in the dining room. The employees, especially the wait staff, could tell who were the good guys and who were the bad ones. Whenever someone from the front of the house came into the kitchen and said, 'So-and-So is a jerk,' you knew it was true.

"Ronald Reagan was the most impressive man. When he came to Le Cirque, the world stopped. Woody Allen would be there three nights a week, ordering really great French white wines and a striped bass or turbot for two. King Juan Carlos was wonderful. Oscar de la Renta is one of the most gracious humans beings on the planet—polite, kind, and respectful of everyone. Carolina Herrera was the most elegant. When Sinatra came, he was still singing; I was shocked at how small a man he was. Jerry Zipkin was hard on everybody— guys like that wore Sirio down. Still, most people are usually on their best behavior at Le Cirque. For two hours, even the worst assholes turned into bearable assholes."

Like Geofffey Zakarian, Michael Lomonaco didn't start out wanting to be a chef; he spent eight years trying to be an actor. "I started my career late in life, at the age of twenty-seven. I went to the New York City College of Technology and studied hospitality. It's the same school that Michael Romano [Union Square Café], Julian Niccolini [The Four Seasons], and the late Patrick Clark attended. I was a struggling actor driving a cab and picked up Patrick. We started taking about the restaurant business. That's what put the idea in my mind.

"I was a home cook but was looking for a creative outlet at which I could make a living. I asked Renato Palmieri what he thought about my becoming a chef. I was living in Brooklyn, in an Italian-American neighborhood, and was a friend of Frank Palmieri, Renato's son. I looked up to Renato—everybody did. He was one of the captains at the Colony, then became maître d' at Le Cirque. His niece was Egidiana Maccioni, Sirio's wife.

"From Renato, I knew about pasta with white truffles and about foie gras, about tableside cooking and celebrity clients. It all sounded so glamorous. Out of love—I was like another son—Renato tried

to talk me out of going into the business. He told me about the long hours and the sacrifices I would have to make."

Lomonaco couldn't be discouraged. When he graduated from City Tech (which was part of NYU), Renato offered to introduce him to Alain Sailhac. "I was working at a private club called Club 101 on 41st Street. Alain had my resume. After three months, he called me. I started in what is called the prep kitchen (where the Spaghetti Primavera was prepared as well as specials of the day and the food for private parties in the Orangerie).

"Those in the prep kitchen were trained by Alain himself. We weren't yet on the line—that was the next step. There were always three or four in the prep kitchen, hoping for an opening on the line." Le Cirque followed the *brigade de cuisine*, the hierarchy conceived by French chef Auguste Escoffier in the late nineteenth century. For Lomonaco, it was exactly the method that he craved: "In a classic French kitchen, you have the *légumier* in the vegetable station. The *poissonnier* preps the fish; the *boucher* takes care of the meat. It is a terrific training ground for any chef.

"When you walked into Le Cirque, there were food displays—wild mushrooms, special forages, *tartufi bianchi* from Italy, ingredients that no other restaurant in New York had. Le Cirque had a locavore vibe before the word existed. All of a sudden I was working at a place I'd heard about almost all of my life.

"I stayed there for a year and a half, which was like working for three years anyplace else. Sirio was a terrific taskmaster. Sailhac was a gifted chef with a light hand for classic French food. Geoffrey Zakarian was sous chef. After Alain left, I worked under Daniel for nine months. Nouvelle cuisine had become a major trend in the late seventies and early eighties. Every nouvelle cuisine chef from France—Vergé, Bocuse, Chapel—came to Le Cirque and were often in the kitchen. Daniel was one of the most knowledgeable individuals when it came to ingredients, locality, and seasonality.

"All of us in the kitchen knew everybody who was in the room. All the orders were handwritten dupes. Each captain thought his table was the most important. It seemed like every table had a boldfaced name. The king of Spain sat at table three. There was the shah of Iran, Hollywood stars, Texas ladies. Mick Jagger

would come for dinner, which truly surprised me. We had John Fairchild and all of the *WWD* people and the fashion crowd. Woody Allen sat at the most important table—the same one where the Schneiders sat earlier in the evening. He loved having a baked potato with white truffles.

"The food at Le Cirque was very sensuous. It was essential to both Alain and Daniel to make original, creative, highly flavored food. The menu was big and then there were all those dishes that were off the menu, including daily specials—*bollito misto, jarret de veau*, which was like osso buco. Sirio, too, had a deep interest and knowledge of food. He knew how to cook, and we in the kitchen knew that. Anything I know, especially about precision cooking, I learned at Le Cirque." His training served him well. Lomonaco went on to cook at the "21" Club, then at Windows on the World in the World Trade Center, where he was one of a few survivors after September 11. (Before showing up for work as usual that morning, he stopped at the optometrist's; talk about fate.) He's now in charge of Porter House in the Time Warner Center in Columbus Circle.

Opposite, clockwise from top left: Jacques Torres and Marco Maccioni (photo: Kris Kruid); with Fredy Girardet and Dieter Schorner; David Bouley and Daniel Boulud; Alain Allegretti and Geoffrey Zakarian. *Above:* The fellowship of Le Cirque—chefs, servers, and family members gather on East 65th Street (photo: Norman Parkinson).

Above: Gathering at Palace Hotel in 2000 (photo: Jerry Ruotolo). At center left, in tuxedo, is Mario Wainer, maître d'hôtel. *Opposite:* The staff of East 65th Street at the ready, 1979. At center is Bruno Dussin, maître d'hôtel.

MASTER CLASS

In any important restaurant, there is an intricate choreography that occurs at least twice a day to prepare for lunch and for dinner. It begins before the first guest walks in and ends well after the last dessert is served. At Le Cirque, the choreography could rival that of a Balanchine ballet. For one thing, you get the sense that a great deal of training and rehearsal have taken place. For another, each person—from captain to dishwasher—knows his or her role thoroughly. Mistakes may occur, but rarely, and they are not to be repeated. This is not to say that Le Cirque is a dictatorship run by a tyrant. In fact, it seems to be a pleasant atmosphere in which to work. Nonetheless, expectations of every employee are high.

Linens are changed at least twice daily—more if a table is turned during a meal. The settings are exacting, with napkins folded in one way and one way only; the crystal and flatware must be placed with precision. That's merely the preparation. During the meal, the servers must be cordial but not overfriendly. There is a certain rhythm that is abided and a coordination with each other and with

the kitchen that is required. The expression "fancy footwork" springs to mind. While every table pretty much looks like another, each is regarded by the captain, the waiters, and bussers as *sui generis.*

Supervising the action is the maître d'hôtel—French for "master of the hotel." In today's world, it refers to the individual in charge of the dining room, usually the first person a customer encounters and the one who leads the way to the table. But a maître d' is much more than a meeter and greeter. He or she oversees the servers, assigns them to their areas of responsibility, and, above all, makes sure that civility reigns.

To do this job well requires uncommon grace and subtlety. Joseph Garni, Francois Latapie, Romeo De Gobbi, and Benito Sevarin each held the position for long periods of time, their faces as familiar to patrons as Sirio's. Mario Wainer is now the maître d' at Le Cirque. His counterpart across town at Osteria del Circo is Bruno Dussin, previously at Le Cirque.

Wainer started working at Le Cirque about twenty-four years ago. Born in Buenos Aires, he came to Le Cirque directly from Regine's nightclub, where he was maître d' for almost ten years. His is a very demanding job, from 10:30 in the morning very often until 1 A.M., six days a week. "You have to be on your toes from the moment you arrive," says Wainer. "You're dealing with so many customers and each thinks he is the only one.

"Everything has to be flexible and correct. If someone doesn't like something, we change it right away. We never argue with the customer. By the time the customer leaves, he will be mostly happy."

Bruno Dussin, the maître d' at Circo, was born in Asolo, in the Veneto. He got his early experience working on the Italian line transatlantic ships—the *Michelangelo,* the *Raffaello,* and the *Leonardo da Vinci.* "I was always in first class," he says with pride. Dussin was working for La Pace restaurant in Hackensack, New Jersey, when Tony May, its owner, suggested he seek out Sirio, who was opening a new restaurant on 65th Street. "When I met Sirio, he said, 'You start tomorrow as a waiter.' After two weeks, he said, 'I think you should be captain. You're too good to be a waiter.'

"After two years I was put on the 'royal station'—where Jerry Zipkin, Frank Sinatra, Kirk Douglas,

Betsy Bloomingdale, and Richard Nixon would sit. That was near the door."

The maître d' back then was Joseph Garni, who had been with Sirio at the Colony. When Garni left, Sirio chose Dussin to succeed him. "I was proud, but I was also afraid," admits Dussin. Sirio assured him he could do the job. "I was young and I was stubborn. Sirio and I had many fights, but I understood him and he understood me. We were a team.

"We had difficult customers at Le Cirque, but the more difficult they were, the more I wanted to please them. That was the way I learned. It was just a matter of understanding people. After all, we are all in the same boat—with small problems and big problems."

THE DISHES

Daniel Boulud and Sirio toast at table
(photo: Slim Aarons).

JEAN VERGNES
1974 to 1978

Art by Tim Flynn.

CHAMPAGNE MEDICATO

The recipe for this cure-all cocktail, in the "Flutes" category of the drinks list, shines a spotlight on Le Cirque's ringmaster: "Champagne and whatever Sirio wants."

1 SERVING

½ ounce St-Germain liqueur, Chambord liqueur, or Fragoli wild strawberry liqueur

4 ounces Champagne

Pour the liqueur into a Champagne flute. Add the Champagne and serve.

TIPS

If you prefer not to eat raw egg, the satisfyingly pungent vinaigrette will be great without it.

You can either steam or boil the artichokes. Steaming is easier because you don't have to wait for a large pot of water to come to a boil. If boiling, add a lemon half to the water.

VARIATIONS

Use this recipe as a blueprint for leeks or asparagus vinaigrette, reducing the steaming time as needed.

Try adding fresh lemon juice instead of the vinegars to the dressing.

Just before serving, you can stir a small finely chopped shallot, or chopped tarragon, basil, or dill into the vinaigrette.

SERVE WITH

For a sweetly old-fashioned French meal, follow these artichokes with Sole Amandine (page 121) and Floating Islands (page 131).

MAKE AHEAD

The cooked artichokes can be refrigerated for up to 2 days.

The vinaigrette can be refrigerated for up to 4 hours.

ARTICHOKES VINAIGRETTE

In an amusing 1977 piece in New York *magazine called "I Love Le Cirque but Can I Be Trusted?" restaurant critic Gael Greene relates some pillow talk with Jean-Louis Todeschini, the right-hand man of then co-owner and executive chef Jean Vergnes. Greene faults the "artichauts," as they were listed on the menu, for tasting like plastic. Todeschini counters, "The artichoke is not to eat . . . it is a cold table decoration." True, spiky globe artichokes are ornamental, but they are also sublime when freshly steamed or boiled, especially with Le Cirque's creamy, mustardy vinaigrette. And scraping off the velvety flesh with your teeth is fun.*

4 APPETIZER SERVINGS

4 large artichokes, stems trimmed

1 large egg yolk

1 tablespoon sherry vinegar

1 tablespoon red wine vinegar

1 tablespoon Dijon mustard

3 tablespoons canola oil

3 tablespoons extra-virgin olive oil

Salt

1 Set a steamer basket in a large pot over 1 inch of boiling water. Arrange the artichokes, stem side down, in the basket. Cover and steam over medium heat until a knife easily pierces the stem end, 45 minutes to 1 hour. Transfer the artichokes to a cutting board and let cool slightly.

2 Pull the center leaves from the artichokes and, using a melon baller or small spoon, scrape out the hairy chokes. Transfer the artichokes to a platter.

3 In a medium bowl, whisk the egg yolk with the vinegars and mustard. Gradually whisk in the canola oil, then the olive oil, and season with salt. Serve the artichokes warm or lightly chilled with the vinaigrette.

MOULES MARINIÈRE

These mussels steamed in the shell are as delicious today as they were during Jean Vergnes's reign as executive chef in the '70s (and well before that). The briny juices flavor a buttery, aromatic broth of vermouth, onion, and shallots, then freshly ground pepper and chopped parsley, added just before serving, invigorate the mix. And they couldn't be easier. All the ingredients are combined in a pot, and in minutes they're ready to eat.

6 APPETIZER OR 4 ENTRÉE SERVINGS

4 pounds small mussels in the shell (see Tips)

1 large shallot, finely chopped

½ onion, finely chopped

½ cup dry vermouth

2 tablespoons white wine vinegar

4 tablespoons unsalted butter, diced

Freshly ground pepper

2 tablespoons finely chopped parsley

1 In a large pot, combine the mussels, shallot, onion, vermouth, vinegar, and butter. Cover and cook over high heat, stirring once or twice, until the mussels start to open, about 5 minutes. Remove the pot from the heat.

2 Using a slotted spoon, dish the mussels into bowls, discarding any that don't open. Pour some of the cooking broth through a fine-mesh sieve over the mussels. Season with pepper and sprinkle the parsley over the top. Serve hot, passing the remaining broth separately.

TIPS

Farmed mussels require very little work—just a quick rinse, the discarding of any with broken shells, and pulling out the beard, which takes only a few minutes for several pounds of mussels.

Cockles and other small clams are also delicious prepared this way.

VARIATIONS

Add 1 cup crème fraîche to half the cooking liquid, simmer for 2 minutes, and you have mussels in cream sauce.

This classic recipe for steamed mussels lends itself to aromatic riffs. Dry white wine, sparkling cider, beer, or coconut milk can replace the vermouth.

Or arrange the mussels in the half shell in a gratin dish and sprinkle with dry bread crumbs mixed with garlic and parsley. Drizzle with melted butter or olive oil and broil until lightly browned, about 3 minutes.

SERVE WITH

You really don't need much more than a loaf of bread, a bottle of wine, and a green salad for a great casual meal.

FILET DE FLOUNDER GRILLÉ LE CIRQUE

Sirio Maccioni likes to say that this recipe has kept Le Cirque in business since it debuted in 1974. (It was imported from the old high-society mecca the Colony Club, where Sirio was maitre d'.) The reasons for its much-deserved success: thick local fish fillets are dipped in butter and dragged through dry bread crumbs, then broiled until golden. The flounder manages to be moist and crunchy, rich and light, all at the same time. While you admire the fish's brown gorgeousness, a server adds a spoonful of pungent, luscious mustard hollandaise to the plate, leaving the rest of the sauce in easy reach.

4 ENTRÉE SERVINGS

MUSTARD HOLLANDAISE

2 large egg yolks

1 tablespoon warm water

½ cup clarified butter (see Caesar Salad Le Cirque, step 1, page 194)

1 tablespoon fresh lemon juice

1 tablespoon Dijon mustard

Salt and freshly ground pepper

1 tablespoon finely chopped tarragon

1 tablespoon finely chopped parsley

FISH

½ cup clarified butter (see Caesar Salad Le Cirque, step 1, page 194)

1¼ cups fine dry bread crumbs

4 (6-ounce) skinless flounder fillets

Salt and freshly ground pepper

Olive oil, for brushing and drizzling

2 lemons, halved

1 Make the mustard hollandaise: In a medium saucepan, bring 2 inches of water to a simmer. In a medium heatproof bowl, whisk the egg yolks with the 1 tablespoon warm water. Set the bowl over the saucepan and whisk the yolks constantly until thickened slightly and bright yellow, about 1 minute. Remove from the heat.

2 Gently heat the butter; very gradually, whisk it into the yolks until a slightly thick sauce forms. Whisk in the lemon juice and mustard, and season lightly with salt and pepper. Whisk in the tarragon and parsley. Keep warm over the hot water off the heat.

3 Make the fish: Pour the butter and bread crumbs into two separate baking pans. Season 1 fish fillet generously with salt and pepper. Dip in the butter, letting the excess drip back into the pan. Coat generously with the bread crumbs, pressing to help the crumbs adhere. Transfer to a sheet of parchment paper. Repeat with the remaining fillets, stacking them between sheets of parchment paper. Chill for 15 minutes.

4 Position an oven rack 5 inches from the heat source and heat the broiler. Brush a large wire cooling rack with oil. Drizzle 2 fillets on both sides with oil and transfer to the prepared rack. Broil until golden brown, turning or moving the rack if needed for even coloring, 5 to 7 minutes. Using 2 wide spatulas, gently flip the fillets and cook for 2 to 3 minutes longer. Carefully transfer the fillets to a platter or plates. Repeat with the remaining fillets.

5 Serve with the mustard hollandaise and lemon halves.

DOVER SOLE LE CIRQUE

Le Cirque's Dover sole (or "sole de Douvres," as it's listed on a 1989 menu) is prepared whole, meunière-style—seasoned with salt, dusted with a light coating of flour (meunière means "miller's wife"), and pan-fried in clarified butter. It's one of the best and most basic ways to cook spanking-fresh seafood. The technique is terrific for small fish, like sole and trout, and fish fillets, as well as soft-shell crabs (one of Sirio's favorites). A small amount of flour gives the fish (or shellfish) crispness and makes it beautifully brown. If you order this dish at the restaurant, you get the drama of an entire fish displayed on a shiny platter without the bother of bones: a server fillets it tableside.

4 ENTRÉE SERVINGS

½ cup all-purpose flour

4 (1-pound) Dover soles, dark skin peeled, heads and tails removed

Salt

1 cup clarified butter (see Caesar Salad Le Cirque, step 1, page 194)

2 large lemons, peeled and cut in between the membranes into segments, juices reserved (see Lobster Salad Le Cirque, Tips, page 150)

¼ cup finely chopped parsley

1 Spread the flour in a large baking pan. Season 1 sole generously with salt. Dredge in the flour, patting off the excess. Transfer to a sheet of parchment paper. Repeat with the remaining soles, stacking them between sheets of parchment paper.

2 Heat the oven to 200 degrees.

3 In a large skillet, heat ¼ cup of the clarified butter over high heat. Add 1 sole and cook over medium heat until golden brown and opaque throughout, about 4 minutes per side. Transfer to a baking sheet and keep warm in the oven. Scrape the butter into a small glass measuring cup and reserve. Repeat with the remaining clarified butter and soles.

4 Stir the lemon segments and juices into the reserved butter, along with the parsley. Season with salt.

5 Fillet the soles and arrange on plates. Spoon the sauce over the fish and serve.

TIPS

Le Cirque's custom of serving a one-pound sole per person is typically extravagant, and more than some people can comfortably eat. The recipe can easily be cut in half to feed three or four.

One-pound soles are long, so you can probably fit only one at a time in a large skillet.

Try this also with petrale sole, or flounder, which is more fragile than Dover sole, but delicious.

VARIATION

Chef Alain Sailhac created Sole Richard Nixon for the president, who often dined at Le Cirque after he resigned. Sailhac removed the bones and stuffed the fish with sautéed julienne vegetables before sautéing it. This version was sauced with browned butter and lemon juice.

SERVE WITH

Sautéed spinach and steamed, peeled new potatoes with chopped parsley are time-honored side dishes. Or try sumptuous Stuffed Baked Potatoes with Truffles (page 168), which can swing as either accompaniment or starter.

To begin, serve simple Artichokes Vinaigrette (page 116). For an archetypal French menu, finish with Chocolate Soufflés (page 144), Crème Brûlée Le Cirque (page 143), or Crêpes Suzette (page 132).

MAKE AHEAD

The recipe can be prepared through step 1 and refrigerated for up to 4 hours.

SOLE AMANDINE

Most recipes for sole amandine call for sautéing sliced almonds in butter, then pouring them over the golden fish. But here almonds make a lavishly nutty crust, patted on the whole fish after a dip in flour and beaten eggs, then pan-fried. It's a crunchy step up from meunière (page 119).

4 ENTRÉE SERVINGS

½ cup all-purpose flour

2 large eggs, lightly beaten

4 cups sliced blanched almonds

4 (1-pound) Dover soles, dark skin peeled, heads and tails removed

Salt

1 cup clarified butter (see Caesar Salad Le Cirque, step 1, page 194)

2 large lemons, peeled and cut in between the membranes into segments, juices reserved (see Lobster Salad Le Cirque, Tips, page 150)

¼ cup finely chopped parsley

1 Spread the flour, eggs, and almonds in three large separate baking pans. Season 1 sole generously with salt. Dredge in the flour, patting off the excess. Dip in the eggs, letting the excess drip back into the pan. Coat with the almonds, pressing to help them adhere. Transfer to a sheet of parchment paper. Repeat with the remaining soles, stacking them between sheets of parchment paper.

2 Heat the oven to 200 degrees.

3 In a large skillet, heat ¼ cup of the clarified butter over high heat. Add 1 sole and cook over medium heat until golden brown and opaque throughout, about 5 minutes per side. Transfer to a baking sheet and keep warm in the oven. Scrape the butter and any stray almonds into a small glass measuring cup and reserve. Repeat with the remaining clarified butter and soles.

4 Stir the lemon segments and juices into the reserved butter, along with the parsley. Season with salt.

5 Fillet the soles and arrange on plates. Spoon the sauce around the fish and serve.

TIPS
Like Dover Sole Le Cirque (page 119), this recipe can easily be cut in half to feed three or four.

It's tricky to make the almonds stay on the fish. But even if your crust isn't perfect, it's still very tasty.

SERVE WITH
Haricots verts, sautéed with chopped shallots and garlic, and steamed, peeled new potatoes are excellent on the side.

For an appetizer, serve Curried Chicken Salad (page 175). Finish with Chocolate Soufflés (page 144), Crème Brûlée Le Cirque (page 143), or Crêpes Suzette (page 132).

MAKE AHEAD
The recipe can be prepared through step 1 and refrigerated for up to 4 hours.

TIPS
Skate has to be very fresh or
it develops an ammonia taste.
Cook it the day you buy it or
the next.

SERVE WITH
Start with a light first course,
such as Curried Tuna Tartare
(page 172).

MAKE AHEAD
The recipe can be prepared
through step 2 and the fish
refrigerated for up to 4 hours.

SKATE GRENOBLOISE WITH CAULIFLOWER PUREE

A grenobloise preparation is the most complex variation in the continuum that includes meunière and amandine. It starts with the same minimal coating in flour and sautéing in clarified butter. It also has a buttery sauce, sharpened with lemon juice and flavored with chopped parsley. But a grenobloise adds crunchy croutons (replacing the almonds in amandine) and ramps up the acidity with tiny capers that burst in your mouth. Cauliflower puree makes a creamy contrast.

4 ENTRÉE SERVINGS

¾ cup clarified butter (see Caesar
Salad Le Cirque, step 1, page 194)

2 slices of firm white bread, crusts
removed, cut into ¼-inch cubes

½ cup all-purpose flour

4 (6-ounce) skinless skate fillets

Salt

2 large lemons, peeled and cut
in between the membranes into
segments, juices reserved (see Lobster
Salad Le Cirque, Tips, page 150)

2 tablespoons small capers, drained

¼ cup finely chopped parsley

Cauliflower Puree (page 123)

1 In a medium skillet, heat ¼ cup of the clarified butter over high heat. Add the bread cubes and cook over medium heat, stirring, until golden brown on all sides, about 2 minutes total. Remove and drain on paper towels. Wipe out the skillet.

2 Spread the flour in a baking pan. Season 1 skate fillet generously with salt. Dredge in the flour, patting off the excess. Transfer to a sheet of parchment paper. Repeat with the remaining fillets, stacking them between sheets of parchment paper.

3 Heat the oven to 200 degrees.

4 In the same skillet, heat 2 tablespoons of the clarified butter over high heat. Add 1 skate fillet and cook over medium heat until golden brown and opaque throughout, about 3 minutes per side. Transfer to a baking sheet and keep warm in the oven. Scrape the butter into a small glass measuring cup and reserve. Repeat with the remaining clarified butter and fillets.

5 Stir the lemon segments and juices, capers, parsley, and croutons into the reserved butter. Season with salt.

6 Spread some of the cauliflower puree in the center of each plate. Set a skate fillet on the puree, spoon the sauce over the top, and serve.

CAULIFLOWER PUREE

Cauliflower is treated like potatoes to make this velvety puree. The florets are boiled in water and a little milk (to keep the color snowy white) until tender, then drained and pureed with a little cooking liquid and butter.

4 SIDE SERVINGS

½ head of cauliflower, cored and cut into 2-inch pieces

1 cup milk

Salt

4 tablespoons unsalted butter

Freshly ground pepper

1 In a medium saucepan, combine the cauliflower, milk, and enough water to barely cover. Season with salt and bring to a boil over medium-high heat; immediately reduce the heat to a simmer and cook until the cauliflower is very tender, 15 to 20 minutes.

2 Drain, reserving the cooking liquid. Return the cauliflower to the saucepan and add the butter and some of the reserved cooking liquid to moisten. Using an immersion blender or a regular blender, puree until smooth. Season with salt and pepper.

TIPS
Cauliflower needs to be cooked enough so that it can be easily pureed but not so much that it gets smelly.

For extra smoothness, work the puree through a fine sieve or food mill. The blender you use makes a difference. The kitchen at Le Cirque doesn't require a sieve or food mill to get a silky texture; their professional Vitamix blender is so powerful it makes a perfectly smooth puree.

VARIATION
Broccoli can be prepared in the same way.

SERVE WITH
Cauliflower puree makes a delicious accompaniment to all white fish and poultry.

MAKE AHEAD
The puree can be refrigerated for up to 4 hours. Reheat before serving.

Wide, shallow bowls are best for serving spaghetti primavera because they offer room for scattering the pretty array of green vegetables.

VARIATION

While this recipe combines broccoli, zucchini, snow peas, zucchini, asparagus, and peas, you could mix in any spring vegetables you like—sliced baby artichokes (peel off the outer petals) and fava beans (peel off the outer skins), for instance.

SERVE WITH

Spaghetti Primavera is rich, so you might want to start with something light, like Curried Tuna Tartare (page 172).

MAKE AHEAD

This recipe can be prepared through step 3 up to 4 hours in advance.

SPAGHETTI PRIMAVERA

Though full of haute cuisine flourishes (eight different vegetables cooked separately, cream and butter, tableside tossing), Spaghetti Primavera was so controversial in a formal French restaurant in 1977 that it was served only on request. (It is still an off-menu item as a reminder of its disputatious origins.) Yet the popularity it gained at Le Cirque (critic Gael Greene dubbed it "as crisp and beautiful as a Matisse") helped move American cooks beyond spaghetti and meatballs and paved the way for seasonal pasta as it's cooked in Italy.

8 APPETIZER OR 6 ENTRÉE SERVINGS

⅓ cup pine nuts

6 tablespoons extra-virgin olive oil

16 cherry tomatoes, halved

¼ cup plus 1 tablespoon chopped parsley

¼ cup chopped basil

1 teaspoon finely chopped garlic

Salt and freshly ground pepper

2 cups small broccoli florets

8 ounces snow peas, halved crosswise

2 small zucchini, quartered lengthwise and cut into 1½-inch pieces

6 asparagus spears, peeled and cut into 2-inch pieces

1 pound dried spaghetti (see Tips)

8 ounces white mushrooms, thinly sliced

1 cup thawed frozen baby peas

½ cup chicken stock or low-sodium broth

1 cup freshly grated Parmesan cheese

⅔ cup heavy cream

6 tablespoons unsalted butter, diced

1. Heat the oven to 300 degrees. Spread the pine nuts in a pie plate and toast until golden brown, about 12 minutes.

2. In a small skillet, heat 2 tablespoons of the oil until shimmering. Add the tomatoes, ¼ cup of the parsley, the basil, and ½ teaspoon of the garlic and cook over medium heat, stirring, until the tomatoes soften, 2 to 3 minutes. Season with salt and pepper.

3. Bring a large pot of salted water to a boil. Fill a large bowl with ice water. Add the broccoli, snow peas, zucchini, and asparagus to the boiling water, bring back to a boil, and blanch for 1 minute. Using a slotted spoon, transfer the vegetables to the ice water so they cool as quickly as possible, 1 to 2 minutes. Drain and pat dry.

4. Add the spaghetti to the boiling water and cook, stirring occasionally, until almost al dente.

5. Meanwhile, in a large skillet, heat the remaining 4 tablespoons oil until shimmering. Add the mushrooms, the remaining 1 tablespoon parsley, and ½ teaspoon garlic. Cook over medium-high heat, stirring occasionally, until the mushrooms are lightly browned, about 5 minutes. Add the blanched vegetables and the peas and toss over high heat until most of liquid has evaporated and the vegetables are just tender.

6. Reheat the tomatoes. Drain the spaghetti and return it to the pot. Add the stock, cheese, cream, and butter and cook over medium-high heat, stirring and tossing with tongs, until the cheese melts. Add the vegetables and pine nuts, season with salt and pepper, and toss to coat. Transfer the spaghetti to shallow bowls, top with the tomatoes, and serve.

CHÂTEAUBRIAND FOR TWO

Jean Vergnes offered a special category of "Rôtis," large roasts for sharing. If you were patient—the menu specified a thirty-five-minute wait—you could order whole duck and chicken or rack of lamb and have the meat carved in front of you. Alain Sailhac, then Daniel Boulud continued the tradition, expanding the selection to include pigeon, beef rib roast, guinea hen, and red snapper (for four!) and cautioning a "forty-five-minute minimum." There's something so festive and romantic about diners partaking of the same food that the custom persists today at Le Cirque. This châteaubriand pairs perfectly with a robust red wine and demiglace reduction. Sautéed mushrooms add umami depth to the sauce.

2 ENTRÉE SERVINGS

3 tablespoons clarified butter (see Caesar Salad Le Cirque, step 1, page 194)

4 ounces white mushrooms, cut into ½-inch dice

1 cup red wine

1 cup demiglace (see Tips)

1 (20-ounce) center-cut beef tenderloin, tied

Salt and freshly ground pepper

2 tablespoons cold unsalted butter, diced

1 In a small heavy saucepan, heat 1 tablespoon of the clarified butter over high heat. Add the mushrooms and cook over medium heat, stirring often, until lightly browned, about 5 minutes. Add the wine to the pan and boil over medium-high heat until reduced to 2 tablespoons, about 10 minutes. Add the demiglace and boil until the sauce is reduced to ⅔ cup, about 5 minutes.

2 Meanwhile, heat the oven to 425 degrees. Season the tenderloin generously with salt and pepper. In a medium ovenproof skillet, heat the remaining 2 tablespoons clarified butter. Add the tenderloin and cook over medium heat until browned on three sides, 2 to 3 minutes per side. Turn the tenderloin on the fourth side, transfer the skillet to the oven, and roast for 10 minutes. Turn the tenderloin and roast until an instant-read thermometer inserted in the thickest part of the meat registers 130 degrees for medium-rare, about 10 minutes longer. Transfer the tenderloin to a carving board and cover loosely with foil. Let rest for 10 minutes.

3 Bring the sauce to a simmer. Remove the pan from the heat and whisk in the cold butter until it melts creamily. Season with salt and pepper. Discard the butcher's twine, slice the tenderloin ¼ inch thick, and arrange on plates. Spoon some of the sauce over the meat and serve, passing the remaining sauce at the table.

TIPS
The châteaubriand is a small, extravagant roast cut from the thick center of the beef tenderloin.

Demiglace is a rich brown sauce often used as a flavorful base for other sauces. It's available at specialty food stores and from dartagnan.com.

SERVE WITH
At Le Cirque, the châteaubriand is paired with Braised Short Rib–Stuffed Mushrooms (page 128) and crisp Pommes Dauphine (page 130).

MAKE AHEAD
The sauce can be prepared through step 1 and refrigerated overnight.

TIPS
Save the mushroom cooking liquid to make a quick pan sauce for steak.

If the crumb mixture is too soft to stamp out in step 2, freeze it briefly until firm.

VARIATION
Sautéed crumbled pork sausage and a little stock can replace the braised short ribs.

SERVE WITH
At the restaurant, these crisp, rich mushrooms come with Châteaubriand for Two. Try them also with any roast or steak.

MAKE AHEAD
The mushrooms and stuffing can be prepared through step 3 and refrigerated overnight.

BRAISED SHORT RIB–STUFFED MUSHROOMS

Châteaubriand for Two (page 127) comes with an entourage of sizzling mushroom caps, filled with tender wine-braised meat under a buttery blue cheese and Parmesan crust. These beauties also make a wonderful plate of hors d'oeuvres with drinks.

MAKES 16

16 large (about 2 inches) white mushrooms, stems cut off

2 cups chicken stock or low-sodium broth

6 tablespoons unsalted butter, softened

1 cup dry bread crumbs

⅔ cup plus 2 tablespoons freshly grated Parmesan cheese

⅓ cup crumbled blue cheese

1 cup shredded Braised Short Ribs (page 234)

¼ cup braising liquid from Braised Short Ribs (page 234)

1 tablespoon grainy mustard

1 tablespoon snipped chives

1 tablespoon chopped parsley

Salt and freshly ground pepper

1 In a large saucepan, combine the mushroom caps and stock, press a round of parchment paper on top, and cook until tender, about 5 minutes. Let cool, then drain.

2 In a large bowl, using your fingertips, blend the butter with the bread crumbs, ⅔ cup of the Parmesan, and the blue cheese. Roll out this mixture between two nonstick liners or sheets of parchment paper to ¼ inch thick. Using a 2-inch biscuit cutter, stamp out rounds.

3 In a food processor, pulse the short ribs with the braising liquid, remaining 2 tablespoons Parmesan, the mustard, chives, and parsley until coarsely chopped. Season with salt and pepper.

4 Heat the broiler. Lightly oil a baking sheet. Arrange the mushrooms stemmed side up on the sheet. Mound the short rib stuffing on the mushroom caps and set a crumb round on top. Broil the mushrooms until hot and golden brown, about 3 minutes, then serve.

CÔTES DE VEAU MILANAISE

These veal chops, like their name, are a Frenchman's interpretation of veal chop Milanese, a trattoria staple raised to Chef Jean Vergnes's haute cuisine standards. (The title of the 1977 review of Le Cirque in the New York Times *was "French with a Slight Italian Accent.") The chops, which appeared on Le Cirque's first menus under "Spécialités de la Maison," are double thick, and the meat is pounded thin on the bone (a tricky maneuver) before being dunked in a series of flour, egg, and bread crumb baths. The recipe also calls for sautéing the chops in clarified butter—no olive oil here. Today, a version of these chops is served at the Maccioni family's Italian restaurant, Osteria del Circo.*

4 ENTRÉE SERVINGS

½ cup all-purpose flour

2 large eggs, lightly beaten

1¼ cups dry bread crumbs

4 (14- to 16-ounce) veal rib chops, ribs scraped clean, meat pounded ¼ inch thick (see Tips)

Salt and freshly ground pepper

1 cup clarified butter (see Caesar Salad Le Cirque, step 1, page 194)

Lemon wedges, for serving

1 Spread the flour, eggs, and bread crumbs in three separate baking pans. Season 1 veal chop generously with salt and pepper. Dredge in the flour, patting off the excess. Dip in the eggs, letting the excess drip back into the pan. Coat with the bread crumbs, pressing to help the crumbs adhere. Transfer to a sheet of parchment paper. Repeat with the remaining chops, stacking them between sheets of parchment paper. Chill for 15 minutes.

2 Heat the oven to 200 degrees.

3 In a medium skillet, heat ¼ cup of the clarified butter over high heat. Add 1 veal chop and cook over medium heat until golden brown and cooked through, about 3 minutes per side. Transfer to a baking sheet and keep warm in the oven. Discard the butter and repeat with the remaining clarified butter and veal chops.

4 Transfer the chops to a platter or plates and serve with the lemon wedges.

TIPS
Ask the butcher to pound the chops for you, or do the flattening at home with a meat mallet or the bottom of a heavy saucepan.

Even though it takes longer, cooking one chop at a time ensures an evenly browned crust.

VARIATIONS
Combine the bread crumbs with 1 tablespoon chopped sage or oregano or 1 teaspoon dried herbs or ground toasted fennel seeds.

Instead of using all clarified butter, try three parts extra-virgin olive oil and one part clarified butter.

SERVE WITH
Sautéed broccoli rabe is a natural accompaniment for the chops. There's a simple recipe for it in Pan-Roasted Chicken with Red Pepper Puree, Broccoli Rabe, and Parmesan Frico (page 228). Or substitute kale.

For a first course, try a risotto, such as Lobster Risotto (page 153) or Risotto Cristal with Langoustine Carpaccio (page 223).

MAKE AHEAD
The veal chops can be prepared through step 1 and refrigerated for up to 4 hours.

POMMES DAUPHINE

TIPS

In step 4, the dough can also be spooned into a pastry bag fitted with a plain ½-inch tip and piped into the oil in ½-inch pieces.

Drop the dough into the hot oil close to the surface so it doesn't splash.

SERVE WITH

These crisp, creamy potato puffs traditionally accompany Châteaubriand for Two (page 127). Serve them with any elegant roast or steak.

MAKE AHEAD

The dough can be prepared through step 3 and refrigerated overnight. Press a piece of plastic on the dough to keep a crust from forming. Bring the dough to room temperature before frying.

POMMES DAUPHINE

These classic deep-fried marvels are a blend of mashed potatoes and pâte à choux (cream puff dough). Think homemade Tater Tots, but infinitely creamier.

4 SIDE SERVINGS

1 large Idaho (baking) potato (about 1 pound), scrubbed

3 tablespoons unsalted butter, diced

½ teaspoon salt

½ cup all-purpose flour

2 large eggs, 1 lightly beaten

2 tablespoons snipped chives (optional)

Freshly ground pepper

Canola oil, for frying

1 Heat the oven to 350 degrees. Set the potato on a rack in the oven and bake until tender, 45 minutes to 1 hour. Transfer to a wire cooling rack and let cool slightly, about 5 minutes. Halve the potato and scoop out the flesh, then work it through a ricer or food mill into a medium bowl.

2 In a medium saucepan, combine the butter, ½ cup water, and the salt. Bring to a boil over medium-high heat, then remove the pan from the heat. Add the flour and stir vigorously with a wooden spoon until a ball forms. Return the pan to medium heat and cook, stirring, for 3 minutes to evaporate the moisture. Let cool slightly.

3 Beat in the whole egg, then the beaten egg, a little at time, until smooth, shiny, and elastic; you may not need to add all of the second egg. Beat in the potato and chives, if using, and season with salt and pepper.

4 Line a baking sheet with paper towels. In a large pot, heat 2 inches of oil to 375 degrees over medium heat. Working in batches, drop the dough by teaspoonfuls into the oil and fry, stirring occasionally, until golden brown all over, 3 to 5 minutes. Using a slotted spoon, transfer the fritters to the prepared baking sheet. Serve as soon as possible.

FLOATING ISLANDS

In the late 1970s and early '80s, Le Cirque's menu was a jumble of classic French dishes, like oeufs à la neige, and nouvelle cuisine novelties, such as kiwi tart. Restaurant reviewers swooned over the tart's bright green fruit and eggy, vanilla-perfumed custard, but it's the old-school poached meringue afloat in vanilla custard sauce that you still want to eat. The dome-shaped islands were garnished with candy fruits for Christmas in 1981. Today they're embellished with fresh raspberries.

6 SERVINGS

CRÈME ANGLAISE

3½ cups whole milk

½ cup heavy cream

1 vanilla bean, split lengthwise, seeds scraped

⅓ cup sugar

5 large egg yolks

MERINGUE

5 large egg whites

¼ teaspoon cream of tartar

½ cup superfine sugar

½ teaspoon pure vanilla extract

1. Make the crème anglaise: In a medium saucepan, bring the milk, cream, and vanilla bean and seeds to a simmer over medium-high heat. In a medium bowl, whisk the sugar with the egg yolks until combined. Slowly whisk one third of the warm milk mixture into the egg yolks, then whisk this mixture back into the remaining warm mixture in the saucepan.

2. Cook the sauce over medium heat, stirring gently with a wooden spoon or heatproof silicone spatula, until slightly thickened, 2 to 3 minutes. Fill a large bowl with ice water. Set a large glass measuring cup in the ice water, and strain in the sauce. Whisk the sauce often until chilled, about 5 minutes. Cover and refrigerate.

3. Make the meringue: In a large bowl, whip the egg whites with the cream of tartar until foamy. Gradually beat in the superfine sugar at high speed until the whites are glossy and hold soft peaks. Beat in the vanilla extract.

4. Fill a large deep skillet with 1½ inches of water and bring to a bare simmer. Using a large spoon, dollop 6 mounds of the meringue into the simmering water and cook over medium heat until just set on the bottom, about 2 minutes. Gently flip the meringues and cook for 2 minutes longer; do not let the water boil. Using a slotted spoon, transfer the meringues to paper towels to drain.

5. Pour the custard sauce into shallow bowls, add the meringues, and serve.

TIPS
Don't let the crème anglaise get too hot in step 2 or the egg yolks will curdle. The sauce should be as thick as cream. The meringues puff up as they're poached, so use the largest skillet you have.

VARIATION
Floating islands are often served with caramel sauce drizzled over the top.

MAKE AHEAD
For all its delicacy, poached meringue holds up remarkably well. In France, restaurant kitchens prepare île flottante in the morning and serve it for lunch.

Alternatively, the meringue can stand at room temperature, covered with plastic wrap, for 2 hours before poaching.

The crème anglaise can be refrigerated for up to 3 days.

CRÊPES SUZETTE

In the early days of Le Cirque, these orange-infused crêpes were flamed with Grand Marnier as you watched for the princely sum of $3.75. The fanfare of their presentation in a plush restaurant dining room translates easily to the home kitchen. The crêpes and orange sauce can be made well in advance, then reheated and ignited just before rushing them to the table.

4 SERVINGS

CRÊPES

2 large eggs

1 tablespoon sugar

1 cup whole milk

¾ cup all-purpose flour

¼ teaspoon salt

2 tablespoons unsalted butter, melted and cooled, plus more for the pan

1 teaspoon canola oil

ORANGE SAUCE

1 cup fresh orange juice

3 tablespoons sugar

2 tablespoons unsalted butter

Finely grated zest of 1 orange

1 orange, peeled and cut in between the membranes into segments (see Lobster Salad Le Cirque, Tips, page 150)

¼ cup Grand Marnier or another orange liqueur

1   Make the crêpes: In a medium bowl, whisk the eggs and sugar. Whisk in the milk and ¼ cup water, then the flour and salt. Whisk in the butter and oil.

2   Heat an 8-inch skillet over high heat and brush with a little butter. Add 2 tablespoons of the batter and tilt the pan to distribute the batter evenly. Cook over medium heat until the edges begin to brown, about 40 seconds. Using a thin-bladed spatula, flip the crêpe and cook until a few brown spots appear on the bottom, about 15 seconds. Slide the crêpe onto a plate. Repeat with the remaining batter, buttering the pan a few times as needed, and stacking the crêpes.

3   Fold each crêpe in half and in half again to form a triangle. Arrange all the crêpes slightly overlapping in a large skillet.

4   Make the orange sauce: In a small saucepan, bring the orange juice, sugar, and butter to a simmer, then cook over medium-high heat until reduced to ½ cup, about 5 minutes. Add the orange zest and segments. Pour the orange sauce over the crêpes and bring to a simmer. Add the Grand Marnier, then tilt the skillet and, using a long match, carefully ignite it. Serve.

ALAIN SAILHAC
1978 to 1986

Art by Tim Flynn.

RICOTTA AND SPINACH RAVIOLI

While Spaghetti Primavera (page 124) was still being prepared in the dining room to avoid offending the sensibilities in the kitchen, Egi Maccioni, Sirio's wife, was quietly cooking the food of her Tuscan girlhood. She cranked out as many as twenty portions a day of these delicate ravioli in her home kitchen, ferrying them to the restaurant for special customers.

8 APPETIZER OR 6 ENTRÉE SERVINGS

PASTA DOUGH

2 cups all-purpose flour, plus more for sprinkling

3 large eggs

1 teaspoon extra-virgin olive oil

½ teaspoon salt

FILLING AND SERVING

¾ cup fresh ricotta (see Tips)

1 cup freshly grated Parmesan cheese

12 ounces spinach, blanched, drained, squeezed dry, and finely chopped (about ½ cup)

2 tablespoons finely chopped parsley

1 small garlic clove, minced

Freshly grated nutmeg

Salt and freshly ground pepper

6 tablespoons unsalted butter

16 to 20 small sage leaves

1 Make the pasta dough: In a food processor, pulse the flour a few times. Add the eggs, oil, and salt and process until a fairly stiff dough forms. Scrape the dough onto a work surface, flatten into a disk, and wrap in plastic. Let stand at room temperature for at least 30 minutes or up to 2 hours.

2 Meanwhile, make the filling: In a medium bowl, beat the ricotta with ½ cup of the Parmesan, the spinach, parsley, and garlic. Season with nutmeg, salt, and pepper; refrigerate.

3 Cut the dough into 4 equal pieces; work with 1 piece at a time and keep the rest wrapped. Flatten the dough with your hands. Using a pasta machine, roll the dough through at the widest setting. Fold the dough in thirds (like a letter), then run it through the machine at the same setting, folded edge first. Repeat the folding and rolling once more, open edge first. Roll the dough through successively narrower settings, two times per setting; roll the dough once through the narrowest setting. Cut the sheet crosswise in half and hang over the back of a chair so air reaches both sides. Repeat with the remaining dough.

4 Cut the pasta sheets into 3- to 4-inch squares. On a lightly floured work surface, spread 4 pasta squares; keep the rest covered with a damp towel. Place 2 teaspoons of the filling in the center of each square. Moisten the edges with water. Top with 4 more squares, press to remove any air pockets, and then press well around the edges to seal. Transfer to a lightly floured baking sheet and cover loosely with plastic wrap. Repeat with the remaining pasta and filling.

5 Bring a large pot of salted water to a gentle simmer. Add the ravioli to the simmering water and cook, stirring occasionally, until they float. Carefully drain the ravioli, transfer to a large platter or plates, and blot dry with paper towels.

6 In a medium skillet, melt the butter, then add the sage. Pour the sage butter over the ravioli, season with pepper, and serve. Pass the remaining ½ cup Parmesan separately.

TIPS

Sweet and creamy artisanal ricotta is available at most good Italian groceries, cheese purveyors, and some farmers' markets. Calabro's fresh whole-milk ricotta is available at many supermarkets. Made from cow's milk (what you are likely to find) or sheep's milk, fresh ricotta is one of life's simple pleasures.

If the ingredients don't form a dough in step 1, add 2 to 3 teaspoons water and pulse again. On the other hand, if the dough is sticky, add a little flour. The dough needs to be firm enough to pass easily through the rollers of the pasta machine.

It's best to roll out the dough within a couple of hours of when you plan to use it.

When cooking the ravioli, stir very gently only occasionally so they don't tear or stick to each other.

VARIATION

Instead of the sage butter, serve the ravioli with a tomato sauce such as the one in Spaghetti alla Chitarra with Cherry Tomato Sauce and Basil (page 176).

SERVE WITH

Follow this with Côtes de Veau Milanaise (page 129) or Osso Buco (page 184).

MAKE AHEAD

The dough can be refrigerated overnight.

The ravioli can be prepared through step 4 and refrigerated overnight, or frozen for up to 6 months; do not defrost before cooking.

If the ingredients don't form
a dough in step 1, add 2 to
3 teaspoons water and pulse
again. On the other hand, if
the dough is sticky, add a little
flour. The dough needs to be
firm enough to pass easily
through the pasta machine.

It's best to roll out the dough
within a couple of hours of
when you plan to use it.

The cooks at Le Cirque make
their own truffle butter, but
it's available, along with fresh
white truffles, at specialty food
stores and from dartagnan.
com, plantin.com, and urbani.
com. If you want to prepare it
yourself, mash 1 tablespoon
minced black truffle peelings
with 4 tablespoons softened
salted butter. It can be
refrigerated for up to 3 days or
frozen for up to 6 months.

Many chefs peel the firm outer
rind of the truffle and mince it
to use in truffle butter or as a
simple garnish; the rest of the
truffle is thinly sliced.

SERVE WITH
To keep the Italian accent,
serve Osso Buco (page 184)
for a main course.

MAKE AHEAD
The dough can be refrigerated
overnight.

The fettuccine can be
prepared through step 3 and
refrigerated overnight.

FETTUCCINE WITH WHITE TRUFFLES

*Alain Sailhac, drilled in the classic French tradition of black truffles (*Tuber melanosporum*), had never seen a white truffle (*Tuber magnatum*) before Le Cirque, but he was a quick study. Writing in the* New York Times *in 1986, restaurant critic Bryan Miller described this dish, the result of "an annual ritual this time of year [September], when Mr. Maccioni makes his pilgrimage to Alba in northern Italy to hand-pick some of the season's first white truffles. These explosively fragrant truffles, nearly the size of tennis balls, are shaved over a bowl of fettuccine in a light cream sauce. The combination is sheer bliss." (In the same review, Miller awarded Le Cirque three stars.) Like Spaghetti Primavera (page 124), Fettuccine with White Truffles was strictly off-menu but became a favorite of regulars.*

8 APPETIZER OR 6 ENTRÉE SERVINGS

PASTA DOUGH

2 cups all-purpose flour, plus more
for sprinkling

3 large eggs

1 teaspoon extra-virgin olive oil

½ teaspoon salt

SAUCE

1½ cups heavy cream

6 tablespoons freshly grated Parmesan
cheese, plus more for serving

6 tablespoons truffle butter (see Tips)

Salt

2 fresh white truffles (about 1 ounce
each), for shaving (see Tips)

1 Make the pasta dough: In a food processor, pulse the flour a few times. Add the eggs, oil, and salt and process until a fairly stiff dough forms. Scrape the dough onto a work surface, flatten into a disk, and wrap in plastic. Let stand at room temperature for at least 30 minutes or up to 2 hours.

2 Cut the dough into 4 equal pieces; work with 1 piece at a time and keep the rest wrapped. Flatten the dough with your hands. Using a pasta machine, roll the dough through at the widest setting. Fold the dough in thirds (like a letter), then run it through the machine at the same setting, folded edge first. Repeat the folding and rolling once more, open edge first. Roll the dough through successively narrower settings, two times per setting, finishing with the second narrowest setting. Cut the sheet crosswise in half and hang over the back of a chair so air reaches both sides. Repeat with the remaining dough.

3 Feed the sheets of dough through the wide cutters of the pasta machine. Transfer to a lightly floured baking sheet and cover loosely with plastic wrap until all the sheets are cut.

4 Bring a large pot of salted water to a boil. Add the fettuccine to the boiling water and cook, stirring occasionally, until they float. Drain.

5 Meanwhile, make the sauce: In a large skillet, warm the cream and cheese over medium heat. Add the fettuccine and truffle butter, season with salt, and cook, stirring and tossing with tongs, until the butter melts. Transfer to shallow bowls or a serving dish. Shave the truffles over the top and serve. Pass the remaining cheese separately.

BOUILLABAISSE LE CIRQUE

Bouillabaisse, the Provençal fish soup stew, appears on Jean Vergnes's menus, but in a 1980 review in the New York Times, *Mimi Sheraton gushes that Alain Sailhac takes it to "sublime heights [with] a hefty, garlic-perfumed rouille sauce." Sailhac says that what's really important is the broth. He makes it with lobster shells as well as fish bones to give it deep flavor. "It really should have been called Bouillabaisse de l'Atlantique," he says. During his tenure at Le Cirque, he wasn't air-freighting Mediterranean fish and instead used local East Coast seafood.*

6 ENTRÉE SERVINGS

BROTH

¼ cup extra-virgin olive oil

1 pound lobster shells (from 2 lobsters), crushed (see Tips)

1 pound non-oily white fish bones and heads

1 star anise

6 medium tomatoes, cut into chunks

1 onion, chopped

1 small fennel bulb, chopped

1 leek, white and light green parts only, chopped

1 head of garlic, cut in half horizontally

2 quarts fish stock or water

ROUILLE

Salt

2 small new potatoes (about 4 ounces), peeled and halved

1 large egg yolk

2 garlic cloves, finely chopped

1 tablespoon broth

Pinch of saffron threads

¼ cup canola oil

¼ cup extra-virgin olive oil

Freshly ground black pepper

Pinch of ground cayenne

SOUP

¼ cup plus 2 tablespoons extra-virgin olive oil

2 tablespoons anise-flavored liqueur, such as Ricard or Pernod

2 garlic cloves, finely chopped

Pinch of saffron threads

1½ pounds mixed snapper and monkfish fillets, cut into 1½-inch pieces

Salt

1 fennel bulb, trimmed and sliced vertically ¼ inch thick

1 pound cockles or other small clams, scrubbed

1 pound mussels, scrubbed

12 jumbo shrimp in the shell, preferably with heads on, shelled and deveined

1 large tomato, peeled (see Tomato, Bacon, and Saffron Soup à la Minute, Tips, page 209), seeded, and diced

Freshly ground black pepper

18 thin slices baguette, toasted

1 Make the broth: In a large pot, heat the oil until shimmering. Add the lobster shells, fish bones, and heads and cook over medium-high heat, stirring occasionally, until they begin to break down, about 5 minutes; push to one side of the pot. Add the star anise and cook, stirring, for 1 minute. Add the tomatoes and cook, stirring, for 2 minutes. Add the onion, fennel, leek, and garlic, cover, and cook over medium heat, stirring occasionally, until softened, 8 to 10 minutes. Add the stock, bring to a simmer, and cook over medium-low heat for 15 minutes. Strain the broth and discard the solids.

2 Make the rouille: In a small saucepan of boiling, salted water, cook the potatoes until tender, about 10 minutes. Drain and transfer to a food processor. Add the egg yolk, garlic, broth, and saffron and process to a puree. Add the canola oil and process briefly until just incorporated, then pulse in the olive oil. Scrape the rouille into a bowl and season with salt, black pepper, and the cayenne. Cover and refrigerate.

3 Make the soup: In a large bowl, combine ¼ cup of the oil with the liqueur, garlic, and saffron. Add the fish, season with salt, and stir to coat. Cover and refrigerate.

4 In a large pot, heat the remaining 2 tablespoons oil until shimmering. Add the fennel and cook over medium heat, turning once, until tender and lightly browned, about 8 minutes; transfer to a plate.

5 Add the broth to the pot and bring to a boil. Add the clams and mussels, cover, and cook over medium heat until they start to open, about 3 minutes. Using a slotted spoon, transfer them to a large bowl, discarding any that don't open. Add the shrimp to the broth and cook just until they turn pink, about 3 minutes. Using a slotted spoon, transfer them to the bowl. Add the tomato and fish and marinade to the broth and simmer until the fish is just opaque, 2 to 3 minutes. Using a slotted spoon, transfer the fish to the bowl. Season the broth with salt and pepper.

6 Spoon the seafood into shallow bowls and ladle the broth on top. Garnish with the fennel slices and serve. Pass the toasts and rouille at the table.

CÔTES D'AGNEAU CHAMPVALLON

Most versions of this earthy gratin bury shoulder lamb chops between layers of sliced potatoes and onions and add stock to braise them. But Alain Sailhac folds the potatoes into the onions and lays double-thick rib chops on top, roasting them while basting occasionally until they turn burnished brown.

4 ENTRÉE SERVINGS

SERVE WITH
For a simple first course, serve Tomato, Bacon, and Saffron Soup à la Minute (page 209). Braised Lacinato Kale (page 235) makes a stellar accompaniment.

MAKE AHEAD
The recipe can be prepared through step 3 and refrigerated for up to 4 hours.

1 tablespoon clarified butter (see Caesar Salad Le Cirque, step 1, page 194)

8 double-rib lamb chops (about 5 ounces each)

Salt and freshly ground pepper

1 cup dry white wine

3 tablespoons fresh unsalted butter, plus more for brushing

3 medium onions (about 1 pound), thinly sliced

2 pounds Yukon Gold potatoes, peeled and very thinly sliced, preferably on a mandoline

2 garlic cloves, finely chopped

2 teaspoons chopped thyme leaves, plus thyme sprigs for garnishing

2 bay leaves, halved

Freshly grated nutmeg

1 cup chicken or beef stock or low-sodium broth

1 In a medium skillet, heat the clarified butter over high heat. Season the lamb chops with salt and pepper. Add the lamb to the skillet in 2 batches and brown over medium heat on 3 sides, about 2 minutes per side. Transfer the lamb to a large plate. Discard any fat in the skillet, add the wine, and boil over medium-high heat, scraping up the browned bits from the bottom, until reduced to ¼ cup, about 5 minutes; pour into a glass measuring cup.

2 Heat the oven to 350 degrees. In the same skillet, melt the fresh butter over high heat. Add the onions, season with salt and pepper, and cook over medium heat, stirring occasionally, until they start to soften, about 10 minutes. Reduce the heat to low and cook the onions until tender, about 5 minutes. Scrape the onions into a large bowl. Fold in the potatoes, garlic, thyme, and bay leaves and season with salt, pepper, and nutmeg.

3 Brush a 9- by 13-inch gratin dish with butter. Spread the potato mixture in the dish. Pour in the stock and cover the dish with foil.

4 Bake in the upper third of the oven for 45 minutes. Uncover the gratin dish, arrange the lamb chops on top, and increase the oven temperature to 400 degrees. Return the dish to the oven and bake, brushing the chops often with the reserved wine, until the potatoes are tender and an instant-read thermometer inserted in the center of the meat registers 125 to 130 degrees for medium-rare, 15 to 20 minutes. Let the dish rest for 10 minutes. Garnish with thyme sprigs and serve.

HERB-CRUSTED RACK OF LAMB

The New York Times *1980 review of Le Cirque singles out Alain Sailhac's roast rack of lamb with a gilded crust as "delicious." The genius of Sailhac's crust is that he makes a spinach-and-herb butter, blends in dry bread crumbs, and rolls it out. After the lamb is roasted, he sets a rectangle of the green crust on top, like a lid, and slides it under the broiler until golden.*

2 ENTRÉE SERVINGS

5 tablespoons unsalted butter, 4 tablespoons softened

2 garlic cloves, finely chopped

2 ounces baby spinach (about 1 packed cup)

2 tablespoons chopped parsley

Salt and freshly ground pepper

½ cup dry bread crumbs

1 tablespoon chopped thyme

1 tablespoon chopped rosemary

1 tablespoon extra-virgin olive oil

1 (2½-pound) rack of lamb, fat trimmed and ribs scraped clean

1 In a medium skillet, melt 1 tablespoon of the butter over high heat. Add the garlic and cook over medium heat until fragrant, about 1 minute. Add the spinach and parsley and cook, stirring, until wilted, 1 to 2 minutes. Season with salt and pepper. Transfer to a cutting board and chop.

2 In a medium bowl, using your fingertips, blend the 4 tablespoons softened butter with the bread crumbs, spinach mixture, thyme, and rosemary. Roll out this mixture between 2 nonstick liners or parchment paper ¼ inch thick. Refrigerate or freeze until firm.

3 Heat the oven to 400 degrees. In a medium skillet, heat the oil until shimmering. Season the lamb with salt and pepper. Add the lamb to the skillet, fat side down, and cook over medium heat until richly browned, about 3 minutes. Turn the lamb fat side up and cook for 2 minutes longer. Transfer the skillet to the oven and roast the rack until an instant-read thermometer inserted in the center of the meat registers 125 to 130 degrees for medium-rare, 15 to 20 minutes. Remove the skillet from the oven and trim the fat off the lamb.

4 Heat the broiler. Trim the herb crust to a rectangle just large enough to cover the meat. Set the herb crust on the lamb and broil until lightly golden, 3 to 5 minutes. Transfer the lamb to a cutting board and let rest for 5 minutes. Carve the lamb and serve.

TIPS

In true Le Cirque style, the lamb servings are very generous. This recipe easily serves three, or even four, as part of a multicourse meal. Cover the bones with foil when broiling the lamb if they start to get too dark.

To carve a rack of lamb, sharpen a large chef's knife. Cut in between the individual chops until you reach the bottom, then feel around with the tip of the knife for the joint between the bones and cut through it.

VARIATIONS

You can vary the spinach-and-herb-crust mixture, adding sorrel (look for it at farmers' markets) or Swiss chard leaves instead of spinach, or different herbs, or by playing around with the proportions.

SERVE WITH

For an appetizer, try Tomato Tatin (page 196) or Heirloom Tomato Salad with Gorgonzola Mousse and Arugula (page 211). It's hard to imagine a better side dish than potatoes au gratin, buttery mashed potatoes, or the herbed potato, onion, and stock gratin that's the base of Alain Sailhac's Côtes d'Agneau Champvallon (page 140). For something a little different, try Craig Hopson's Mashed Sunchokes (page 235) or Cauliflower Puree (page 123).

MAKE AHEAD

The herb crust can be refrigerated overnight.

The recipe can be prepared through step 3 up to 2 hours in advance.

CRÈME BRÛLÉE LE CIRQUE

Before Alain Sailhac took over the back of the house, Le Cirque had no pastry kitchen. He carved one out of part of his office and brought in pastry chef Dieter Schorner and his lieutenant, Francisco Gutierrez. Schorner and Gutierrez perfected the iconic egg custard under a lid of caramelized sugar. (For more on the story, see page 57.) The recipe, which is more than thirty years old, is still so popular it's stenciled on the bottom of the ramekin in which the dessert is served.

4 SERVINGS

2 cups heavy cream

1 vanilla bean, split lengthwise, seeds scraped (see Tips)

Pinch of salt

4 large egg yolks

½ cup granulated sugar

8 teaspoons sugar in the raw, for glazing (see Tips)

1 Heat the oven to 300 degrees. In a medium saucepan, heat the cream with the vanilla bean, seeds, and salt over medium heat until bubbles appear around the edge.

2 In a large glass measuring cup, blend the egg yolks and granulated sugar with a wooden spoon. Slowly add the hot cream mixture, stirring gently. Remove the vanilla bean.

3 Arrange 4 shallow 4½-inch-long ramekins in a roasting pan (see Tips). Slowly pour the custard into the ramekins, filling them almost to the top. Set the roasting pan in the center of the oven and carefully pour in enough hot water to reach halfway up the sides of the ramekins. Cover the pan loosely with foil and bake until the custards are firm at the edges but still a bit wobbly in the center, about 1 hour.

4 Transfer the ramekins to a rack to cool completely. Cover and refrigerate until cold, at least 3 hours.

5 Heat the broiler. Set the ramekins on a baking sheet and blot the surfaces of the custards to remove any condensation. Using a small sieve, sift 2 teaspoons of the sugar in the raw over each custard in a thin, even layer. Broil the custards on the top rack of the oven until the sugar is evenly caramelized, 30 seconds to 2 minutes. Let cool slightly, then serve at once.

TIPS

At Le Cirque, the chefs use a kitchen torch to caramelize the sugar topping. You can find one at Williams-Sonoma stores.

If using deeper 6-ounce ramekins, bake the custards for about 20 minutes longer and reduce the sugar topping to 1 teaspoon per custard.

A fresh vanilla bean that's been used once still has a lot of flavor. Rinse the bean and then let it dry at room temperature before wrapping and refrigerating. Used beans rehydrate when added to poaching liquid or milk to make a sauce. They can also be added to the sugar jar to make vanilla sugar.

VARIATIONS

Pastry chefs love to play around with the flavorings in Crème Brûlée, infusing the cream in step 1 with toasted fennel seeds, coffee beans, strips of orange or lemon zest, or cardamom seeds. Or you can spread fresh raspberries in the ramekins before adding the custard—the possibilities are almost endless.

MAKE AHEAD

The crème brûlées can be refrigerated, covered, for up to 2 days.

CHOCOLATE SOUFFLÉS

Although Jean Vergnes had established the tradition of serving individual soufflés at the restaurant, it was Alain Sailhac's pastry chef, Dieter Schorner, who wowed the critics with these intense, almost bitter, chocolate soufflés, adding four times as many egg whites as yolks for extra buoyancy.

6 SERVINGS

Unsalted butter, softened, for brushing

⅓ cup granulated sugar, plus more for coating

6 ounces bittersweet chocolate, chopped

2 large egg yolks

8 large egg whites

¼ teaspoon cream of tartar (optional)

Confectioners' sugar, for dusting

1 Position a rack in the center of the oven. Heat the oven to 375 degrees. Generously brush six 8-ounce ramekins, including the rims, with butter. Add a little granulated sugar to each ramekin and turn to lightly coat the bottom and sides, tapping out any excess; refrigerate.

2 In a medium stainless-steel bowl set over a medium saucepan of simmering water, heat the chocolate until just melted. Remove the bowl from the heat and stir the chocolate until smooth. Let cool slightly, then beat in the egg yolks.

3 In a large stainless-steel bowl set over a medium saucepan of simmering water, whip the egg whites with the granulated sugar at medium speed until slightly thickened and foamy, 1 to 2 minutes. Remove the bowl from the heat, add the cream of tartar, and whip at medium speed until the whites hold firm peaks. Beat one fourth of the egg whites into the chocolate mixture, then gently fold this lightened mixture into the remaining whites. Spoon the soufflé mixture into the ramekins and smooth the tops.

4 Transfer the ramekins to a roasting pan or shallow baking dish and fill the pan with ½ inch of hot water. Bake until the soufflés have risen, 10 to 12 minutes for a soft center. Dust the tops with confectioners' sugar and serve.

Gradually whisking hot milk into an egg yolk mixture before placing it on the heat prevents the eggs from scrambling.

Pastry cream traditionally uses flour or a mixture of flour and cornstarch as a thickener, but using all cornstarch makes a lighter cream that is still firm enough for piping.

For extra smoothness, push the pastry cream through a fine sieve to remove cooked egg.

VARIATIONS

To make a delightful vanilla custard, reduce the cornstarch in the pastry cream to 2 tablespoons. Serve with crisp butter cookies.

It's easy to vary the flavor of pastry cream. Whisk in about 1 teaspoon of a liqueur just before using the cream. Be sure to add the liqueur slowly and taste often. Adding too much will make the pastry cream runny. Alternatively, the pastry cream can be flavored with strips of orange zest or lemon verbena sprigs; add these flavorings when heating the milk in step 1.

MAKE AHEAD

The puff pastry pieces can be stored in an airtight container for up to 2 days.

The raspberry puree and pastry cream can be refrigerated for up to 2 days. Press a piece of plastic wrap directly on the pastry cream to prevent a skin from forming.

The napoleons can be assembled and refrigerated for up to 6 hours. Plate them just before serving.

NAPOLEON LE CIRQUE

Over the years, the brittle puff pastry layers of Le Cirque's Napoleon have been garnished with "a fluffy mortar of faintly sweetened whipped cream" (Bryan Miller's 1986 description), with pastry cream (as here), or both. Whatever the filling, it remains "so light it should come with fishing weights to hold it down," as Miller suggested after tasting it again in 1987.

4 SERVINGS

PASTRY CREAM

2 cups whole milk

½ cup sugar

1 vanilla bean, split, seeds scraped

3 tablespoons cornstarch

4 large egg yolks

2 tablespoons unsalted butter, diced

LAYERS AND SERVING

All-purpose flour, for dusting

8 ounces cold all-butter puff pastry dough

¼ cup light corn syrup, thinned with 2 tablespoons water

1 cup raspberries

2 cups mixed berries, such as blackberries, raspberries, sliced strawberries, and blueberries

1 pint raspberry sorbet

Small mint sprigs, for garnishing

1 Make the pastry cream: In a medium saucepan, bring the milk and ¼ cup of the sugar to a simmer over medium-high heat. Add the vanilla bean and seeds. Remove from the heat, cover, and let stand for 15 minutes. Strain the milk into a heatproof measuring cup.

2 In a medium bowl, whisk the cornstarch with the remaining ¼ cup sugar. Whisk in the egg yolks until smooth. Gradually whisk in the hot milk. Pour the mixture into the saucepan and cook over medium heat, whisking constantly, until the pastry cream is very thick, about 4 minutes. Whisk in the butter. Scrape the pastry cream into a bowl and refrigerate until cold.

3 Make the layers: Heat the oven to 425 degrees. Line a large baking sheet with a nonstick liner or parchment paper.

4 On a lightly floured surface, roll out the puff pastry ⅛ inch thick. Trim to a 12- by 16-inch rectangle and transfer to the baking sheet. Top with another liner and another baking sheet and bake on the middle rack for 8 minutes.

5 Remove the baking sheet from the oven and reduce the oven temperature to 375 degrees. Remove the top sheet and liner and lightly brush the pastry with the corn syrup mixture. Lay the liner back on the glazed pastry and flip over. Remove the liner from what was the bottom of the dough and lightly brush with the corn syrup; remove the liner. Return the pastry to the oven, uncovered, and bake until lightly browned, doubled in height, and dry, about 15 minutes.

6 Slide the liner and pastry onto a rack and let cool. Cut the pastry lengthwise into 3 equal strips, then crosswise into twelve 3½-inch squares.

7 In a blender or food processor, puree the raspberries, then work through a sieve to remove the seeds.

8 Arrange 8 of the pastry squares on a work surface. Scoop the pastry cream into a pastry bag fitted with a plain medium tip and pipe the cream in 9 mounds on the squares. Stack 2 pastry cream squares, then set a plain square on top.

9 Transfer each napoleon to a plate. Mound some of the berries next to the pastry and more on top. Set a small scoop of raspberry sorbet on top next to the berries. Decorate the plates with dots of the raspberry puree, garnish with the mint, and serve.

FINE TARTE AUX POMMES

Nouvelle cuisine pastry chefs transformed the clunky apple tart into a chic pastry disk. They covered the pastry with apples sliced X-ray thin on a mandoline, brushed them with butter, and baked them until lightly caramelized. The individual tarts practically melt in your mouth. "We sold a ton of those things," says Alain Sailhac. They still sell like hotcakes.

4 SERVINGS

8 ounces cold all-butter puff pastry dough

2 Granny Smith apples, peeled, cored, halved, and sliced lengthwise ⅛ inch thick on a mandoline

2 tablespoons unsalted butter, melted and cooled

¼ cup light brown sugar

1 Line 2 baking sheets with a nonstick liner or parchment paper. On a lightly floured surface, roll out the puff pastry ¹⁄₁₆ inch thick. Using a plate or a pan lid as a guide, cut the dough into 4 rounds about 6 inches across. Transfer the rounds to the baking sheets and prick the dough all over with a fork. Chill until firm, at least 15 minutes.

2 Heat the oven to 350 degrees. Arrange the apple slices on the dough rounds, rounded sides out, in concentric circles. Overlap the slices so the dough is completely covered. Brush the apples with the butter and sprinkle with the brown sugar.

3 Bake the tarts until the apples are tender and the pastry is crisp, about 30 minutes. Serve hot.

BREAD PUDDING

Is bread pudding too homey a dessert for Le Cirque? Not when it's made this way: You bake cubes of brioche in what is essentially the restaurant's decadent crème brûlée mixture. Critic Mimi Sheraton called it "the world's best bread pudding."

6 SERVINGS

2½ cups heavy cream

1 vanilla bean, split lengthwise, seeds scraped

1 teaspoon ground cinnamon

½ teaspoon salt

2 large eggs

1 large egg yolk

½ cup sugar

Unsalted butter, softened, for brushing

12 ounces brioche, cut into 1½-inch cubes

1 In a medium saucepan, heat the cream with the vanilla bean, seeds, cinnamon, and salt over medium heat until bubbles appear around the edge.

2 In a large glass measuring cup, blend the eggs, egg yolk, and sugar with a wooden spoon. Slowly add the hot cream mixture, stirring gently. Remove the vanilla bean.

3 Heat the oven to 350 degrees. Generously butter a 7- by 11-inch baking pan. Spread the brioche cubes in the pan. Pour the custard over the brioche and let soak for 5 minutes.

4 Bake on the upper rack of the oven until puffed and set in the center, about 45 minutes. Serve warm.

DANIEL BOULUD
1986 to 1992

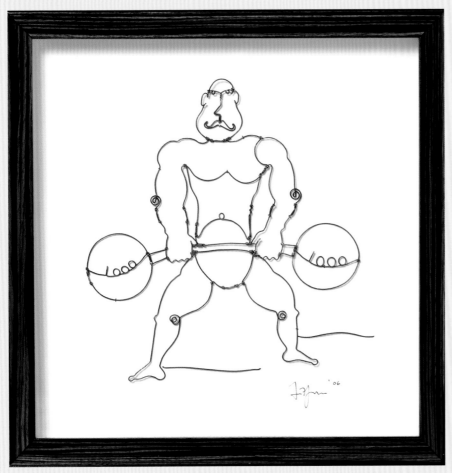

Art by Tim Flynn.

LOBSTER SALAD LE CIRQUE

If you combined in one dish everything Sirio wants Le Cirque's food to be, you'd get this composed lobster salad: abundant luxury ingredients prepared simply and arranged precisely and artfully on the plate. Alain Sailhac introduced a lobster salad with samphire, in 1978, but Daniel Boulud created this winning version with its mix of fresh vegetables and truffle dressing. Each flavor is bright, distinct, amazing. The restaurant serves an entire 1½-pound lobster per person as a first course. It is a complete introduction to the restaurant and its pleasures.

4 APPETIZER SERVINGS

LOBSTER SALAD

Kosher salt

2 ounces haricots verts

12 asparagus spears, 2 inches of tips only

2 medium fingerling potatoes, peeled

2 live (1½-pound) lobsters

8 small bibb lettuce leaves

1 medium tomato, cut into thin wedges

½ avocado, peeled and thinly sliced

½ pink grapefruit, peeled and cut in between the membranes into segments (see Tips)

Fleur de sel (see Tips)

Snipped chives, for garnishing

BLACK TRUFFLE VINAIGRETTE

1 tablespoon sherry vinegar

1 tablespoon extra-virgin olive oil

1 tablespoon canola oil

1 tablespoon black truffle oil (see Tips)

½ tablespoon canned black truffle juice (see Tips)

1 teaspoon black truffle peelings (see Tips), minced (optional)

Salt and freshly ground pepper

LEMON VINAIGRETTE

3 tablespoons extra-virgin olive oil

1 tablespoon fresh lemon juice

Salt and freshly ground pepper

1   Make the lobster salad: Bring a large pot of water to a boil. Season with kosher salt. Fill a medium bowl with ice water. Add the haricots verts and asparagus, separately, to the boiling water and cook until crisp-tender, about 2 minutes. Using a slotted spoon, transfer them to the ice water to cool as quickly as possible, about 1 minute. Using a slotted spoon, transfer to a thick kitchen towel, roll up, and refrigerate.

2   Add the potatoes to the boiling water and cook until tender, about 15 minutes. Using a slotted spoon, transfer to a cutting board. Pat dry and thinly slice.

3   Add the lobsters to the boiling water, cover, and bring to a boil, then uncover and cook over high heat for 8 minutes. Fill a very large bowl with ice water. Using tongs, transfer the lobsters to the ice water and let them cool slightly. Transfer to a cutting board and remove the rubber bands from the claws. Crack the claws and knuckles and remove the meat. Using scissors, slit the tail shells, top and bottom, and remove the meat. Cut the tails lengthwise in half and remove the dark intestinal veins.

4   Make the black truffle vinaigrette: In a medium bowl, whisk the vinegar with the oils, truffle juice, and truffles. Season with salt and pepper. Add the lobster meat and toss to coat.

5   Make the lemon vinaigrette: In a medium bowl, whisk the oil and lemon juice and season with salt and pepper. Add the haricots verts, asparagus, and potatoes, separately, to the vinaigrette; stir to coat and, using a slotted spoon, transfer each batch of vegetables to a plate.

6   Nestle 2 lettuce leaves in the center of each plate to form a bowl and arrange the meat from ½ lobster on top. Mound the haricots verts, asparagus tips, potatoes, tomato, avocado, and grapefruit in small piles around the plates. Add a spoonful of truffle vinaigrette to the plates. Sprinkle with fleur de sel, garnish the potatoes with chives, and serve.

LOBSTER RISOTTO

As soon as Sirio bought out his French partner, Jean Vergnes, Italian dishes like risotto put in a more frequent appearance at Le Cirque. In addition to chunks of fresh lobster and lobster-infused sauce américaine, Daniel Boulud boosted the shellfish flavor with a butter mashed with the lobster's green tomalley.

6 APPETIZER OR 4 ENTRÉE SERVINGS

SAUCE AMÉRICAINE

3 tablespoons extra-virgin olive oil

1 pound raw lobster shells, crushed (see Tips)

1 large onion, finely chopped

1 medium carrot, finely chopped

2 garlic cloves, crushed

2 tablespoons Cognac or brandy

½ cup dry white wine

1 tablespoon tomato paste

1 bouquet garni (see Tips)

1 large tarragon sprig

Salt

Ground cayenne

TOMALLEY BUTTER

4 tablespoons softened unsalted butter

2 tablespoons raw lobster tomalley (see Tips)

LOBSTER RICE

3 to 4 cups chicken stock

6 tablespoons unsalted butter

1 small onion, finely chopped

1 large garlic clove, finely chopped

Salt and freshly ground pepper

1¼ cups Vialone Nano rice (see Tips)

½ cup dry white wine

¼ cup freshly grated Parmesan cheese

8 ounces cooked lobster meat, cut into ½-inch dice

1 tablespoon finely chopped rosemary

1 Make the sauce américaine: In a large pot, heat the oil until shimmering. Add the lobster shells and cook over medium-high heat, stirring, until red, 2 to 3 minutes. Add the onion, carrot, and garlic and cook over medium heat, stirring occasionally, until the vegetables are softened, about 5 minutes. Add the Cognac and bring to a boil, then tilt the pot and, using a long match, carefully ignite it. When the flames subside, add 2 cups water, the wine, tomato paste, bouquet garni, and tarragon. Bring to a simmer and cook over medium-high heat until reduced to 2 cups, about 20 minutes.

2 Discard the herbs and lobster shells from the pot. Using an immersion blender, puree the sauce. Scrape it into a medium saucepan. For extra smoothness, push the sauce through a fine sieve or a food mill into a saucepan. Season with salt and cayenne.

3 Make the tomalley butter: In a mini food processor, puree the butter with the lobster tomalley; refrigerate.

4 Make the lobster rice: In a medium saucepan, bring the stock to a simmer. Keep warm.

5 In a large saucepan, melt the butter over medium-high heat. Add the onion and garlic, season with salt and pepper, and cook over medium heat, stirring occasionally, until softened, about 5 minutes. Add the rice and cook over medium-high heat for 1 minute, stirring to coat. Add the wine and cook, stirring, until nearly absorbed. Add 1 cup of the stock and cook over medium heat, stirring constantly, until nearly absorbed. Continue adding the stock, ½ cup at a time, stirring constantly until it is nearly absorbed between additions. The risotto is done when the rice is al dente, 15 to 20 minutes total.

6 Remove the pan from the heat and stir in the cheese, lobster meat, tomalley butter, and rosemary. Season with salt and pepper. Spoon the risotto into shallow bowls, drizzle some of the sauce américaine over the top, and serve. Pass the remaining sauce separately.

TIPS

To make a bouquet garni, tie 3 thyme sprigs, 6 parsley stems, 1 bay leaf, and 3 leek or scallion greens in a bundle with kitchen string.

The lobster's dark green tomalley is available from lepicerie.com.

Vialone Nano's short, plump grains don't overcook as easily as Arborio or Canaroli rice.

Instead of using raw lobster shells to make the sauce américaine, you can substitute the shells (including the head and legs) from 2 boiled lobsters, reserved from, say, Lobster Salad Le Cirque (page 150). Add them to the pot with the vegetables.

The recipe for sauce américaine makes more than enough for four servings, but it freezes well. Extra sauce is a good incentive for making Lobster Thermidor (page 225). Or serve the leftover sauce another time with sautéed monkfish fillet—the classic lotte à l'américaine.

SERVE WITH

For a main course, try Daurade en Croûte de Sel (page 157) or Braised Veal Shank for Two (page 166).

MAKE AHEAD

The sauce américaine and lobster tomalley butter can be refrigerated overnight. The lobster tomalley butter can be frozen for up to 3 months.

BLACK TIE SCALLOPS

Critic Bryan Miller judged Daniel Boulud's "sea scallops fantasy in black tie" (its name on a 1987 menu) "unforgettable . . . an individual silver casserole dish of exquisite sliced sea scallops layered with black truffles, moistened with buttery vermouth and truffle juice." The recipe evolved into one of Boulud's iconic creations; ultimately, the chef wrapped each whole Maine sea scallop (layered with truffles) in spinach leaves and baked it in a crisp puff-pastry shell. It may require a lot of labor, but for home cooks it's entirely doable, and just as memorable.

8 APPETIZER OR 4 ENTRÉE SERVINGS

All-purpose flour, for dusting

8 ounces cold all-butter puff pastry dough

Salt

12 large spinach or Swiss chard leaves, stems and thick ribs removed

8 large sea scallops (see Tips)

Freshly ground pepper

1 fresh black truffle (about 1 ounce), sliced paper-thin, trimmings reserved (see Tips)

1 large egg beaten with 1 teaspoon water

1 tablespoon extra-virgin olive oil

3 tablespoons ruby port

2 tablespoons demiglace (see Tips)

2 tablespoons unsalted butter, diced

1 On a lightly floured work surface, roll out the puff pastry dough 1/16 inch thick. Using a 2½-inch biscuit cutter, stamp out 8 rounds slightly larger than the scallops. Cut out eight 2½-by 7-inch rectangles. Transfer to a lightly floured baking sheet and refrigerate.

2 Bring a medium saucepan of water to a boil. Salt the water. Fill a medium bowl with ice water. Line a baking sheet with a kitchen towel. Add the spinach to the boiling water and blanch for 30 seconds to 1 minute. Drain and transfer to the ice water so it cools as quickly as possible, about 1 minute. Drain, shaking off the water. Carefully unfurl each leaf on the towel, without overlapping. Pat dry with paper towels.

3 Make 2 parallel horizontal cuts in each scallop, cutting almost but not all the way through. Season each cut with salt and pepper and insert a truffle slice. Set a stuffed scallop on a spinach leaf and wrap the scallop, using additional leaves if needed. Reserve the remaining truffle slices.

4 Remove the dough from the refrigerator. Brush 1 narrow end of a pastry rectangle with the egg wash. Set a wrapped scallop on its side at the opposite end and roll up the scallop. Brush 1 pastry round with egg wash, set the scallop horizontally on top, and press the rectangle and round together to seal. Pinch the dough on top to seal like a dumpling. Trim the bottom pastry to neaten. Repeat with the remaining scallops. Refrigerate for at least 15 minutes. Refrigerate the remaining egg wash.

5 Heat the oven to 450 degrees. Line a baking sheet with a nonstick liner or parchment paper. Brush the scallop rounds with the remaining egg wash and transfer to the prepared baking sheet. Bake until puffed and golden brown, 7 to 10 minutes. Transfer the baking sheet to a wire cooling rack.

TIPS

Buy "dry" scallops. "Wet" scallops are soaked in a solution that plumps and whitens them and extends their shelf life. They never brown properly (they exude quantities of liquid) and don't have any flavor.

Truffles are available at specialty food shops and from dartagnan.com, plantin.com, and urbani.com. Many chefs peel the firm outer rind of the truffle and mince it to use in truffle butter or truffle salt; the rest of the truffle is thinly sliced.

Instead of the demiglace, you can use ¼ cup chicken stock or low-sodium broth reduced to 2 tablespoons.

Daniel Boulud used spinach leaves, but Swiss chard leaves are larger and sturdier for wrapping the scallops.

VARIATION

Without the pastry, this is an easy dish—scallops, black truffle shavings, a hint of spinach, and deeply flavored sauce.

SERVE WITH

Creamed spinach and glazed baby turnips are perfect accompaniments.

MAKE AHEAD

The recipe can be prepared through step 4 and refrigerated overnight.

6 Finely chop all the remaining truffle pieces. In a medium
saucepan, heat the oil until shimmering. Add the truffle and
cook over medium-low heat, stirring occasionally, until fragrant,
about 2 minutes. Add the port and demiglace, bring to a simmer,
and cook over medium-high heat until reduced by half, about 2
minutes. Remove the pan from the heat and whisk in the butter
until the sauce thickens creamily. Season with salt and pepper.

7 Using a serrated knife, cut each scallop in half. Spoon a little
of the sauce in the center of each plate. Arrange 4 scallop
halves with their layered insides facing out, and serve.

DAURADE EN CROÛTE DE SEL

When Daniel Boulud took over the kitchen at Le Cirque, in 1986, the critics went crazy. "He was just another well-trained technician, running the kitchen at Le Regence," Gael Greene wrote in a 1989 review. "Now at Le Cirque, toiling in the vortex of Sirio Maccioni's consuming obsession with perfection, chef Boulud is flying." The reviewers, however, continued to gripe about all the French in the menu—for instance, this dish. It's still on the menu, en français, *but asking a question or two and discovering whole daurade baked in a salt crust is so worth it. The simple technique is matchless. The fish emerges pristine, moist-fleshed. It's served with sauce vierge—that is, lemon vinaigrette flavored with chopped tomatoes and herbs.*

2 ENTRÉE SERVINGS

1 lemongrass stalk, pale core only, sliced

1-inch piece of ginger, sliced

1 (2-pound) whole daurade or black bass, cleaned and scaled

2 tablespoons extra-virgin olive oil, plus more for rubbing

1 pound kosher salt

1 large egg white, lightly beaten

1 small tomato (about 4 ounces), peeled (see Tomato, Bacon, and Saffron Soup à la Minute, Tips, page 209), seeded, and diced

2 tablespoons finely chopped parsley or a mix of tender herbs

1 tablespoon fresh lemon juice

Table salt and freshly ground pepper

1 Heat the oven to 350 degrees. Stuff the lemongrass and ginger in the fish cavity. Rub the fish all over with oil. In a large bowl, combine the salt with the egg white and 2 teaspoons water. On a large rimmed baking sheet, using half of the salt mixture, spread a shallow fish-shaped pile. Set the fish on the pile and cover completely with the remaining salt, pressing to adhere.

2 Bake the fish for 45 minutes.

3 Meanwhile, in a medium bowl, combine the tomato, oil, parsley, and lemon juice; season with salt and pepper.

4 Using a knife and fork, break the top crust into pieces and remove. (The skin usually peels off with the salt.) Fillet the fish and arrange on plates. Spoon the sauce over the fish and serve.

TIPS

The salt mixture looks like wet sand before it's baked.

Surprisingly, for a fish baked in a salt crust, the flesh is perfectly seasoned. The skin keeps it from absorbing too much salt.

Sauce vierge can be used on almost any fish, and it can be flavored with almost any herb you happen to have on hand.

VARIATIONS

At Le Cirque, the kitchen wraps the fish in blanched cabbage leaves before packing it in the salt crust. A server then breaks the crust and peels away the cabbage to reveal a perfect skin-on fish. To get this result, cut out the large ribs of 4 large cabbage leaves. Blanch the leaves in a large pot of boiling water until tender, drain, and cool in a bowl of ice water. Drain again and pat dry, then wrap the fish.

Stuffing the fish with lemongrass and ginger is Chef Craig Hopson's twist. The aromatics can be added or not.

SERVE WITH

Grilled vegetables make an excellent accompaniment to the fish. Pass lemon halves at the table for squeezing over the vegetables. You can never have too much lemon juice.

SERVE WITH

To make a menu of Boulud's greatest hits, serve Black Tie Scallops (page 154) as an appetizer and Jacques Torres's Caramel-Walnut Soufflés (page 186) for dessert.

MAKE AHEAD

The recipe can be prepared through step 3 and refrigerated for up to 2 hours.

CRISP PAUPIETTES OF BLACK BASS IN BAROLO SAUCE

In 1987, Bryan Miller waxed lyrical about Daniel Boulud's now-mythic bass recipe: "One world-class dish, if one can be so effusive about a fish, is the roasted black sea bass wrapped in diaphanous sheets of sliced potatoes, all golden crackling, set in a concentrated Barolo wine sauce brightened with shallots and thyme." In the same review, he awarded Le Cirque four stars.

4 ENTRÉE SERVINGS

FISH

4 skinless 4-ounce black bass or black cod fillets

Salt and freshly ground pepper

1 teaspoon chopped thyme

2 large Idaho (baking) potatoes

5 tablespoons clarified butter (see Caesar Salad Le Cirque, step 1, page 194)

3 large leeks, white parts only, thinly sliced

1 tablespoon minced chives

BAROLO SAUCE

1 tablespoon canola oil

½ cup chopped shallots

½ cup sliced white mushroom caps

1 small thyme sprig

1 cup chicken stock or clam juice

3 cups Barolo or other full-bodied dry red wine

1 tablespoon heavy cream

½ cup (1 stick) cold unsalted butter, diced

Pinch of sugar

Salt and freshly ground pepper

1 Make the fish: Trim each of the bass fillets into a 5- by 1½-inch rectangle. Season with salt, pepper, and the thyme.

2 Using a knife, slice each potato lengthwise to remove the rounded portions and make a block shape; do not cut off the tips of the potatoes, but do peel them. Using a mandoline, slice the potatoes lengthwise paper-thin. Brush the slices on both sides with 1 tablespoon of the butter and season with salt.

3 For each paupiette, on a 10-inch sheet of wax paper, arrange 8 slightly overlapping potato slices to form a 5-inch-wide rectangle. Center a fish fillet horizontally in the rectangle and wrap the potatoes around the fillet to enclose it completely. Use the wax paper to help seal the potato wrap; remove the paper. Repeat to form the remaining paupiettes. Cover and refrigerate.

4 Make the sauce: In a medium saucepan, heat the oil until shimmering. Add the shallots, mushrooms, and thyme and cook over high heat, stirring frequently, for 10 minutes. Add the stock and boil until the pan is almost dry. Stir in the wine and boil until reduced to 2 tablespoons, about 30 minutes. Stir in the cream and bring to a boil over low heat. Whisk in the butter and sugar, then season with salt and pepper. Strain the sauce through a fine sieve, pressing on the solids, and keep warm.

5 In a medium skillet, melt 2 tablespoons of the clarified butter over medium heat. Add the leeks and cook, stirring, until softened, about 5 minutes. Season with salt and pepper and keep warm.

6 In a large nonstick skillet, heat the remaining 2 tablespoons clarified butter over medium-high heat. Add the paupiettes and cook until the potatoes are tender and golden brown, turning once with a large spatula, 8 to 10 minutes per side.

7 Mound the leeks on plates and spoon the Barolo sauce around them. Set the paupiettes on the leeks and serve.

NAVARIN OF LAMB

Daniel Boulud perfumed the classic spring lamb and vegetable stew with unexpected orange zest and rosemary—Provençal accents—as an homage to Roger Vergé, the great nouvelle cuisine chef of Le Moulin de Mougins in southern France. New York Times *critic Bryan Miller found it "lighter and daintier than a thick-sauced home version, but the verdant flavors come rolling through."*

4 ENTRÉE SERVINGS

½ cup all-purpose flour

3 tablespoons extra-virgin olive oil

2 pounds boneless lamb shoulder, cut into 1½- to 2-inch pieces

Salt and freshly ground pepper

1 cup chopped onion

½ cup chopped carrot

½ cup chopped celery

1 head of garlic, cut in half horizontally

4 thyme sprigs, plus more for garnishing

4 rosemary sprigs, plus more for garnishing

1 orange, zested (see Tips) and juiced

4 cups veal or chicken stock or low-sodium broth

8 small new potatoes, halved

8 baby carrots, peeled, tops trimmed to ½ inch, or 2 regular carrots, peeled and sliced on the diagonal ¾ inch thick

½ cup snow peas

3 scallions, cut into 3-inch pieces

Cherry tomatoes, halved, for garnishing (optional)

Basil sprigs, for garnishing (optional)

1 Heat the oven to 350 degrees. Spread the flour in a baking pan. In a large enameled cast-iron casserole, heat 2 tablespoons of the oil until shimmering. Season the lamb generously with salt and pepper and dredge in the flour, patting off the excess. Working in two batches, add the lamb to the pot and cook over medium heat until browned on all sides, about 10 minutes per batch; transfer to a large bowl. Discard the fat.

2 Add the onion, chopped carrot, celery, garlic, thyme, rosemary, and remaining 1 tablespoon oil to the pot. Cook over medium heat, stirring occasionally, until softened, about 5 minutes.

3 Add the orange juice to the pot and bring to a simmer, scraping up the browned bits on the bottom. Return the lamb to the pot along with the orange zest and stock, cover, and bring to a simmer. Transfer to the oven and cook until the lamb is tender, about 1½ hours.

4 Meanwhile, bring a medium saucepan of salted water to a boil. Add the potatoes and cook over medium-high heat until tender, 10 to 15 minutes. Using a slotted spoon, transfer to a bowl. Add the baby carrots to the boiling water and cook until tender, 8 to 10 minutes; transfer to the potatoes. Add the snow peas and scallions to the boiling water and cook until crisp-tender, about 1 minute. Drain and rinse under cold water. Add to the potatoes.

5 Remove the pot from the oven and transfer the lamb to a bowl. Strain the braising liquid into a medium saucepan; discard the vegetables. Bring the braising liquid to a boil over medium-high heat and cook until slightly thickened and flavorful, about 10 minutes. Add the lamb to the pan.

6 Spoon the stew into shallow bowls, garnish with the potatoes, carrots, snow peas, scallions, cherry tomatoes and basil if using, thyme, and rosemary, and serve.

TIPS
Use a vegetable peeler to remove the orange zest in long strips, leaving behind as much of the bitter white pith as possible.

The navarin can also be braised on top of the stove over low heat.

VARIATIONS
Tender spring peas, carrots, onions, and potatoes are the classic vegetables that are blanched and stirred into a navarin just before serving to give the stew a fresh taste. Young turnips, snap peas, white or green asparagus tips, fiddlehead ferns, artichoke bottoms, and morel mushrooms would also be terrific additions.

SERVE WITH
For accompaniments, serve an herbed rice pilaf and fresh peas. You can never have enough peas when they first arrive at the market in early spring. Start the meal with Spring Pea Soup with Parmesan Frico (page 210).

MAKE AHEAD
The navarin can be prepared through step 3 and refrigerated for up to 2 days.

SYLVAIN PORTAY
1992 to 1996

Art by Tim Flynn.

COCOTTE DE LÉGUMES MIJOTÉS

In this cross between a warm salad and a stew, each of a variety of vegetables is quickly sautéed, then simmered with the others until lightly cooked and served with a dollop of fresh cheese and a drizzle of peppery olive oil. When Sylvain Portay first prepared the dish at the restaurant Louis XV in Monaco, he included sixteen different vegetables, and instead of using bacon for flavor, as here, he added black truffles.

4 ENTRÉE SERVINGS

1 bacon slice, cut into 4 pieces

8 teaspoons extra-virgin olive oil, plus more for drizzling

4 baby turnips, peeled and halved or quartered if large, tops trimmed to ½ inch

4 baby carrots, peeled, tops trimmed to ½ inch, or 1 regular carrot, peeled and sliced on the diagonal ¾ inch thick

8 snow peas

8 radishes, halved

1 (6-ounce) zucchini, halved lengthwise and sliced crosswise ¼ inch thick

4 asparagus spears

½ cup shelled peas (2½ ounces)

½ cup cooked shell beans (2½ ounces or 8 ounces in the pod), such as cranberry beans or lima beans (see Tips)

1 romaine lettuce heart, quartered lengthwise

1 cup chicken stock or low-sodium broth

¾ cup fresh goat cheese or ricotta (3½ ounces)

Flaky salt and freshly ground pepper

1 In a medium skillet, cook the bacon over medium heat until lightly browned, about 5 minutes. Transfer the bacon to a dish. Add 1 teaspoon of the oil to the skillet and heat until shimmering. Add the turnips and carrots and cook over medium heat, stirring, for 3 minutes; transfer to a bowl. Repeat with the snow peas, radishes, zucchini, asparagus, peas, beans, and lettuce, cooking each vegetable separately in 1 teaspoon of the oil for 1 to 2 minutes and adding it to a second bowl.

2 In a medium enameled cast-iron casserole, combine the turnips, carrots, and stock. Press a piece of parchment paper on top, cover, and bring to a simmer, then cook over medium-low heat until al dente, about 5 minutes. Add all the remaining vegetables except the lettuce, bring to a simmer, and cook until just tender, about 4 minutes.

3 Spoon the vegetables, a little of the broth, and the bacon into shallow bowls. Set a dollop of cheese on the vegetables, drizzle with oil, and season with flaky salt and pepper. Serve warm.

TIPS
New-crop shelling beans (as opposed to dried beans) are available in the fall. To cook them, remove the beans from their pods, cover with water, and add 1 sliced onion, 1 garlic clove, and 1 rosemary sprig; season with salt. Simmer over medium heat until tender, about 30 minutes. While they are in season, cook up as many as you have time to shuck; these creamy seasonal beans are fantastic warm with a drizzle of olive oil.

VARIATIONS
This is one of those dishes where, really, anything goes. Experiment with other vegetables, cauliflower or broccoli florets, for instance, or sugar snap peas.
It can easily be made vegetarian by omitting the bacon and substituting vegetable stock for the chicken stock. Stir in 2 tablespoons chopped mixed herbs, such as tarragon, parsley, basil, and chives, and 1 teaspoon fresh lemon juice into the stew just before serving.

SERVE WITH
Portay's John Dory in Bouillabaisse Sauce with Basil and Olives (page 165) would make a great main course.

SERVE WITH

Sylvain Portay tosses young salad greens with more of the lemon vinaigrette and arranges the salad on the plate next to the salmon.

MAKE AHEAD

The ratatouille salad can be prepared through step 2 and refrigerated for up to 4 hours.

BACON-WRAPPED SALMON WITH RATATOUILLE SALAD

Even though Sylvain Portay was born in Evian-les-Bains on the French-Swiss border and grew up in Paris, his cuisine was deeply affected by cooking at the Negresco Hotel in Nice and helming the kitchen at Alain Ducasse's restaurant Louis XV in Monaco. He brought the Provençal influence with him to Le Cirque in dishes like this pan-seared salmon paired with a warm chopped salad composed of the vegetables you traditionally find in a ratatouille stew—zucchini, bell pepper, onion, eggplant. Dressed with a lemony vinaigrette, the bright-flavored salad contrasts beautifully with the rich fish and smoky bacon.

4 ENTRÉE SERVINGS

½ cup plus 1 teaspoon extra-virgin olive oil

2 tablespoons fresh lemon juice

Salt and freshly ground pepper

1 (6-ounce) zucchini, cut into ¼-inch dice

1 red bell pepper, cut into ¼-inch dice

1 onion, cut into ¼-inch dice

4 ounces eggplant, cut into ¼-inch dice

4 (6-ounce) skinless salmon fillets

4 bacon slices

1 small tomato (about 4 ounces), peeled (see Tomato, Bacon, and Saffron Soup à la Minute, Tips, page 209), seeded, and cut into ¼-inch dice

1. In a medium bowl, whisk 6 tablespoons of the olive oil and the lemon juice, and season with salt and pepper.

2. In a medium skillet, using 1 teaspoon of the oil for each vegetable, cook the zucchini, red pepper, onion, and eggplant, separately, over medium heat, stirring occasionally, until al dente, 5 to 7 minutes each. Add to the lemon vinaigrette.

3. In a large skillet, heat the remaining 1 tablespoon oil until shimmering. Season the salmon fillets with salt and pepper and wrap each one in a slice of bacon. Add to the skillet and cook over medium heat until the fillets are golden brown and just opaque throughout, about 4 minutes per side.

4. Add the tomato to the lemon vinaigrette and toss to coat. Mound some of the ratatouille salad in the center of each plate. Set a salmon fillet on top, drizzle with a little lemon vinaigrette, and serve. Pass the remaining salad separately.

JOHN DORY IN BOUILLABAISSE SAUCE WITH BASIL AND OLIVES

"When you live in the South of France, bouillabaisse becomes part of your vocabulary," says Sylvain Portay. In this dish, the chef rethinks the classic fish stew, sautéing the fish separately and whipping up a quick tomato-y, fennel-scented fish broth, which he reduces and emulsifies with olive oil to make a glossy sauce. To compare Portay's version with a more traditional recipe, see Alain Sailhac's Bouillabaisse Le Cirque (page 138).

4 ENTRÉE SERVINGS

½ cup extra-virgin olive oil

1 onion, chopped

1 leek, white and light green parts only, chopped

1 fennel bulb, chopped

2 (2-pound) whole John Dory, each cut into 2 fillets, heads and bones reserved (see Tips)

2 medium tomatoes, chopped

Salt and freshly ground pepper

Niçoise olives, for garnishing

Tiny basil sprigs, for garnishing

1. In a large saucepan, heat 2 tablespoons of the oil until shimmering. Add the onion, leek, fennel, and reserved fish heads and bones and cook over medium heat, stirring occasionally, until the vegetables are softened, about 5 minutes; push to one side of the pan. Add the tomatoes and cook, stirring, for 2 minutes. Add 2 cups water, cover, and bring to a simmer. Cook over low heat for 30 minutes. Strain into a medium saucepan and discard the solids.

2. Bring the broth to a simmer and cook over medium-high heat until reduced to 1 cup, about 20 minutes. Add 2 tablespoons of the oil and simmer until emulsified. Season with salt and pepper.

3. Heat the oven to 200 degrees. In a medium skillet, heat 1 tablespoon of the oil until shimmering. Season 1 fish fillet with salt and pepper and cook over medium heat until opaque throughout, 2 to 3 minutes per side. Transfer to a baking sheet and keep warm in the oven. Wipe out the skillet and repeat with the remaining fillets.

4. Transfer the fillets to plates. Spoon the sauce over the fish, garnish with olives and basil, and serve.

TIPS
The John Dory fish, called St. Pierre in French (it's common on European tables), is recognized by its long spines and the large dark spot on its side. Any flat white-fleshed whole fish that serves two can be used here—for instance, fluke or turbot.

Or you can substitute 4 (6-ounce) white fish fillets plus 1 pound heads and bones for the whole fish.

VARIATION
Sylvain Portay studs the thick fish fillets with pitted olives wrapped in basil leaves. Slice the olives crosswise if needed to make them the same thickness as the fillets.

SERVE WITH
Keep the spirit of the Riviera: sauté diced zucchini, fennel, and red bell peppers in olive oil as an accompaniment. Serve steamed rice to soak up the juices.

MAKE AHEAD
The broth can be prepared through step 1 and refrigerated for up to 2 days.

BRAISED VEAL SHANK FOR TWO

Instead of Le Cirque's familiar Osso Buco (page 184), Sylvain Portay wanted to prepare something more unusual, so he introduced a whole glazed veal shank. The joint bubbles gently in veal broth with thyme and aromatic vegetables until melt-in-your-mouth tender. Then the broth is strained, reduced, and sharpened with a little white wine vinegar, and the shank is returned to the oven and basted frequently with the broth. The mahogany shank with its velvety sauce carries on the restaurant's tradition of "Rôtis," sized-for-two cuts of meat.

2 ENTRÉE SERVINGS

1 (3½-pound) veal shank

1 carrot, halved

1 onion, halved

1 large celery rib, halved

1 large thyme sprig

Salt

1 teaspoon whole black peppercorns

1 cup veal stock, chicken stock, or low-sodium broth

2 tablespoons white wine vinegar

Freshly ground pepper

1 Heat the oven to 350 degrees. In a large oval enameled cast-iron casserole, combine the veal shank, carrot, onion, celery, and thyme and season with salt and the peppercorns. Add the stock and water to barely cover. Cover and bring to a simmer, then transfer to the oven and cook, turning the shank every 30 minutes, until tender, 1½ to 2 hours.

2 Transfer the shank to a large roasting pan. Strain the braising liquid into a large saucepan, bring to a simmer, and cook over medium-high heat until reduced by half, about 30 minutes.

3 Increase the oven temperature to 400 degrees. Stir the vinegar into the braising liquid, pour over the shank, and bake, basting often, until the shank is coated with a light syrupy glaze, 20 to 30 minutes.

4 Transfer the shank to a cutting board and slice the meat off the bone. Arrange the meat on plates and season with salt and ground pepper. Season the sauce with salt and pepper. Spoon a little of the sauce over the meat and serve. Pass the remaining sauce separately.

VARIATIONS

Top each potato with a poached egg (see Brandade Fraîche with Softly Poached Egg and Winter Truffles, page 220) before adding the shaved truffles, and serve as an entrée with a green salad.

Instead of shaving truffles over the potatoes before serving, garnish the potatoes with 2 ounces Osetra caviar.

Occasionally in the past the restaurant served an even more luxurious version of this dish, topping it with a seared pavé of foie gras.

SERVE WITH

For a main dish, follow the baked potatoes with Braised Veal Shank for Two (page 166), Entrecôte aux Poivres (page 198), or Chicken Under a Brick (page 182).

MAKE AHEAD

The potatoes can be prepared through step 3 and refrigerated for up to 4 hours.

STUFFED BAKED POTATOES WITH TRUFFLES

After Daniel Boulud's intricate dishes, such as Black Tie Scallops (page 154), in which the shellfish are layered with prized truffles, then wrapped in spinach leaves and puff pastry, Sylvain Portay ushered in a pared-down era of the perfect, occasionally humble, ingredient, simply yet perfectly cooked, alongside Le Cirque's luxe standbys. In this dish, for example, Portay enriches the flesh of a baked potato with browned butter, olive oil, and white truffles, then stuffs the mixture back into the potato skin and returns it to the oven until golden. In fine Le Cirque fashion, more truffles are showered over the top at the table.

4 APPETIZER OR SIDE SERVINGS

4 large Idaho (baking) potatoes (about 14 ounces each), scrubbed

12 tablespoons (1½ sticks) unsalted butter

2 tablespoons extra-virgin olive oil

2 medium fresh white truffles (about 1 ounce each), 1 finely chopped (see Tips)

Salt and freshly ground pepper

1 Heat the oven to 350 degrees. Set the potatoes in a roasting pan and bake until tender, 45 minutes to 1 hour. Transfer to a wire cooling rack and let cool slightly, about 5 minutes.

2 Meanwhile, in a small saucepan, cook 8 tablespoons of the butter over medium heat until the milk solids turn dark golden, about 4 minutes. Strain through a fine sieve into a small glass measuring cup.

3 Cutting horizontally, slice off the top quarter of each baked potato. Scoop out the potato flesh from the bottoms, leaving a thin but sturdy shell, and put in a medium bowl. Scoop out the potato from the tops and add to the bowl; discard the top skin. Press the potatoes through a ricer or food mill into another medium bowl and stir in the browned butter, the remaining 4 tablespoons fresh butter, the oil, and chopped truffle. Season with salt and pepper. Spoon the stuffing back into the shells, mounding slightly.

4 Transfer the potatoes to a roasting pan and bake until heated through and lightly browned, 10 to 15 minutes. Transfer the stuffed potatoes to plates, shave the remaining 1 truffle over the tops, and serve.

SOTTHA KHUNN
1996 to 2000

Art by Tim Flynn.

BLUE ROOM

After the move to the New York Palace Hotel, Billy Ghodbane, who has bartended at Le Cirque for fifteen years, invented this fruity blue Curaçao cocktail, named after the dining room where the bar was located. It was a favorite drink of socialite Anne Slater, famous for her cobalt-blue tinted eyeglasses (see photo, page 39).

1 SERVING

Ice cubes

1½ ounces peach vodka

1 ounce fresh pineapple juice

½ ounce blue Curaçao

½ ounce fresh lemon juice

Fill a cocktail shaker with ice. Add the peach vodka, pineapple juice, Curaçao, and lemon juice and shake well. Strain into a chilled martini glass and serve.

CURRIED TUNA TARTARE

Sottha Khunn first joined Le Cirque as one of Daniel Boulud's sous chefs in the 1980s when fish tartares had become trendy restaurant fare. Khunn's fusion version mirrors his own international background: curry seasoning from his Cambodian heritage and precise technique (brunoise = 1/8-inch dice) from training in such gastronomic temples as France's Troisgros and L'Archestrate. Each mouthful is the perfect balance of tiny crunchy vegetables, smooth cool tuna, and subtly spiced mayonnaise.

4 APPETIZER SERVINGS

CURRY MAYONNAISE

1 large egg yolk (see Tips)

Salt

1/2 cup canola oil

1 1/2 tablespoons fresh lemon juice

2 teaspoons Madras curry powder

TARTARE

12 ounces sushi-grade tuna fillet, cut into 1/4-inch dice (see Tips)

2 tablespoons celery brunoise (see Tips)

2 tablespoons shallot brunoise

2 tablespoons radish brunoise, plus finely julienned radish for garnishing

1 tablespoon snipped chives

Salt and freshly ground pepper

Fresh lemon juice

Canola oil, for brushing

Small celery leaf sprigs, for garnishing

1 Make the curry mayonnaise: In a blender, puree the egg yolk with a pinch of salt. With the machine on, slowly add the oil. Scrape the mayonnaise into a bowl and whisk in the lemon juice and curry powder; refrigerate.

2 Make the tartare: In a medium bowl, toss the tuna with the vegetable brunoise and chives. Fold in 1/4 cup of the curry mayonnaise. Season with salt, pepper, and lemon juice.

3 Brush a 4- or 6-ounce ramekin with oil. Pack one fourth of the tartare in the ramekin and turn it out in the center of a plate. Repeat with the remaining tartare. Garnish the tops with the radish julienne and celery sprigs. Decorate the plates with dots of the remaining curry mayonnaise and serve.

TIPS

If you prefer not to eat raw egg, stir the lemon juice and curry powder into 1/2 cup prepared mayonnaise.

This homemade mayonnaise is thinner than store-bought.

Freezing the tuna slightly, about 20 minutes, makes for easy dicing. Transfer the diced tuna to a bowl and set it in a larger bowl of ice water.

To cut the celery into a brunoise, slice it lengthwise into 1/8-inch strips, then cut crosswise into 1/8-inch dice. For the shallot and radish, slice them 1/8 inch thick first.

VARIATIONS

In step 2, you can double the chives or add a mix of chopped tender herbs, such as chives, cilantro, and mint.

This tuna tartare recipe makes delicate tuna burgers: Fold 2 tablespoons dry bread crumbs into the mixture in step 2, or as much as needed so it barely holds together. Shape into 4 patties, dust with all-purpose flour, and fry them in 2 tablespoons olive oil over medium heat until browned, about 2 minutes per side. Serve with lemon wedges.

SERVE WITH

This tartare would be delicious with something crunchy like plantain chips or Yuca Chips (page 224).

MAKE AHEAD

The curry mayonnaise can be refrigerated overnight.

The tartare can be refrigerated, covered, for up to 4 hours.

CURRIED CHICKEN SALAD

"Today most ladies just eat at the computer," says Sottha Khunn. Yet in the '70s and '80s, women in New York's high society came to Le Cirque for a light, leafy lunch after a morning of shopping. Khunn created this dish as an alternative to the Salad Le Cirque (greens tossed with shaved seasonal vegetables). To flavor the mayonnaise, Khunn simmers orange juice with curry powder, saffron, and other spices, a technique that delivers zing without bitterness.

4 APPETIZER OR 2 ENTRÉE SERVINGS

CHICKEN SALAD

4 cups chicken stock or low-sodium broth

1 onion, unpeeled, quartered

1 celery rib, chopped

4 garlic cloves, halved

6 parsley sprigs

3 thyme sprigs

2 bay leaves

6 whole black peppercorns

2 (8-ounce) boneless, skinless chicken breasts (see Tips)

1 tablespoon desiccated coconut, toasted, plus more for sprinkling

1 tablespoon snipped chives, plus more for garnishing

Salt

Golden raisins, for sprinkling

Small bibb lettuce leaves, sliced banana, mango chutney, and sour cream, for garnishing

CURRY MAYONNAISE

1 cup orange juice

2 tablespoons Madras curry powder

Pinch of saffron threads

1 whole clove

1 cinnamon stick

¼ teaspoon coriander seeds

¼ cup mayonnaise

1 Make the chicken salad: In a medium saucepan, combine the stock, onion, celery, garlic, parsley, thyme, bay leaves, and peppercorns. Cover and bring to a boil, then remove the lid and simmer over medium heat for 5 minutes. Add the chicken, cover, and simmer over medium-low heat for 7 minutes. Remove the pan from the heat and let the chicken cool in the liquid for 1 hour. Remove the chicken from the poaching liquid and let cool completely. Cut into ¼-inch dice.

2 Meanwhile, make the curry mayonnaise: In a small saucepan, combine the orange juice, curry powder, saffron, clove, cinnamon, and coriander seeds. Bring to a boil, then simmer over medium heat until reduced to ¼ cup, about 10 minutes. Strain into a medium bowl and let cool completely. Whisk in the mayonnaise.

3 Add the chicken, coconut, and chives to the mayonnaise and stir to coat.

4 Mound one fourth of the chicken salad on each plate. Sprinkle with coconut and raisins. Garnish the plates with the lettuce leaves, banana, chutney, sour cream, and chives and season with salt. Serve.

TIPS

The method for poaching chicken in step 1 produces tender, delicately flavored meat that can be used in any chicken salad or poached chicken recipe.

The flavorful poaching liquid can be strained and used to prepare chicken soup or reduced to make a sauce.

If you have cooked chicken left over from another recipe, you'll need about 3 cups (12 ounces), diced, to make this salad.

For a more chef-y presentation, brush a 4- or 6-ounce ramekin with canola oil. Pack one fourth of the salad in the ramekin and turn it out in the center of each plate.

VARIATION
Instead of the coconut, you can add sliced almonds.

SERVE WITH
To keep the meal light, follow the chicken salad with Salmon Fillet, Baby Carrots, Parsley, and Orange Jus (page 226).

MAKE AHEAD
The chicken can be refrigerated in the stock for up to 2 days.

The strained poaching liquid can be refrigerated for up to 3 days.

SPAGHETTI ALLA CHITARRA WITH CHERRY TOMATO SAUCE AND BASIL

By the time the Maccioni family opened Osteria del Circo, in 1996, homespun Italian cooking, such as this house-made pasta, had gained enough prestige to appear on Le Cirque's elegant menu. A chitarra, which resembles the guitar you play, is a kitchen tool used for cutting sheets of pasta into spaghetti-like noodles. Le Cirque's spaghetti is served with a beautifully balanced tomato sauce. It contains cherry tomatoes for sweetness, vine-ripened tomatoes for acidity and freshness, and canned tomatoes, which give it body.

8 APPETIZER OR 6 ENTRÉE SERVINGS

PASTA DOUGH

1½ cups semolina flour

½ cup all-purpose flour, plus more for sprinkling

3 large eggs

1 teaspoon extra-virgin olive oil

½ teaspoon salt

TOMATO SAUCE

¼ cup extra-virgin olive oil

½ large onion, coarsely chopped

2 garlic cloves, sliced

½ pint cherry tomatoes, halved

8 ounces vine-ripened tomatoes, chopped

1 (14-ounce) can diced tomatoes with juice

2 large basil sprigs, plus small sprigs for garnishing

Salt

¼ cup freshly grated Parmesan cheese, plus more for serving

1 Make the pasta dough: In a food processor, pulse the flours a few times. Add the eggs, oil, and salt and process until a fairly stiff dough forms. Scrape the dough onto a work surface, flatten into a disk, and wrap in plastic. Let stand at room temperature for at least 30 minutes or for up to 2 hours.

2 Meanwhile, make the tomato sauce: In a large saucepan, heat the oil until shimmering. Add the onion and garlic and cook over medium heat, stirring occasionally, until softened, about 5 minutes. Add the cherry tomatoes, vine-ripened tomatoes, diced tomatoes, and large basil sprigs and season with salt. Bring to a simmer, then cook over medium heat until the sauce thickens, 20 to 30 minutes. Discard the basil. Using an immersion blender, puree the sauce until smooth.

3 Cut the dough into 4 equal pieces; work with 1 piece at a time and keep the rest wrapped. Flatten the dough with your hands. Using a pasta machine, roll the dough through at the widest setting. Fold the dough in thirds (like a letter), then run it through the machine at the same setting, folded edge first. Repeat the folding and rolling once more, open edge first. Roll the dough through successively narrower settings, two times per setting, finishing with the third narrowest setting. Cut the sheet crosswise in half and hang over the back of a chair so air reaches both sides. Repeat with the remaining dough.

4 Bring a large pot of salted water to a boil. Feed the sheets of dough through the narrow cutters of the pasta machine. Transfer to a lightly floured baking sheet and cover loosely with plastic wrap.

VARIATION

To make a rustic mushroom-tomato sauce, soak ½ cup dried porcini mushrooms in ¾ cup boiling water for 10 minutes. Lift the mushrooms out of the water, coarsely chop them, and add to the pan with the tomatoes in step 2. Pour the soaking water into the pan, leaving the grit behind. Do not puree the sauce.

SERVE WITH

If serving the spaghetti as a first course, follow it with Osso Buco (page 184) or Braised Veal Shank for Two (page 166).

MAKE AHEAD

The recipe can be prepared through step 2 and refrigerated overnight. Both the spaghetti and the sauce can be frozen for up to 6 months. Do not defrost the spaghetti before boiling.

5 Add the spaghetti to the boiling water and cook, stirring occasionally, until they float. Drain, reserving 1 cup of the pasta cooking water. Add the spaghetti, cheese, and a little of the pasta water to the tomato sauce (if needed to loosen). Cook over medium heat, stirring and tossing with tongs, until the spaghetti is al dente. Season with salt and transfer to shallow bowls or a serving dish. Garnish with basil sprigs and serve. Pass the remaining cheese separately.

CHICKEN WITH GINGER

"Sirio asked me to make something from Asia, and I love chicken with ginger," says Sottha Khunn. "For me it's like what a hamburger or a hot dog is to an American. My mother used to make it." You might be expecting a stir-fry, but with Khunn's classic training, the dish is a hybrid: Asian ingredients and French technique. Khunn browns pieces of bone-in chicken on the stovetop, then adds julienned vegetables and finishes the cooking in the oven. He builds a complex-tasting pan sauce with an avalanche of ginger, vinegar, brandy, and chicken stock, then strains it as Escoffier would.

4 ENTRÉE SERVINGS

1 (3½-pound) chicken, cut into 8 pieces

2 garlic cloves, finely chopped

1 cup finely chopped ginger

Salt and freshly ground pepper

1 tablespoon canola oil

8 ounces shiitake mushrooms, caps only, sliced ½ inch thick

2 cups julienned bell peppers, preferably a mix of yellow, red, and green

1 red onion, cut into julienne strips

3 scallions, cut into julienne strips

2 tablespoons honey

¼ cup red wine vinegar

2 tablespoons brandy or port (optional)

1½ cups chicken stock or low-sodium broth

1. In a large bowl, combine the chicken, garlic, and ⅓ cup of the ginger. Season with salt and pepper and toss to combine. Cover and refrigerate for 20 minutes.

2. Heat the oven to 350 degrees. In a large flameproof roasting pan, heat the oil until shimmering. Add the chicken, skin side down, and cook over medium heat until lightly browned, about 5 minutes.

3. Turn the chicken over, transfer to the oven, and bake for 5 minutes. Add the mushrooms, bell peppers, onion, and scallions and bake until tender, about 20 minutes. Remove the pan from the oven and brush the chicken with the honey. Return to the oven and bake for 5 minutes.

4. Remove the pan from the oven and transfer the chicken and vegetables to a platter or plates.

5. Set the pan over high heat, add the vinegar and brandy, if using, and cook, stirring up the browned bits on the bottom. Add the stock and remaining ginger and cook until reduced by half, about 5 minutes. Strain the pan sauce into a small bowl and season with salt and pepper. Spoon the sauce around the platter or plates and serve.

VARIATION
In one adaptation of Khunn's dish, the julienned vegetables are stir-fried with ginger, garlic, red wine vinegar, and honey and served on top of Chicken Under a Brick (page 182).

SERVE WITH
Make a dish of steamed jasmine rice.

MAKE AHEAD
The chicken needs to marinate for 20 minutes, so plan ahead.

CHICKEN DIABLE

Poulet grillé diable appears on Jean Vergnes's menus at Le Cirque in the '70s. In a 1981 review in the New York Times, *Mimi Sheraton called Alain Sailhac's version of grilled chicken diable "proof of his dedication to perfection with simple, classic preparations." This later variation pairs the traditional ingredients with a Tuscan technique: fiery Dijon mustard is slathered on Chicken Under a Brick (see page 182) and crusted with bread crumbs, then browned under the broiler.*

3 OR 4 ENTRÉE SERVINGS

2 tablespoons extra-virgin olive oil, plus more for drizzling

1 (3-pound) chicken, split and semi-boned (see Tips)

Salt

2 tablespoons Dijon mustard

¼ teaspoon ground cayenne

½ cup dry bread crumbs

⅔ cup chicken stock or low-sodium broth

2 teaspoons grainy mustard

Freshly ground black pepper

1 In a large heavy skillet, heat the oil over high heat until smoking. Season the chicken generously with salt. Add the chicken, skin side down, to the skillet and set another large heavy skillet on top. Cook the chicken over medium heat until browned and crisp on the bottom, about 15 minutes. Remove the top skillet, turn the chicken over, and cook for 3 minutes.

2 Meanwhile, in a small bowl, combine the Dijon mustard with ⅛ teaspoon of the cayenne. Season the bread crumbs with salt and the remaining ⅛ teaspoon cayenne and toss to combine.

3 Heat the broiler. Slather the chicken with the mustard mixture. Sprinkle the crumbs on top. Drizzle with oil. Broil the chicken on the top rack of the oven until the crumbs are golden brown, about 3 minutes. Transfer the chicken to a cutting board, crumb side up, and let rest for 5 minutes.

4 Meanwhile, discard most of the fat and crumbs in the skillet. Add the stock and bring to a simmer over medium-high heat, scraping up the browned bits on the bottom, and cook until slightly thickened, about 3 minutes. Remove the skillet from the heat and stir in the grainy mustard. Season with salt and black pepper. Cut the chicken into serving pieces and arrange on a platter or plates. Spoon the pan sauce around the chicken and serve.

TIPS

Ask your butcher to split the chicken in half, remove the backbones, trim the wings to the second joint, and debone the breasts and thighs.

The second skillet that sits on top of the chicken should cover the bird as much as possible to get maximum skin contact with the hot surface.

If the top skillet is not especially heavy, add another skillet or a couple of cans to weight it down.

SERVE WITH

Today at Le Cirque, Chicken Diable is served with stir-fried vegetables, such as peppers, zucchini, shiitake mushrooms, and snow peas, seasoned with ginger, red wine vinegar, and honey.

TIPS

Is it necessary to say that Le Cirque uses only tasty chickens that have lived a good life?

Ask your butcher to split the chicken in half, remove the backbones, trim the wings to the second joint, and debone the breasts and thighs. But don't waste the bones; take them home and use them to make stock.

The second skillet that sits on top of the chicken should cover the bird as much as possible so the skin gets maximum contact with the hot surface.

If the top skillet is not especially heavy, add another skillet or a couple of cans to weight it down.

VARIATIONS

You can rub the chicken with olive oil and chopped rosemary and garlic, cover, and refrigerate for at least 20 minutes or overnight.

Or stuff the chicken under the skin with a blend of pancetta or bacon finely chopped in the food processor with softened unsalted butter, shallots, and sage.

Poussins (baby chickens) and Cornish hens can also be prepared in the same way; adjust the cooking time. Each 1-pound bird makes one serving.

SERVE WITH

For side dishes, try stir-fried vegetables or roasted new potatoes and Luca Banfi's sweet and tart peperonata, a component in his Seared Scallops with Peperonata and Yuca Chips (page 224).

CHICKEN UNDER A BRICK

Sirio first fell in love with this Tuscan classic as it was served at Ristorante Cecco in the town of Pescia. The dish has a history in that region, where it is said that originally the locally made, curved terra cotta roof tiles were used to weigh down the chicken. Some recipes still call for wrapping real bricks in foil to give it perfectly crisp, golden skin. Le Cirque's version substitutes a heavy skillet for the bricks. It's extraordinarily simple: sear chicken on one side, turn, and sear the other side, but its success depends so much on the particular skillets (top and bottom) and stovetop used that's it's hard to write one-size-fits-all instructions. To get that crunchy skin and juicy meat will probably require some fiddling. You may need to move the chicken around in the skillet, or move the skillet around on the heat, or add canned goods (or bricks) to the top skillet, or play around with the heat. Follow these directions the first time, then adjust. Once you get it right, you will make it forever.

3 OR 4 ENTRÉE SERVINGS

2 tablespoons extra-virgin olive oil

1 (3-pound) chicken, split and semi-boned (see Tips)

Salt

⅔ cup chicken stock or low-sodium broth

Freshly ground pepper

1 In a large heavy skillet, heat the oil over high heat until smoking. Season the chicken generously with salt. Add the chicken, skin side down, to the skillet and set another large heavy skillet on top. Reduce the heat to medium and cook the chicken until browned and crisp on the bottom, about 15 minutes.

2 Remove the top skillet, turn the chicken over, and cook for 3 to 5 minutes. Transfer the chicken to a cutting board, skin side up. Cover loosely with foil and let rest for 5 minutes.

3 Meanwhile, discard most of the fat in the skillet. Add the stock and bring to a simmer over medium-high heat, scraping up the browned bits on the bottom. Cook until slightly thickened, about 3 minutes. Season with salt and pepper. Cut the chicken into serving pieces and arrange on a platter or plates. Spoon the pan sauce around the chicken and serve.

PAN-ROASTED VEAL CHOPS WITH WINTER ROOT VEGETABLES

Veal chops are a splurge, so when you buy them you want to know the best way to get them richly browned on the outside and barely pink inside. Sottha Khunn sears them first on the stove, then finishes them in the oven. He serves the chops with an intensely flavored veal sauce and buttery braised salsify, carrots, and celery root.

4 ENTRÉE SERVINGS

5 tablespoons canola oil

1 pound veal trimmings and scraps (see Tips)

5 shallots, halved and thinly sliced

3 thyme sprigs

1 head of garlic, cut in half horizontally

1 cup Cognac or brandy

1 cup tawny port

4½ cups veal stock, chicken stock, or low-sodium broth

½ pound salsify, peeled and sliced on the diagonal ½ inch thick (see Tips)

2 carrots, peeled and sliced on the diagonal ½ inch thick

1 small celery root (about 12 ounces), thickly peeled and cut into 1-inch cubes

½ cup chicken stock or low-sodium broth

4 tablespoons unsalted butter, diced

Salt and freshly ground pepper

4 veal rib chops (14 to 16 ounces each), ribs scraped clean and tied with butcher's twine

Chervil sprigs, for garnishing

1. In a large saucepan, heat 1 tablespoon of the oil until shimmering. Add the veal trimmings and cook over medium heat, stirring occasionally, until browned, about 10 minutes. Transfer to a bowl. Add the shallots, thyme, and garlic to the pan and cook until the shallots are softened, 2 to 3 minutes. Return the veal trimmings to the pan and add the Cognac, then bring to a simmer over medium-high heat and cook, scraping up the browned bits on the bottom. Add the port and cook until reduced to ½ cup, about 20 minutes. Add 4 cups of the veal stock and cook until the sauce lightly coats a spoon, about 20 minutes.

2. In a large skillet, heat 2 tablespoons of the oil. Add the salsify and carrots and cook over medium-high heat, stirring occasionally, for 5 minutes. Add the celery root, chicken stock, and remaining ½ cup veal stock and cook over medium heat until tender, about 15 minutes. Remove the skillet from the heat and whisk in 2 tablespoons of the butter until it melts creamily. Season with salt and pepper.

3. Meanwhile, heat the oven to 425 degrees. In a large ovenproof skillet, heat the remaining 2 tablespoons oil until shimmering. Season the veal chops generously with salt and pepper, add to the skillet, and cook until richly browned, about 3 minutes per side. Transfer the skillet to the oven and roast, turning the chops halfway through, until they are just pink in the center, about 15 minutes. Transfer the chops to a platter and cover loosely with foil.

4. Strain the sauce into a small saucepan and bring to a simmer. Remove the pan from the heat and whisk in the remaining 2 tablespoons butter until it melts creamily. Season with salt and pepper.

5. Mound the vegetables on plates and top with a veal chop. Garnish with the chervil sprigs, spoon a little of the sauce around the plates, and serve. Pass the remaining sauce separately.

TIPS

When scraping the veal ribs clean, reserve the meat for making the sauce in step 1.

Salsify's white flesh quickly turns brown when peeled. You can rub it with a lemon half if it bothers you.

VARIATIONS

Khunn varied the dish according to the seasons. In the spring, you can replace the cold-weather roots with tender vegetables such as peas, asparagus, baby turnips, scallions, and quartered heads of bibb lettuce. In the summer, swap in diced red bell peppers, tomatoes, and zucchini.

To make a lighter sauce, substitute chicken necks, wings, and backs and chicken stock for the veal trimmings and veal stock in step 1.

MAKE AHEAD

The sauce can be refrigerated overnight.

To make a large bouquet
garni, tie 6 thyme sprigs, 6
rosemary sprigs, 1 bay leaf,
and 1 teaspoon whole white
peppercorns in a bundle with
cheesecloth.

Use a vegetable peeler to
remove the orange zest in
long strips, leaving behind as
much of the bitter white pith as
possible.

After the first 45 minutes of
braising, check to see that
the liquid is not boiling in the
oven. It should be simmering
slowly. It may be necessary to
reduce or increase the oven
temperature.

The osso buco can also be
braised on top of the stove
over low heat.

VARIATION

For a more rustic sauce,
work the vegetables with the
braising liquid through a food
mill in step 4.

SERVE WITH

Khunn suggests creamy
polenta and sautéed
broccoli rabe or kale as
accompaniments.

MAKE AHEAD

The stew can be prepared
through step 3 and
refrigerated for up to 2 days.
Remove the congealed fat,
then reheat the jellied stew
before proceeding.

OSSO BUCO

When Sottha Khunn prepares this hearty Italian veal stew, you can see the French fingerprints. For instance, he deglazes the pot with Armagnac, adds a teaspoon of tomato paste at the end of cooking for color, and enriches the sauce with butter.

4 ENTRÉE SERVINGS

4 tablespoons extra-virgin olive oil

4 (2-inch-thick) center-cut veal shanks

Salt and freshly ground pepper

5 shallots, halved

1 large onion, cut into 6 pieces

1 large carrot, cut into thirds

2 celery ribs, cut into thirds

1 head of garlic, cut in half horizontally

2 medium tomatoes, chopped

1 large bouquet garni (see Tips)

1 orange, zested (see Tips) and juiced

1 cup Armagnac or brandy

1 cup dry white wine

6 cups veal or chicken stock or low-sodium broth

1 teaspoon tomato paste

4 tablespoons unsalted butter, diced

1 Heat the oven to 350 degrees. In a large enameled cast-iron casserole, heat 2 tablespoons of the oil until shimmering. Season the veal shanks generously with salt and pepper. Add the shanks to the pot and cook over medium heat until browned on all sides, about 12 minutes; transfer to a large bowl. Discard the fat.

2 Add the shallots, onion, carrot, celery, garlic, and remaining 2 tablespoons oil to the pot. Cook over medium-high heat, stirring occasionally, until lightly browned, about 10 minutes.

3 Add the tomatoes, bouquet garni, orange zest, Armagnac, and wine to the pot, bring to a boil, scraping up the browned bits on the bottom, then tilt the pot and, using a long match, carefully ignite. When the flames subside and the liquid has evaporated, return the shanks to the pot along with the orange juice and stock, cover, and bring to a simmer. Transfer to the oven and cook until the meat is tender, about 1½ hours.

4 Remove from the oven and transfer the shanks to a platter. Strain the braising liquid into a large saucepan; discard the vegetables. Whisk the tomato paste into the braising liquid, bring it to a boil over medium-high heat, and cook until the sauce is slightly thickened and flavorful, about 20 minutes. Remove the pan from the heat, whisk in the butter, and season with salt and pepper.

5 Transfer each shank to a shallow bowl, spoon some of the sauce over it, and serve. Pass the remaining sauce separately.

CARAMEL-WALNUT SOUFFLÉS

Pastry wizard Jacques Torres's eleven-year run at Le Cirque lasted through three executive chefs, including Daniel Boulud, Sylvain Portay, and Sottha Khunn. It was a chapter filled with flashy, whimsical desserts that sometimes looked more like toys than pastry. His signature dessert was a chocolate stove whose oven door opened to reveal an opera cake. Two white-chocolate saucepans on top of the stove contained raspberry and mango coulis, which were poured over the cake. This fall soufflé requires slightly less technical expertise. Torres folds walnut caramel into Italian meringue—egg whites whipped with a sugar syrup cooked to the hard-ball stage—which makes a sturdy yet ethereal mixture that can be held for up to two hours before baking. It's a caramel lover's dream dessert.

8 SERVINGS

CARAMEL-WALNUT BASE

1 cup sugar

½ cup heavy cream

½ cup whole milk

1¾ cups chopped walnuts

Splash of rum (if needed)

SOUFFLÉS

Unsalted butter, softened, for brushing

¾ cup plus 1 tablespoon sugar, plus more for coating

¼ cup light corn syrup

13 large egg whites

½ cup meringue powder (optional; see Tips)

Juice of ½ lemon

1 Make the caramel-walnut base: In a heavy medium saucepan, cook the sugar over medium-high heat, stirring occasionally with a wooden spoon, until the sugar melts and turns a light caramel color. Watch it carefully; once the sugar begins to caramelize, it can burn very quickly. Slowly and carefully stir in the cream until smooth. Add the milk and mix thoroughly. Stir in the walnuts and cook until the mixture reaches 225 degrees on a candy thermometer. At this point, the caramel will have thickened and darkened slightly. Pour the filling into a heatproof bowl. Let cool.

2 Make the soufflés: Position a rack in the center of the oven. Heat the oven to 375 degrees. Generously brush eight 8-ounce ramekins, including the rims, with butter. Add a little sugar to each ramekin and turn to lightly coat the bottom and sides, tapping out any excess; refrigerate.

3 In a medium bowl set over a medium saucepan of simmering water, heat 1½ cups of the caramel-walnut base until warm. If the base is too thick (having the consistency of peanut butter), add the rum to loosen it slightly.

4 In a medium saucepan, combine 2 tablespoons water, the sugar, and corn syrup. Cook over medium-high heat until the mixture reaches 250 degrees. Remove from the heat.

5 In a large bowl, whip the egg whites with the meringue powder and lemon juice until slightly thickened and foamy, 1 to 2 minutes. Increase the speed to medium-high and gradually pour the hot sugar down the side of the bowl into the whites. Be careful not to pour the hot sugar directly onto the beaters, or it will splatter. Continue to whip the meringue until stiff and glossy, about 5 minutes.

6 Beat one fourth of the egg whites into the caramel-walnut base, then gently fold this lightened mixture into the remaining whites. Spoon the soufflé mixture into the ramekins and smooth the tops. Bake until the soufflés have risen and are lightly browned, about 20 minutes for a soft center. Serve immediately.

BOMBOLONI

When the Maccioni family was developing the menu for Osteria del Circo, Sirio sent his pastry chef Francisco Gutierrez along with Jacques Torres, to Montecatini on a recon mission to learn about Tuscan desserts. Jacques didn't like the way the Italians made their doughnuts. "I wanted something richer, so I took brioche dough and deep-fried it." This is a streamlined version of the original bombolini, but just as buttery.

MAKES ABOUT 7 DOZEN

1 (.6-ounce) cube fresh yeast (see Tips)

¼ cup warm water

3½ cups bread flour, plus 1 tablespoon more if needed

4 large eggs

⅓ cup sugar, plus ¾ cup for coating

1½ teaspoons salt

14 tablespoons unsalted butter, diced

Canola oil, for deep frying

Warmed raspberry jam, for serving (optional)

1 In a stand mixer fitted with the paddle, dissolve the yeast in the warm water. Add the flour, eggs, the ⅓ cup sugar, and the salt and mix at low speed until the dough forms a ball, about 2 minutes. Add the butter and beat at medium speed, scraping down the bowl occasionally, until the dough no longer sticks to the side of the bowl, 5 to 7 minutes. If the dough is very sticky, add the 1 tablespoon flour. Remove the paddle and pat the dough into a ball. Cover with plastic wrap and let rise in a warm place for 2 hours.

2 In a large pot, heat 2 inches of oil to 325 degrees over medium heat. Spread the remaining ¾ cup sugar in a baking pan.

3 Working in batches, drop the dough by heaping teaspoons in the oil and fry, turning occasionally, until golden brown, 3 to 5 minutes. Using a slotted spoon, transfer to a paper towel–lined plate to drain. While they are still hot, roll the bombolini in the sugar to coat, then transfer to a platter. Serve hot, with the raspberry jam.

TIPS
Fresh yeast can be found in the dairy section of many supermarkets. Alternatively, you can use 1 packet active dry yeast, which needs to be proofed: In step 1, let the yeast and water mixture stand until foamy, about 5 minutes, then proceed with the recipe.

VARIATIONS
Jacques Torres originally filled each doughnut with pastry cream using a pastry bag and plain tip. Try the pastry cream recipe in Napoleon Le Cirque (page 146); reduce the quantity of cornstarch to 2 tablespoons for a softer filling.

For a warmly spicy note, season the sugar for coating the fried bombolini with 1 teaspoon ground cardamom or cinnamon (or a mix) and a pinch of kosher salt.
Instead of raspberry jam, you can serve the bombolini with warm chocolate sauce for dipping such as the one served with Chestnut Dacquoise Cake (page 190).

SERVE WITH
Jacques Torres used to serve these deep-fried pastries with crème anglaise. Try the vanilla-scented custard sauce in the recipe for Floating Islands (page 131.) Without the sauce, the bombolini make a breakfast treat served hot with a cup of coffee.

MAKE AHEAD
The bombolini can be prepared through step 1 and refrigerated overnight.

Store any leftover bombolini in an airtight container overnight and reheat in a toaster oven.

CHESTNUT DACQUOISE CAKE

When Sirio requested a holiday dessert flavored with chestnuts, Jacques Torres presented him with this magnificent layer cake: rounds of crunchy pine nut meringue stacked with chestnut ice cream and topped with ganache, all glazed with chocolate sauce. Each wedge of cake came with a garnish of candied chestnuts, a seasonal favorite of French and Italian cooks alike. "Sirio has an instinct," Jacques Torres says. "He knows his clientele. If you please him, you're going to please everyone." This is still the dessert Sirio requests for his birthday every year.

10 SERVINGS

MERINGUES

6 large egg whites

1 cup confectioners' sugar

1 cup granulated sugar

¼ cup pine nuts

GANACHE

1 cup chopped bittersweet chocolate

1 cup heavy cream

2 tablespoons unsalted butter, softened

CHOCOLATE SAUCE

¼ cup sugar

½ cup unsweetened cocoa powder

2 tablespoons dry milk powder

1 pint chestnut ice cream

Candied chestnuts, for garnishing (optional)

1 Make the meringues: Heat the oven to 300 degrees. Using a round 8-inch springform pan as a template, trace one 8-inch circle on each of three sheets of parchment paper. Line three baking sheets with the parchment.

2 In a large bowl, whip the egg whites at low speed until slightly thickened and foamy, about 2 minutes, then whip at medium-high speed until they begin to form stiff peaks. Gradually add the confectioners' sugar at high speed, until the peaks are stiff and shiny. Using a spatula, fold in the granulated sugar and pine nuts.

3 Transfer the meringue to a pastry bag fitted with a plain ½-inch tip and pipe out disks ½ inch smaller than the rounds traced on the parchment. Transfer the baking sheets to the oven, immediately reduce the oven temperature to 200 degrees, and bake until the meringues are dry all the way through, 3 to 4 hours. Remove from the oven and let cool on racks. Remove the paper.

4 Make the ganache: Put the chocolate in a large heatproof bowl. In a small saucepan, heat the cream over high heat until bubbles appear around the edge. Pour the hot cream over the chocolate and let stand for 30 seconds. Slowly whisk the mixture until almost smooth. Let the mixture stand for 5 minutes, then whisk in the butter until the ganache is shiny and smooth. Let cool to room temperature.

5 Make the chocolate sauce: In a small saucepan, bring 1 cup water and the sugar to a boil. Remove the pan from the heat and add the cocoa powder and dry milk powder, then return it to the heat and bring to a boil. Remove from the heat.

6 Set 1 meringue disk in the bottom of an 8-inch springform pan. Using an offset spatula, spread one third of the ice cream in a layer on top. Repeat layering meringue and ice cream, finishing with a layer of ice cream. Transfer to the freezer for at least 3 hours or overnight.

7 Set the pan on a wire cooling rack over a sheet of parchment paper. Pour the ganache on the cake and, using an offset spatula, spread it evenly over the top and sides. Return the cake to the freezer until the ganache sets.

8 Remove the sides of the pan. Using a serrated knife, slice the cake; wipe the blade clean between cuts. Transfer the slices to plates, garnish with candied chestnuts, if using, drizzle with the chocolate sauce, and serve.

PIERRE SCHAEDELIN
2000 to 2006

Art by Tim Flynn.

TARTE FLAMBÉE

Most people now know this crisp-crusted bacon-and-onion pizza from Alsace, in eastern France. But when Pierre Schaedelin, an Alsace native, put it on Le Cirque's bar menu, it was exotic. Schaedelin got the recipe from his mentor, Paul Haeberlin, who served it as an amuse-bouche at his legendary restaurant, l'Auberge de l'Ill, in Illhaeusern. Haeberlin's dough contains no yeast; when baked it's similar to a cracker.

4 APPETIZER SERVINGS

DOUGH

1 cup all-purpose flour

2 tablespoons canola oil

¼ teaspoon salt

TOPPINGS

12 bacon slices, finely chopped

1 tablespoon canola oil

1 large onion, halved and thinly sliced

4 ounces fromage blanc, crème fraîche, or sour cream

1 large egg

1 tablespoon heavy cream

½ tablespoon milk

Salt and freshly ground pepper

1 Position a pizza stone or upside-down sturdy baking sheet in the center of the oven and heat the oven to 500 degrees.

2 Make the dough: In a food processor, pulse the flour a few times. Add ⅓ cup water, the oil, and salt and process until a dough forms. On a lightly floured work surface, roll out the dough to a rectangle about 1/16 inch thick. Let the dough dry for 10 minutes per side. Transfer the dough to a baking sheet and put in the freezer.

3 Make the toppings: In a medium skillet, cook the bacon over medium heat, stirring occasionally, until lightly browned, about 5 minutes. Using a slotted spoon, transfer to a paper towel–lined plate.

4 Wipe out the skillet and heat the oil until shimmering. Add the onion and cook over medium heat, stirring occasionally, until softened, about 5 minutes.

5 In a medium bowl, whisk the fromage blanc with the egg, cream, and milk and season with salt and pepper.

6 Spread the fromage blanc mixture over the dough, then scatter the onion and bacon over the top. Transfer the tart to the pizza stone and bake until the pastry is crisp and spotted with brown on the bottom, 3 to 4 minutes. Cut the tart into 4 squares and serve hot.

TIPS

For a shortcut, chop the bacon in a food processor after you've made the dough.

The tart can also be baked on a room-temperature baking sheet. Set the sheet on the floor of the oven and bake until the pastry is crisp and spotted with brown on the bottom, 5 to 7 minutes.

VARIATIONS

Scatter 1 cup shredded Gruyère cheese over the tart just before baking.

The tart can be cut into bite-size pieces and served as finger food.

SERVE WITH

Tarte flambée also makes a light meal with tossed greens or a tomato salad in a mustardy vinaigrette.

Follow this with more regional specialties from Alsace, Rabbit à la Moutarde (page 230) and Mustard-Tarragon Spaetzle (page 232).

MAKE AHEAD

The recipe can be prepared through step 5 and refrigerated for up to 4 hours before baking.

If you prefer not to eat raw
egg, the dressing will still be
tasty without it.

Clarified butter is ideal for
frying because it doesn't burn.
It's available at specialty food
stores, South Asian groceries
(as ghee), and online.
However, it's easy to prepare
at home, if you start with at
least 16 tablespoons (2 sticks,
or 8 ounces) unsalted butter.
This is more than you need
for frying the toasts in this
recipe but it keeps well, so
you'll have some on hand for
another recipe. Refrigerated
in a tightly covered container,
it will keep for months. If you
clarify unsalted butter, it can
be used in either sweet or
savory dishes.

VARIATION

For a more rustic salad,
you can stack whole tender
romaine lettuce leaves. Swap
the white bread croutons for
slices of a country loaf (crust
on); brush them with olive
oil and toast on a baking
sheet in a 400-degree oven
until golden brown, about 10
minutes.

SERVE WITH

For a main course, serve
Chicken Diable (page 180).

MAKE AHEAD

Clarified butter can be
refrigerated for up to 1 month.
Melt it before using.

The Caesar dressing can be
refrigerated overnight.

CAESAR SALAD LE CIRQUE

"I have to tell you at the time I wasn't really happy about making a Caesar salad,"
Pierre Schaedelin admits. "That's why I made it a bit fancier than the original. But
looking back, it's a great dish." Instead of tossing romaine leaves with an egg-rich
dressing, cheese, and croutons, he meticulously layers rectangles of lettuce brushed
with the pungent dressing and grated Parmesan and serves an egg fried in a round
crouton (aka toad in the hole) on the side. Robert De Niro liked it so much he always
called ahead to order one for himself and his wife. Schaedelin's elegant Caesar salad
is still a favorite.

4 APPETIZER SERVINGS

16 tablespoons (2 sticks) unsalted
butter (see Tips)

2 romaine lettuce hearts, leaves
separated

¼ cup freshly grated Parmesan cheese

2 oil-packed anchovy fillets, drained
and sliced crosswise in half, then
lengthwise in half

Small parsley sprigs, for garnishing

4 slices of firm white bread

4 large eggs

Flaky salt and freshly ground pepper

CAESAR DRESSING

1 large egg yolk (see Tips)

2 tablespoons red wine vinegar

2 tablespoons fresh lemon juice

1 tablespoon Dijon mustard

Dash of Worcestershire sauce

2 oil-packed anchovy fillets

1 garlic clove, chopped

1 shallot, chopped

½ cup canola oil

½ cup freshly grated Parmesan cheese

Salt and freshly ground pepper

1 In a small saucepan, melt the butter over high heat. Remove
the pan from the heat and, using a spoon, skim off the
foam. Pour the remaining butter into a bowl, leaving behind the
whitish milk solids at the bottom; discard the milk solids.

2 Make the Caesar dressing: In a blender, puree the egg yolk
with the vinegar, lemon juice, mustard, Worcestershire
sauce, anchovies, garlic, and shallot. With the machine on, slowly
add the oil. Pulse in the cheese. Season with salt and pepper.

3 Stack four piles of 5 lettuce leaves and trim to 5- to 6-inch
rectangles. For each salad, arrange a leaf on one side of
a plate and, using a pastry brush, spread with the dressing.
Sprinkle with cheese. Continue layering the lettuce, dressing,
and cheese, finishing with a sprinkling of cheese. Garnish with
2 anchovy strips and parsley sprigs.

4 Using a 4- to 5-inch round pastry cutter, stamp the bread
slices into rounds. Using a 2- to 3-inch round pastry cutter,
stamp out a hole in each round. In a large skillet, heat ¼ cup of
the clarified butter over high heat. Add the bread rings and cook
over medium heat until golden brown on the bottom, about 2
minutes. Turn the rings, break 1 egg into each, and cook until the
egg whites are set but the yolks are still soft, about 3 minutes.
Using a spatula, transfer the egg toasts to paper towels.

5 Set an egg toast next to the salad and season with flaky
salt and pepper. Serve, passing the remaining dressing
separately.

TOMATO TATIN

Pierre Schaedelin calls these individual tarts "tomato tatins" because he arranges confit tomatoes rounded side up on a puff pastry disk, resembling the classic upside-down apple tart. Hiding under the densely flavored tomatoes is ricotta seasoned with shallot, scallion, and parsley.

4 APPETIZER SERVINGS

8 small tomatoes (4 ounces each), peeled, halved, and seeded (see Tomato, Bacon, and Saffron Soup à la Minute, Tips, page 209)

Salt and freshly ground pepper

2 garlic cloves, thinly sliced

16 small thyme sprigs

2 tablespoons extra-virgin olive oil

8 ounces cold all-butter puff pastry dough

½ cup fresh ricotta

1 large shallot, finely chopped

1 scallion, finely chopped

2 tablespoons finely chopped parsley

Fava Bean, Red Pepper, and Olive Salad (page 197)

1 Heat the oven to 250 degrees. Line a baking sheet with foil and spread the tomatoes, cut side up, on the sheet. Season with salt and pepper. Scatter the garlic and thyme on top, drizzle with 1 tablespoon of the oil, and bake until the tomatoes are semi-dry, 1½ to 2 hours. Remove and let cool.

2 Meanwhile, line two baking sheets with a nonstick liner or parchment paper. On a lightly floured surface, roll out the puff pastry 1/16 inch thick. Using a plate or a pan lid as a guide, cut the dough into 4 rounds about 6 inches across. Transfer the rounds to the baking sheets and prick the dough all over with a fork. Chill until firm, at least 15 minutes.

3 Increase the oven temperature to 375 degrees. Bake the pastry rounds until golden brown, about 15 minutes.

4 Meanwhile, in a medium bowl, beat the ricotta with the shallot, scallion, parsley, and remaining 1 tablespoon oil. Season with salt and pepper; refrigerate.

5 Spread one fourth of the ricotta mixture on each pastry round. Arrange 4 tomato confit halves, round side up, on top. Bake for 15 minutes. Transfer the tomato tarts to plates, spoon some of the fava bean salad around the tart, and serve. Pass the remaining salad separately.

TIPS

In step 1, after the first hour, check the tomatoes every 15 minutes. The tomatoes on the edges will be ready before the ones in the center. Remove them from the baking sheet as they are done.

You may need to overlap the tomatoes to fit when arranging them on the pastry.

VARIATIONS

Add a few toasted pine nuts to each tart just before serving, or drizzle with a little pesto sauce.

SERVE WITH

A simple green salad garnished with a few black olives would hit the same fresh note as the fava bean salad.

MAKE AHEAD

The oven-dried tomatoes can be refrigerated for up to 1 week or frozen for up to 6 months.

The tarts can be prepared through step 4 up to 4 hours in advance.

FAVA BEAN, RED PEPPER, AND OLIVE SALAD

In a fancy restaurant, you need more than green salad as a garnish for a tomato tart, so Pierre Schaedelin created this Mediterranean mix of crisp and tender vegetables.

4 SIDE SERVINGS

1 large red bell pepper, quartered lengthwise, stemmed, and seeded

Salt

1 cup shelled fava beans (4 ounces, or 1 pound in the pod)

2 tablespoons extra-virgin olive oil

1 tablespoon balsamic vinegar

2 teaspoons sherry vinegar

Freshly ground pepper

24 pitted Kalamata olives, quartered lengthwise

2 scallions, thinly sliced on the diagonal

1 Heat the broiler. Line a baking sheet with foil. Arrange the red pepper on the sheet skin side up and broil about 4 inches from the heat until the skin is very charred, 10 to 15 minutes. Remove from the oven and wrap the pepper in the foil to steam the skin loose, 10 to 15 minutes. Peel off the skin and cut the flesh into ⅜-inch dice.

2 Meanwhile, bring a medium saucepan of salted water to a boil. Fill a medium bowl with ice water. Add the fava beans to the boiling water and blanch for 1 minute. Drain and add to the ice water to cool as quickly as possible, 1 to 2 minutes. Drain and peel.

3 In a medium bowl, whisk the oil with the vinegars and season with salt and pepper. Add the red pepper, fava beans, olives, and scallions and toss to coat. Serve.

VARIATION
Instead of the fava beans, Pierre Schaedelin sometimes adds diced cooked artichoke bottoms.

SERVE WITH
You could add this dish to a cold buffet of marinated salads. Or try it as an accompaniment to grilled chicken or fish.

MAKE AHEAD
The salad can be refrigerated for up to 4 hours.

ENTRECÔTE AUX POIVRES

Entrecôte au poivre vert (strip steak with green peppercorns) appeared under the house specials on the earliest Le Cirque menus. Pierre Schaedelin revived this bistro classic by adding two kinds of peppercorns: the dried black variety, which are crushed and pressed onto the steak before sautéing, plus pickled young green peppercorns, which add a kick to his rich Cognac-spiked pan sauce.

4 ENTRÉE SERVINGS

¼ cup extra-virgin olive oil

4 (10-ounce) boneless strip steaks, about 1 inch thick

Salt

2 tablespoons whole black peppercorns, crushed (see Tips)

2 tablespoons unsalted butter

¼ cup chopped shallot

2 tablespoons green peppercorns in brine, drained and chopped (see Tips)

6 tablespoons Cognac or brandy, plus a splash (optional)

½ cup dry white wine

½ cup demiglace

2 tablespoons crème fraîche or heavy cream

1 In a large skillet, heat the oil until shimmering. Season both sides of the steaks with salt and black peppercorns, pressing them into the surface of the steaks. Add the steaks to the skillet and cook over medium heat until browned on the bottom, about 4 minutes. Turn and cook until medium rare, about 3 minutes. Transfer the steaks to a platter and cover loosely with foil.

2 Pour off the fat in the skillet. Add the butter, swirling the skillet, until the butter melts. Set the skillet over medium-high heat, add the shallot and green peppercorns, and cook until the shallot is softened, about 1 minute. Add the Cognac and cook until the skillet is almost dry, 2 to 3 minutes. Add the wine and cook until skillet is almost dry, about 3 minutes.

3 Add the demiglace and cook until reduced by half, about 2 minutes. Stir in the crème fraîche and a splash of Cognac, if desired. Transfer the steaks to plates, spoon the sauce over them, and serve.

CHRISTOPHE BELLANCA
2006 to 2008

Art by Tim Flynn.

You might find that one of these ravioli per person is sufficiently indulgent.

Feathery hen-of-the-woods mushrooms are also called maitake mushrooms.

Strain the dried mushroom soaking liquid and save it for a sauce or stew.

Soy sauce is the stealth ingredient in this duxelles recipe, adding incredible umami to the mushroom mixture.

Truffles, truffle oil, and truffle juice are available at specialty food stores and from dartagnan.com, plantin.com, and urbani.com. Many chefs peel the firm outer rind of the truffle and mince it to use in truffle butter or truffle salt; the rest of the truffle is chopped or thinly sliced, as here.

Fresh, raw foie gras is available at some specialty food stores and from dartagnan.com and hudsonvalleyfoiegras.com.

The foie gras ravioli should be slightly larger than Champagne corks.

Soy lecithin helps hot liquids to foam. It's available at health-food stores and many grocery stores in the nutritional supplements section.

SERVE WITH
An entrée of equal extravagance is called for here, say Châteaubriand for Two (page 127).

MAKE AHEAD
The recipe can be prepared through step 6 and refrigerated overnight.

FOIE GRAS RAVIOLI

After Le Cirque's move to the Bloomberg Tower on East 58th Street, in 2006, Christophe Bellanca helped win back three stars for the restaurant with these knockout ravioli. In the game-changing 2008 review, Times *restaurant critic Frank Bruni described them as "swollen with an addictive substance outlawed in an entire swath of the country, by which I mean foie gras"—an ingredient still under siege. The ravioli, which also contain a mound of woodsy mushroom duxelles and chopped truffles, are shaped like top hats and set on a creamy bed of Savoy cabbage ("less vegetable than opiate," according to Bruni). Its crowning opulence: truffle foam. The surprise here is that a recipe so clearly designed for the experienced hands of a three-star chef can be executed by a layman.*

4 APPETIZER SERVINGS

PASTA DOUGH

1⅓ cups all-purpose flour, plus more for sprinkling

2 large eggs

½ teaspoon extra-virgin olive oil

¼ teaspoon salt

MUSHROOM DUXELLES

2 tablespoons unsalted butter

1 large shallot, finely chopped

1 garlic clove, finely chopped

4 ounces mixed mushrooms, such as white, shiitake, and hen-of-the-woods, sliced

1 tablespoon mixed dried mushrooms, such as porcini and shiitake, soaked in boiling water and drained (see Tips)

Salt

2 tablespoons Madeira

2 tablespoons veal stock, chicken stock, or low-sodium broth

¼ teaspoon soy sauce

1 tablespoon heavy cream

Freshly ground pepper

1 Make the pasta dough: In a food processor, pulse the flour a few times. Add the eggs, oil, and salt and process until a fairly stiff dough forms. Scrape the dough onto a work surface, flatten into a disk, and wrap in plastic. Let stand at room temperature for at least 30 minutes or for up to 2 hours.

2 Meanwhile, make the mushroom duxelles: In a small saucepan, melt the butter over high heat. Add the shallot and garlic and cook over medium heat, stirring occasionally, until softened, 2 to 3 minutes. Add the fresh and dried mushrooms, season with salt, and cook over medium-high heat, stirring constantly, until the water they release has evaporated, 3 to 4 minutes. In a food processor, finely chop the mushroom mixture and return it to the pan. Add the Madeira and cook until dry. Add the stock and soy sauce and reduce until dry. Add the cream and cook until slightly thickened. Season with salt and pepper.

3 Make the cabbage: In a large pot of boiling salted water, blanch the cabbage until tender, 8 to 10 minutes. Fill a large bowl with ice water. Drain the cabbage and add to the ice water to cool as quickly as possible, 1 to 2 minutes. Drain again, transfer to a thick kitchen towel, and roll up.

4 In a medium sauté pan, simmer the cream over medium-high heat until slightly thickened, 5 to 10 minutes. Add the cabbage and cook, stirring, until the cream lightly coats the cabbage. Stir in 1 tablespoon of the chopped truffles and season with salt.

CABBAGE AND RAVIOLI

Salt

½ head of Savoy cabbage, leaves separated, thick ribs removed, leaves sliced into ¼-inch ribbons

1 cup heavy cream

2 tablespoons chopped fresh black truffles (about 1 ounce), plus 8 fresh black truffle slices (see Tips)

1 pound fresh foie gras (see Tips), cut into 8 (2-ounce) cylinders, each about 1 by 2 inches

Canola oil, for brushing

½ cup truffle juice (see Tips)

½ cup duck stock or chicken stock

½ cup milk

1 tablespoon soy lecithin (see Tips)

5 Make the ravioli: Cut the dough into 4 equal pieces; work with 1 piece at a time and keep the rest wrapped. Flatten the dough with your hands. Using a pasta machine, roll the dough through at the widest setting. Fold the dough in thirds (like a letter), then run it through the machine at the same setting, folded edge first. Repeat the folding and rolling once more, open edge first. Roll the dough through successively narrower settings, two times per setting, finishing with the second narrowest setting. Cut the sheet crosswise in half and hang over the back of a chair so air reaches both sides. Repeat with the remaining dough.

6 On a lightly floured work surface, spread 1 pasta sheet. Stand 1 cylinder of foie gras near one end of a pasta sheet. Mound a heaping teaspoon of duxelles on top of each cylinder, then a little of the remaining chopped truffles. Moisten the dough around the cylinder with water. Drape another pasta sheet over the cylinder, pressing to remove any air pockets, and then press well around the base to seal. Using a biscuit cutter, stamp out the ravioli slightly larger than the filling, transfer to a lightly floured baking sheet, and cover loosely with plastic wrap. Repeat with the remaining pasta and filling.

7 Bring 1 inch of water to a boil in a steamer. Brush the perforated insert lightly with oil. Stand the ravioli in the insert, cover, and steam for 5 to 7 minutes.

8 Meanwhile, in a small saucepan, bring the truffle juice, duck stock, and milk to a simmer. Add the soy lecithin, remove from the heat, and foam with an immersion blender.

9 Spread the cabbage in shallow bowls. Add the ravioli and top each with a truffle slice. Spoon the truffle foam and sauce around the ravioli and serve.

COMTÉ CHEESE SOUFFLÉS

Le Cirque wouldn't be Le Cirque without its roster of classics. For every voguish recipe like Foie Gras Ravioli (page 200), Christophe Bellanca also offered a timeless dish, like these soufflés. What makes Bellanca's special? "We used Comté," he says, instead of ordinary Gruyère. "The best Comté," he specifies. And he added twice as many egg whites as yolks, making an often stolid dish especially light.

6 APPETIZER OR ENTRÉE SERVINGS

4 tablespoons unsalted butter, plus more, softened, for brushing

½ cup all-purpose flour, plus more for coating

2 cups whole milk

Salt and freshly ground pepper

Pinch of freshly grated nutmeg

4 large egg yolks

1½ cups shredded Comté or Gruyère cheese (6 ounces; see Tips)

8 large egg whites

¼ teaspoon cream of tartar (optional)

1 Position a rack in the center of the oven. Heat the oven to 400 degrees. Generously brush six 8-ounce ramekins, including the rims, with butter. Add a little flour to each ramekin and turn to lightly coat the bottom and sides, tapping out any excess; refrigerate.

2 In a medium saucepan, melt the butter over medium heat. Whisk in the flour and cook, stirring, over low heat for 2 to 3 minutes. Add the milk and bring to a simmer, whisking. Season with ¼ teaspoon salt, ⅛ teaspoon pepper, and the nutmeg and cook until thick, 3 to 5 minutes. Remove the pan from the heat. Beat in the egg yolks, then the cheese.

3 Whip the egg whites with the cream of tartar and ¼ teaspoon salt at medium speed until they hold firm peaks. Beat one fourth of the egg whites into the cheese mixture, then gently fold this lightened mixture into the remaining whites.

4 Spoon the soufflé mixture into the prepared ramekins and smooth the tops. Set on a baking sheet and bake until the soufflés are risen and browned, 15 to 20 minutes. Serve immediately.

TIPS

Comté cheese (also known as Gruyère de Comté) is a nutty, firm cow's-milk cheese from the Franche-Comté region in eastern France.

Beating the egg whites with a little salt and cream of tartar gives them more volume.

Fold the cheese mixture into the whipped egg whites delicately. Use a rubber spatula or large spoon so the egg whites stay puffy.

To help the soufflés rise evenly, run a fingertip around the edge of the ramekins, making a groove in the mixture.

VARIATIONS

There are dozens of ways to tweak this basic soufflé. Instead of the Comté or Gruyère, try any semisoft melting cheese, such as Cheddar, Gouda, or Cantal.

In step 2, in addition to the cheese, you can stir in chopped herbs, a little shredded ham or prosciutto, sautéed mushrooms, leftover cooked greens, or other vegetables.

SERVE WITH

Try these soufflés for lunch alongside an assertive arugula, endive, frisée, watercress, or radicchio salad.

Or serve as an entrée, and begin the meal with Tomato, Bacon, and Saffron Soup à la Minute (page 209).

MAKE AHEAD

The soufflés can be refrigerated for up to 2 hours before baking.

CREAMY SCRAMBLED EGGS WITH CAVIAR

Christophe Bellanca's decadent oeufs brouillés, flavored with precious black truffles, caviar, and lots of butter, were inspired by nouvelle cuisine master Michel Guérard's version. The lightly beaten eggs are cooked over low heat for a long time, producing a creamy emulsion. They are saucier than curdlike scrambled eggs. Bellanca used to make them for Nancy Reagan, when he was at L'Orangerie in Los Angeles. "One day she came to Le Cirque and I did it for her," he says. "Then we put it on the menu."

4 APPETIZER SERVINGS

10 large eggs

3 tablespoons unsalted butter

3 tablespoons truffle butter (see Tips) or unsalted butter, diced

1 small shallot, finely chopped

1 tablespoon snipped chives

Salt and freshly ground pepper

2 ounces Osetra caviar

1 In a medium bowl, lightly beat the eggs.

2 In a medium saucepan, melt the unsalted butter over medium heat. Set the pan in a larger saucepan of barely simmering water. Pour in the eggs and cook very gently, whisking constantly, until the eggs thicken but remain soft and moist, at least 15 minutes.

3 Remove the pan from the heat. Whisk in the truffle butter, shallot, and chives and season with salt and pepper.

4 Spoon the eggs into shallow bowls. Mound the caviar on top and serve.

TIPS
The cooks at Le Cirque make their own truffle butter, but it's available, along with fresh truffles, at specialty food stores and from dartagnan.com, plantin.com, and urbani.com. If you want to prepare it yourself, mash 2 teaspoons minced black truffle peelings with 3 tablespoons softened salted butter. It can be refrigerated for up to 3 days or frozen for up to 6 months.

VARIATIONS
The caviar can be replaced with 2 shaved black or white truffles (about 2 ounces).

For a more elegant presentation, spoon the eggs into a 3- to 4-inch ring mold (or clean tuna can ring) set on a plate, remove the ring, and proceed.

Michel Guérard served his oeufs brouillés in emptied eggshells: Using a serrated knife, remove ½ inch of the eggshell from the pointed end. Pour the egg into a bowl. Wash the eggshells and turn upside down to dry. Place the eggshells in eggcups, fill each three-quarters full of cooked egg, then spoon in the caviar, mounding slightly. Top with the egg lids.

SERVE WITH
Bellanca used to serve the eggs with toast points, which offer a crunchy contrast. Cut slices of crustless white bread into triangles and fry in clarified butter (see Caesar Salad Le Cirque, step 1, page 194) over medium heat until golden brown. Drain on paper towels.

CRAIG HOPSON
2008 to 2011

Art by Tim Flynn.

CUCUMBER BASIL SMASH

Billy Ghodbane's drinks list has evolved in the fifteen years he has presided over Le Cirque's bar. "People want something healthy today," he says. Cuing the zeitgeist, he created this refreshing, low-proof cocktail.

1 SERVING

Ice cubes

3 or 4 cucumber slices

3 or 4 basil leaves

1½ ounces Hendrick's gin

1 ounce ginger liqueur

½ ounce fresh lemon juice

½ ounce elderflower syrup (see Tips)

Club soda

Fill a highball glass with ice. In a cocktail shaker, muddle the cucumber slices and basil. Add ice and the gin, ginger liqueur, lemon juice, and elderflower syrup and shake well. Strain into the glass, top off with club soda, and serve.

TIPS
Elderflower syrup is a floral-scented sweetener made from the extract of elderflower blossoms.

CORN SOUP WITH SHRIMP FRITTERS

Any one of this dish's multiple components is worth making on its own merit. The soup is an ode to summer. The pillowy fritters are studded with corn, scallions, and crunchy cornmeal. The deep green basil oil is intense and easier to prepare than most herb oils (no blanching the basil leaves).

4 APPETIZER SERVINGS

SOUP

6 ears of yellow corn, husked

1 medium onion, quartered

Salt

2 tablespoons unsalted butter

Reserved basil stems from basil oil

Freshly ground pepper

Small basil sprigs, for garnishing (optional)

BASIL OIL

2 (2-ounce) bunches of basil, leaves picked (about 4 cups), stems reserved

1 cup canola oil

Pinch of salt

SHRIMP FRITTERS

Canola oil, for frying

⅓ cup cornmeal

3 tablespoons all-purpose flour

1 teaspoon salt

½ teaspoon baking soda

¼ cup milk

1 large egg, lightly beaten

4 ounces medium shrimp, shelled, deveined, and cut into ¼-inch pieces

6 tablespoons cooked corn kernels reserved from the soup, chopped

2 tablespoons chopped scallion greens

1 Make the soup: In a large pot, combine the corn, onion, and 8 cups water and season with salt. Bring to a boil, then reduce the heat to medium-low and cook until the corn is very tender, about 1 hour.

2 Meanwhile, make the basil oil: In a blender, puree the basil leaves with the oil and salt. Scrape into a small saucepan. Bring to a simmer and cook over medium-low heat for 5 minutes. Strain the oil through a mesh coffee filter into a small bowl. Let cool.

3 Transfer the corn to a cutting board; reserve the corn broth and discard the onion quarters. Cut the corn kernels off the cobs; discard the cobs. Reserve 6 tablespoons of the corn for the fritters. In a medium saucepan, melt the butter. Add the remaining corn and cook, breaking up the kernels, for 2 to 3 minutes. Add 4 cups of the reserved corn broth, bring to a simmer, and cook over medium-low heat for 30 minutes.

4 Remove the soup from the heat. Add the basil stems, cover, and let steep for 20 minutes. Discard the basil. Using an immersion blender or a regular blender, puree the soup. Strain the soup through a medium sieve or food mill into another medium saucepan. Season with salt and pepper.

5 Make the fritters: Line a baking sheet with paper towels. In a large pot, heat 2 inches of oil to 350 degrees over medium heat. Meanwhile, in a medium bowl, whisk the cornmeal with the flour, salt, and baking soda. Add the milk and egg and whisk until the batter is smooth. Stir in the shrimp, corn, and scallions.

6 Working in batches, drop teaspoons of the batter into the oil and fry, stirring occasionally, until golden brown all over, about 1 minute. Using a slotted spoon, transfer the fritters to the prepared baking sheet.

7 Warm the soup until heated through. Add a few shrimp fritters to each shallow bowl. Drizzle a little basil oil around the fritters. Ladle the soup into the bowls, garnish with the basil sprigs, and serve.

TOMATO, BACON, AND SAFFRON SOUP À LA MINUTE

This supersimple recipe is the anti-pureed-tomatoes tomato soup. It's chunky with tomatoes, onion, and bacon, but the liquid is glossy and smooth. And the saffron, orange, and coriander seeds make it unique.

4 APPETIZER SERVINGS

1 tablespoon extra-virgin olive oil

3 white mushrooms, thinly sliced (about 4 ounces)

2 bacon slices, cut into ¼-inch pieces

1 tablespoon finely diced onion

Pinch of saffron threads (see Tips)

Pinch of ground coriander

3 large ripe beefsteak tomatoes, peeled (see Tips), seeded, and chopped (about 2 pounds)

½ cup orange juice

½ cup chicken stock or low-sodium broth

Salt

In a medium saucepan, heat the oil until shimmering. Add the mushrooms, bacon, and onion and cook over medium heat, stirring occasionally, until softened, about 5 minutes. Add the saffron and coriander and cook, stirring occasionally, until fragrant, about 20 seconds. Add the tomatoes and cook, stirring occasionally, until juicy, about 3 minutes. Add the orange juice and stock, bring to a simmer, and cook for 5 minutes. Season with salt and serve.

TIPS
Le Cirque's saffron, which comes from La Mancha in Spain, is unbelievably fragrant. It's available at tienda.com.

To peel tomatoes easily, cut out the cores and slice a shallow X in the bottoms. Drop into a saucepan of boiling water and simmer just until the skin starts to curl, about 20 seconds. Using a slotted spoon, remove the tomatoes from the water and let cool slightly before peeling.

VARIATION
Omit the bacon and double the onion and mushrooms to make a vegetarian soup.

SERVE WITH
Pass a basket of sliced country bread that's been brushed with olive oil and toasted in the oven.

This soup goes with so many dishes. Try Chicken Under a Brick (page 182), Côtes d'Agneau Champvallon (page 140), or Comté Cheese Soufflés (page 202).

MAKE AHEAD
The soup can be refrigerated for up to 4 hours and reheated.

SPRING PEA SOUP WITH PARMESAN FRICO

This vegetarian puree is for the height of spring. Without chicken stock to muddy the taste, it's as pure as it gets. Raw pea shoots, blended with the soup just before serving, enhance the vibrant pea flavor and green color.

4 APPETIZER SERVINGS

1 cup coarsely shredded Parmesan cheese

4 cups vegetable broth

1 tablespoon extra-virgin olive oil

1 medium shallot, thinly sliced

1 garlic clove, crushed

1 pound shelled peas, ¼ cup reserved for garnish

Salt

3 ounces pea shoots (see Tips)

Small mint sprigs, for garnishing

1 Warm a nonstick medium skillet over medium heat for 1 minute. Sprinkle ¼ cup of the cheese into the skillet in a 4-inch round. Cook the cheese until it melts and becomes a lightly browned disk, about 4 minutes. Using a metal spatula, loosen the frico from the skillet and slide it onto a plate to cool; it will crisp up as it cools. Transfer the frico to a wire cooling rack to cool completely. Repeat to make 3 more disks.

2 In a large saucepan, bring the broth to a simmer. In another large saucepan, heat the oil until shimmering. Add the shallot and garlic to the oil and cook over medium-low heat, stirring occasionally, until softened, about 1 minute. Add the peas and season with salt. Cover and cook until tender, about 4 minutes.

3 Add the hot broth, bring to a simmer, and cook for 3 minutes. Fill a large bowl with ice water.

4 Using an immersion blender or a regular blender, puree the soup with the pea shoots. Strain the soup through a sieve or food mill into a medium bowl set in the ice water. Transfer to the refrigerator until serving.

5 In a large saucepan, warm the soup until heated through just before serving. Ladle into shallow bowls and garnish with the reserved peas and mint. Serve with the frico.

HEIRLOOM TOMATO SALAD WITH GORGONZOLA MOUSSE AND ARUGULA

In the summertime, fresh tomatoes are one of Craig Hopson's favorite ingredients. Rather than crumbling Gorgonzola over a tomato salad, he turns the cheese into a creamy mousse and adds a dollop (technically, a quenelle) to the plate.

6 APPETIZER SERVINGS

GORGONZOLA MOUSSE

1 gelatin sheet (see Tips)

1 cup heavy cream

¾ cup crumbled Gorgonzola cheese (3½ ounces)

½ tablespoon honey

¼ teaspoon salt, if needed

SALAD

¼ cup extra-virgin olive oil

2 tablespoons balsamic vinegar

Salt and freshly ground pepper

1½ pounds mixed heirloom tomatoes, cut into random shapes

Baby arugula, for garnishing

1 Make the Gorgonzola mousse: Soak the gelatin sheet in a medium bowl of ice water until softened, about 3 minutes. Drain and squeeze out as much water as possible.

2 In a medium saucepan, heat the cream until bubbles appear around the edge. Remove the pan from the heat and add the cheese and honey. Using an immersion blender, puree the mixture. Season with the salt if needed. Blend in the gelatin. Scrape into a medium bowl and refrigerate overnight.

3 The next day, whip the mousse until firm, about 2 minutes.

4 Make the salad: In a medium bowl, whisk the oil and vinegar and season with salt and pepper. Add the tomatoes to the vinaigrette, toss to coat, and spread on plates. Add the arugula to the vinaigrette and toss to coat lightly. Set a small scoop of the mousse on the tomatoes, garnish with the arugula, and serve. Pass the remaining mousse separately.

TIPS

Chefs like to use sheet gelatin because it yields a better texture than the powdered variety. Sheet gelatin is available in the baking section of specialty markets and from surfasonline.com.

Gorgonzola is especially creamy, but other blue cheeses, such as Roquefort, can be used. Taste for seasoning in step 2 before adding salt.

In the Le Cirque kitchen, the mousse is molded into a perfect egg shape using two soupspoons dipped in hot water before being set on the plate.

VARIATIONS

Instead of using the arugula as a garnish, you can make a bed of it for the tomatoes.

When tomatoes aren't in season, the Gorgonzola mousse is fabulous with a shaved celery or endive salad, or Waldorf salad.

SERVE WITH

Follow the salad with another summery dish, such as Bacon-Wrapped Salmon with Ratatouille Salad (page 164).

MAKE AHEAD

At Le Cirque the Gorgonzola mousse is refrigerated overnight before using, but you can make it early in the day you will be serving it. In three to four hours, it will be chilled and sufficiently set in time for dinner that evening.

If you can't find bay scallop
shells, try Asian porcelain
soupspoons. But you don't
need spoons; the scallops can
be served on plates.

Mustard seed oil is available at
Indian food shops.

Verjus is the tart juice of unripe
grapes.

Make sure everything is very
cold so the jelly doesn't melt.

VARIATION

You can use Taylor or Mexican
bay scallops but they won't be
as sweet.

SERVE WITH

Since this is a light first course,
how about a heavier entrée,
such as Braised Veal Shank
for Two (page 166) or Braised
Short Ribs with Mashed
Sunchokes and Lacinato Kale
(page 235)?

MAKE AHEAD

The apple gelée can be
refrigerated overnight.

NANTUCKET BAY SCALLOPS CRUDO WITH GREEN APPLE GELÉE AND MUSTARD SEEDS

December is bay scallop season, the perfect moment for serving the sweet, delicate shellfish raw. To add zing, Craig Hopson makes a vinaigrette with mustard oil, complemented by a garnish of colorful yellow and brown mustard seeds. The apple gelée and julienne has a cooling effect.

4 APPETIZER SERVINGS

APPLE GELÉE

1 Granny Smith apple, unpeeled, cored
and coarsely chopped

1 tablespoon verjus (see Tip)

1 tablespoon fresh lemon juice

¼ teaspoon sugar

⅛ teaspoon citric acid

1 gelatin sheet (see Heirloom Tomato
Salad with Gorgonzola Mousse and
Arugula, Tips, page 211)

SCALLOPS

1½ tablespoons mustard seed oil
(see Tips)

1 tablespoon extra-virgin olive oil

2 teaspoons sherry vinegar

Salt

20 Nantucket Bay scallops, plus
20 bay scallop shell halves, cleaned

1 teaspoon yellow mustard seeds

1 teaspoon brown mustard seeds

Micro parsley leaves, for garnishing

1 Granny Smith apple, unpeeled,
cut into julienne strips

1. Make the apple gelée: In a food processor, puree the chopped apple with ¼ cup water, the verjus, lemon juice, sugar, and citric acid for 5 minutes. Strain through a fine sieve into a small glass measuring cup, then through a mesh coffee filter.

2. Meanwhile, soak the gelatin sheet in a small saucepan of ice water until softened, about 3 minutes. Drain and squeeze out as much water as possible.

3. Fill a medium bowl with ice water. Add 2 tablespoons of the apple puree to the softened gelatin and melt over low heat. Stir into the remaining apple puree and set in the ice water to chill, stirring frequently. Refrigerate until set, about 2 hours.

4. Make the scallops: In a medium bowl, whisk the oils with the vinegar and season with salt. Add the scallops and toss to coat; refrigerate for up to 2 hours.

5. Spoon a little apple gelée into each scallop shell and set a scallop on top. Sprinkle with the yellow and brown mustard seeds and garnish with the parsley and apple julienne. Arrange 5 scallops on each plate, and serve very cold.

MARINATED TUNA WITH CLEMENTINES AND AVOCADO TAPENADE

To make this not-exactly-raw French-Mediterranean starter, Craig Hopson marinates fresh tuna with a pungent blend of anchovies, chile powder, and herbs in a plastic bag. The mix is briefly submerged in hot tap water before being chilled in an ice bath. Then the tuna and slices of clementine are arranged on seeded crackers and set on a dice of avocado spiked with olives, capers, olive oil, and lemon juice.

4 APPETIZER SERVINGS

MARINATED TUNA

1 tablespoon coriander seeds

1 tablespoon fennel seeds

2 cups extra-virgin olive oil

6 white anchovy fillets

2 tablespoons chopped rosemary

2 tablespoons chopped thyme

1½ tablespoons piment d'Espelette (see Tips)

1 garlic clove, crushed

2 teaspoons salt

8 ounces sushi-grade tuna fillet

4 rectangular seeded flatbread crackers

1 clementine, peeled and cut in between the membranes into segments, segments cut lengthwise in half (see Lobster Salad Le Cirque, Tips, page 150)

1 watermelon or other radish, cut into fine julienne strips

1 tablespoon radish sprouts

AVOCADO TAPENADE

1 large avocado, halved, pitted, and cut into ¼-inch dice

1 tablespoon chopped parsley or cilantro

1 tablespoon extra-virgin olive oil

2 teaspoons fresh lemon juice

1 teaspoon chopped white anchovy fillet

1 teaspoon chopped Kalamata olives

1 teaspoon chopped capers

Salt and freshly ground pepper

1 Make the marinated tuna: In a small skillet, toast the coriander and fennel seeds over medium heat until fragrant, 30 seconds to 1 minute. Pour into a bowl and let cool completely.

2 In a blender, puree the oil with the toasted coriander and fennel seeds, anchovies, rosemary, thyme, piment d'Espelette, garlic, and salt. Scrape the marinade into a large sturdy resealable bag. Add the tuna, squeeze out the air, and seal.

3 Transfer the bag to a large heatproof bowl. Cover with hot tap water and weight it down. Let stand, moving the bag occasionally, for 15 minutes. Transfer the bag to the counter and let stand at room temperature for 15 minutes.

4 Fill a medium bowl with ice water. Transfer the bag to the ice water, weight it down, and refrigerate.

5 Make the avocado tapenade: In a small bowl, using a rubber spatula, fold the avocado with the parsley, oil, lemon juice, anchovy, olives, and capers. Season with salt and pepper. Cover and refrigerate.

6 Remove the tuna from the marinade and cut into ⅛-inch-thick ribbons. Mound one fourth of the avocado tapenade in a rectangle in the center of each plate. Lightly press a flatbread cracker on top. Curl 3 or 4 slices of tuna on the cracker. Garnish with the clementine segments, radish julienne, and radish sprouts. Drizzle the plates with the marinade and serve.

WARM SALAD OF NEW POTATOES, PEAR, REBLOCHON, CIPOLLINE, AND MÂCHE

This elegant, wintry salad was inspired by the rustic tartiflette, a potato-and-Reblochon cheese tart from the French Alps. Craig Hopson first sampled it when he was working at the Parisian restaurant Lucas-Carton, and one of the staffers, from Haute-Savoie, shared it with the kitchen. "I've always loved that cheese and potato combination," says Hopson. "But it's heavy. I wanted to rework the same flavors but make it lighter. The pear introduces a sweet note, and pear and cheese are natural partners."

4 APPETIZER SERVINGS

2 tablespoons extra-virgin olive oil

1 tablespoon balsamic vinegar

8 small cipolline onions, peeled

Salt

12 ounces small multicolored new potatoes, scrubbed

1 ripe Bartlett pear, peeled, cut lengthwise into eighths, and cored (see Tips)

½ cup dry white wine

2 tablespoons sugar

3 ounces Reblochon cheese, thinly sliced (see Tips)

Baby mâche, for garnishing

1   In a medium skillet, heat the oil and vinegar over medium heat. Add the onions, cover, and cook over medium-low heat, stirring occasionally, until tender, 20 to 30 minutes. Transfer the onions to a cutting board and slice in half; season with salt.

2   Meanwhile, in a medium saucepan of salted water, add the potatoes, cover, and bring to a boil. Cook until tender, about 10 minutes. Drain, transfer to a cutting board, and slice in half.

3   In a small saucepan, combine the pear, wine, and sugar. Cover, bring to a simmer, and cook over medium-low heat until tender, 5 to 8 minutes; drain.

4   Heat the broiler. Arrange the potatoes on heatproof plates. Drape the cheese over the potatoes and broil until melted, 2 to 3 minutes. Add the pears and onions to the plates and drizzle with the oil and vinegar from the onions. Garnish with the mâche and serve.

TIPS

To test pears for ripeness, press with your thumb at the pear's neck. If it yields to gentle pressure, it's ready to eat.

Mild and creamy Reblochon from the French Alps is a cow's-milk cheese shaped into a flattened disk with an orange rind. Other Alpine cheeses like French raclette or Comté and Italian fontina would also be good choices.

In step 4, you can melt the cheese over the potatoes in a large gratin dish, then transfer them to plates, or serve from the gratin dish.

VARIATIONS

To make a more substantial salad, add thinly sliced prosciutto and toasted hazelnuts or Marcona almonds to the plate before serving.

Substitute small roasted beets for some of the potatoes.

SERVE WITH

Have this cool-weather salad as an appetizer before Braised Veal Shank for Two (page 166) or Braised Short Ribs with Mashed Sunchokes and Lacinato Kale (page 235).

Or serve it as a side dish with pork chops, baked ham, or roast chicken. It would also be fantastic alongside a radicchio, celery, and curly endive salad, dressed with sherry vinegar and walnut oil.

MAKE AHEAD

This salad can be prepared through step 3 up to 4 hours in advance.

The onions can be refrigerated overnight; reheat before serving.

SAUTÉED SHRIMP WITH CARROT CONFIT AND KAFFIR LIME SABAYON

Craig Hopson loves the combination of carrots and lime. "And I wanted to do a sautéed shrimp dish," he says. "But I was looking for a more classical way of integrating the carrot and lime flavors." He decided to turn the lime into a sabayon, whisking fragrant lime leaf oil into a lime-juice and egg-yolk base. Carrots appear as both contrasting sauce and tender vegetable confit. It's delicious and beautiful.

4 APPETIZER SERVINGS

KAFFIR LIME SABAYON

½ cup canola oil

5 kaffir lime leaves, coarsely chopped

1-inch piece of ginger, coarsely chopped

3 large egg yolks

¼ cup fresh lime juice

CARROT SAUCE

½ cup carrot juice

1 kaffir lime leaf, crushed

¼ teaspoon cornstarch

1 tablespoon grapeseed oil

1 teaspoon fresh lime juice

¼ teaspoon sugar

¼ teaspoon salt

CARROTS AND SHRIMP

3 tablespoons extra-virgin olive oil

1 pound baby carrots, peeled, tops trimmed to ½ inch, or regular carrots, peeled and sliced on the diagonal ¾ inch thick

Salt

20 large shrimp (about 1 pound), shelled and deveined

Freshly ground pepper

Small cilantro sprigs, for garnishing

1. Start the kaffir lime sabayon: In a small saucepan, combine the oil, lime leaves, and ginger. Warm over medium heat, then remove from the heat, cover, and let steep for 20 minutes. Strain this lime leaf oil through a fine sieve set over a small bowl. Let cool.

2. Make the carrot sauce: In a small saucepan, combine the carrot juice and lime leaf, bring to a simmer over medium-high heat, and cook until reduced to ¼ cup, 3 to 5 minutes; discard the lime leaf. Using an immersion blender, blend in the cornstarch until the sauce thickens slightly. Remove from the heat and blend in the grapeseed oil in a thin stream. Add the lime juice, sugar, and salt and let cool.

3. Make the carrots: In a large skillet, heat 2 tablespoons of the oil until shimmering. Add the carrots, cover, and cook over medium-low heat until tender, 20 to 30 minutes. Using a slotted spoon, transfer the carrots to a bowl and season with salt.

4. Finish the kaffir lime sabayon: In a medium heatproof bowl set over a saucepan of barely simmering water, whisk the egg yolks with the lime juice until thick and pale yellow, 3 to 5 minutes. Remove the bowl from the saucepan and whisk in the lime leaf oil in a thin stream.

5. Make the shrimp: In another large skillet, heat the remaining 1 tablespoon oil until shimmering. Add the shrimp and cook over medium heat until white throughout, about 1½ minutes per side. Season with salt and pepper.

6. Drizzle some of the lime sabayon on each plate. Drizzle some of the carrot sauce in the same fashion. Scatter the carrots on top, then the shrimp. Garnish with the cilantro and serve. Pass the remaining sauces separately.

TIPS

When whisking the egg yolks and lime juice over the hot water in step 4, don't let the bottom of the bowl get too hot or the yolks will curdle. You need only an inch or two of water in the saucepan.

Kaffir lime leaf, used in many dishes throughout Southeast Asia and Indonesia, provides a unique floral, citrusy flavor.

VARIATIONS

Spoon this tangy, fluffy kaffir lime sabayon over other seafood like seared salmon, halibut, or scallops.

Or spread the sabayon over seared seafood in a gratin dish and broil on the top rack of the oven until lightly browned, about 3 minutes.

SERVE WITH

For a Mediterranean-Asian-inflected main course, try Halibut Poached in Coconut Milk with Chanterelles and Dried Tomatoes (page 227).

MAKE AHEAD

The lime leaf oil can be refrigerated, tightly covered, for up to 1 week.

BRANDADE FRAÎCHE WITH SOFTLY POACHED EGG AND WINTER TRUFFLES

Le Cirque's mission statement could easily be: How can we use luxury ingredients in new ways? This supremely delicious recipe is heir to such dishes as Creamy Scrambled Eggs with Caviar (page 203) and Stuffed Baked Potatoes with Truffles (page 168). Truffles love eggs as well as potatoes, and here Craig Hopson combines all three, creating a soft, light brandade—a blend of mashed potatoes and quick-cured salt cod—as a vehicle for poached eggs with powerfully aromatic truffles shaved over the top. In a nod to the toast soldiers traditionally served with eggs, Hopson folds in crunchy croutons and passes Parmesan-crusted brioche fingers on the side.

8 APPETIZER SERVINGS

BRANDADE

6 tablespoons kosher salt

1¼ pounds skinless cod fillet

3 cups whole milk

1 cup chicken stock or low-sodium broth

3 garlic cloves, crushed

1 thyme sprig

1 bay leaf

10 ounces Yukon Gold potatoes, peeled and cut into 1½-inch chunks

3 to 6 tablespoons extra-virgin olive oil

1 to 3 tablespoons heavy cream

1 tablespoon white wine or distilled white vinegar

8 large eggs

½ cup clarified butter (see Caesar Salad Le Cirque, step 1, page 194)

8 slices of brioche loaf, crust removed, 4 slices cut into ½-inch cubes, 4 slices cut into 4- by ½-inch rectangles

2 tablespoons freshly grated Parmesan cheese

Snipped chives, for sprinkling

2 tablespoons chopped fresh black truffles (about 1 ounce), plus 1 fresh black truffle (about 1 ounce) for garnishing (see Tips)

2 tablespoons chopped scallion greens

TRUFFLE SAUCE

⅓ cup heavy cream

¼ cup milk

¼ cup reserved cooking liquid

3 tablespoons truffle juice (see Tips)

½ tablespoon soy lecithin (see Tips)

SERVE WITH
Continue the Mediterranean
theme with Bouillabaisse Le
Cirque (page 138). Or follow
with Seared Scallops with
Peperonata and Yuca Chips
(page 224).

MAKE AHEAD
Poached eggs can be kept
in cold water, refrigerated,
overnight.

The brandade can be
prepared through step 4
and refrigerated overnight. It
thickens on standing, so add
a little olive oil and cream if
needed to make it smoother.

1 Make the brandade: Spread 3 tablespoons of the salt on a large plate. Set the cod on the plate and sprinkle the remaining 3 tablespoons of salt on top. Cover the cod with another large plate and weight it down with a heavy can. Let the cod stand at room temperature for 30 minutes.

2 Meanwhile, in a large saucepan, combine the milk, stock, garlic, thyme, bay leaf, and potatoes, cover, and bring to a boil over high heat. Uncover and cook over medium heat until the potatoes are partly tender, about 10 minutes.

3 Rinse the cod and pat dry. Add to the saucepan and cook over medium heat until the fish flakes with a fork, about 10 minutes. Drain, reserving the cooking liquid. Discard the thyme and bay leaf.

4 In a food processor, pulse the cod mixture until combined. Add the oil, cream, and 2 tablespoons of the reserved cooking liquid and pulse until smooth. Scrape the brandade into a medium bowl.

5 Bring a large deep skillet of water to a simmer. Add the vinegar. Crack each egg into a ramekin, then tip into the simmering water. Poach the eggs over medium heat until the whites are set but the yolks are soft, about 3 minutes. Using a slotted spoon, transfer the eggs to a paper towel–lined plate; blot dry. Trim the eggs into neat ovals.

6 In a large skillet, heat ¼ cup of the clarified butter over high heat. Add the brioche cubes and cook over medium heat, stirring, until golden brown on all sides, about 2 minutes total. Remove and drain on paper towels. Wipe out the skillet and repeat with the remaining clarified butter and brioche rectangles; sprinkle these with the cheese and chives.

7 Make the truffle sauce: In a small saucepan, combine the cream, milk, reserved cooking liquid, and the truffle juice and bring to a simmer. Remove from the heat, and using an immersion blender, blend in the soy lecithin until foamy.

8 Reheat the eggs in a shallow bowl of warm water for a few minutes; remove with a slotted spoon to paper towels and pat dry. Stir the bread cubes, chopped truffles, and scallions into the brandade. Mound about ½ cup of the brandade in each bowl and make a hollow in the center. Set a poached egg in the hollow and spoon some of the truffle foam and sauce over the top. Shave the remaining truffle over the sauce and serve with the brioche fingers.

RISOTTO CRISTAL WITH LANGOUSTINE CARPACCIO

Mickey Bhoite, the executive chef at Le Cirque's New Delhi outpost, is clearly having fun, packing in as many extravagant ingredients as possible into his risotto: Champagne, langoustines, caviar. He's brilliantly blended influences, serving the langoustine as a crudo component (French and Italian), stirring in tangy, slightly smoky roasted lime (Indian), and enriching the plump grains of rice with mascarpone as well as Parmesan (Italian).

6 APPETIZER OR 4 ENTRÉE SERVINGS

4 or 6 langoustine tails or jumbo shrimp, shelled, deveined, and butterflied (see Tips)

2 limes, peeled and cut in between the membranes into segments, juices reserved (see Lobster Salad Le Cirque, Tips, page 150)

2 cups light vegetable stock

6 tablespoons unsalted butter

1¼ cups Vialone Nano rice (see Lobster Risotto, Tips, page 153)

½ cup dry white wine

Salt

1 cup Champagne

½ cup freshly grated Parmesan cheese

½ cup mascarpone cheese (about 4 ounces)

Freshly ground pepper

Extra-virgin olive oil, for drizzling

2 ounces Osetra caviar

Small dill sprigs, for garnishing

1 Spread 1 langoustine tail on a sheet of plastic wrap, cover with a second sheet, and, using a meat mallet or the bottom of a heavy saucepan, pound gently until paper-thin. Peel off the plastic and arrange the langoustine on one side of a plate; cover and refrigerate. Repeat with the remaining langoustines.

2 Heat a small skillet over high heat. Add the lime segments and cook until lightly browned, about 20 seconds per side. Remove from the heat, let cool, then juice half of the segments. Reserve the remaining segments.

3 In a medium saucepan, bring the stock to a simmer. Keep warm.

4 In a large saucepan, melt 2 tablespoons of the butter over medium-high heat. Add the rice and cook for 1 minute, stirring to coat. Add the wine and cook over medium heat, stirring, until nearly absorbed. Add 1 cup of the stock and cook, stirring constantly, until nearly absorbed. Continue adding the stock, ½ cup at a time, stirring constantly until it is nearly absorbed between additions. Season with salt and add the Champagne, ½ cup at a time. The risotto is done when the rice is al dente, 15 to 20 minutes total.

5 Remove the pan from the heat and stir in the remaining 4 tablespoons butter, the roasted lime juice, Parmesan, and ¼ cup of the mascarpone. Season with salt and pepper. Drizzle the langoustines with oil and season with salt and pepper. Spoon the risotto next to them, slightly overlapping, and dollop the caviar and remaining mascarpone on the plates. Garnish with the dill and reserved lime segments and serve.

TIPS

To butterfly the langoustine or shrimp tails, cut them lengthwise almost in half and open flat.

VARIATION

Instead of langoustines or shrimp, substitute thinly sliced smoked salmon.

SERVE WITH

For an entrée, serve Pan-Roasted Veal Chops with Winter Root Vegetables (page 183).

MAKE AHEAD

The recipe can be prepared through step 1 and refrigerated overnight.

Yuca, sometimes called cassava, is a starchy root that grows in very warm climates and makes supercrunchy chips. To remove the tough outer skin, use a sharp paring knife rather than a peeler.

Using a mandoline makes it easy to cut the yuca into slices of the same thickness, and the chips will cook evenly.

SERVE WITH

To start, try Marinated Tuna with Clementines and Avocado Tapenade (page 214) or Lobster Risotto (page 153).

VARIATIONS

To make the dish heartier, add a medium diced potato to the peperonata at the same time as the peppers so it can gently cook until tender.

Try the sweet-and-sour peperonata as a side dish with any mild protein, such as chicken, pork, veal, or cod.

Luca Banfi also likes to add a little bit of Brie or St. André cheese into the peperonata for extra richness.

He's also made the peperonata a little saucier by dicing everything smaller and adding more tomato to the recipe and using it as a sauce for pizza or pasta.

MAKE AHEAD

The peperonata and gremolata can be prepared up to 4 hours in advance.

The yuca chips can be stored in an airtight container for up to 3 days.

SEARED SCALLOPS WITH PEPERONATA AND YUCA CHIPS

Luca Banfi, the former executive chef at Le Cirque's branch in the Dominican Republic, mixes Italian, French, and tropical traditions in his peperonata, topping it with sautéed sea scallops and adding crisp yuca chips to the plate.

4 ENTRÉE SERVINGS

PEPERONATA

2 tablespoons extra-virgin olive oil

1 onion, halved and thinly sliced

3 garlic cloves, chopped

¼ cup red wine vinegar

1 tablespoon sugar

Pinch of crushed red pepper

3 small bell peppers, cut into julienne strips

3 medium tomatoes, diced

Salt and freshly ground pepper

1 tablespoon small capers, drained

2 tablespoons chopped basil

2 teaspoons chopped oregano

GREMOLATA

¼ cup chopped parsley

¼ cup extra-virgin olive oil

1 garlic clove, minced

Grated zest of 1 lemon (see Tips)

Salt and freshly ground pepper

YUCA CHIPS AND SCALLOPS

Canola oil, for frying

1 yuca (about 10 ounces), peeled and thinly sliced on a mandoline (see Tips)

Salt

2 tablespoons extra-virgin olive oil

16 sea scallops (see Black Tie Scallops, Tips, page 154)

Freshly ground pepper

1 Make the peperonata: In a medium saucepan, heat the oil until shimmering. Add the onion and garlic, cover, and cook over medium heat, stirring occasionally, until softened but not browned, about 5 minutes. Add the vinegar, sugar, and crushed red pepper and simmer, uncovered, until the vinegar is syrupy, about 5 minutes. Add the bell peppers and tomatoes and season with salt and pepper. Cover and bring to a simmer, then uncover and cook, stirring occasionally, until the peppers are tender and the tomatoes are saucy, 20 to 25 minutes. Remove the pan from the heat and stir in the capers, basil, and oregano. Taste for seasoning.

2 Make the gremolata: In a medium bowl, combine the parsley, oil, garlic, and lemon zest and season with salt and pepper.

3 Make the yuca chips: In a large pot, heat 1½ inches of canola oil to 350 degrees. Line a baking sheet with paper towels. Add the yuca to the oil in batches and stir gently to separate the slices. Fry until golden brown, 1 to 2 minutes. Using a slotted spoon, transfer the chips to the paper towels to drain. Season the chips with salt.

4 In a large skillet, heat the olive oil until smoking. Season the scallops with salt and pepper and add them to the skillet. Cook over medium-high heat until browned on the bottom, 2 to 3 minutes. Turn the scallops and cook for 2 to 3 minutes longer. Remove from the heat.

5 Mound some of the peperonata on each plate and arrange 4 of the scallops on top. Spoon the gremolata on the scallops, garnish with the yuca chips, and serve.

LOBSTER THERMIDOR

This exquisite dish was created in 1894 to honor the play Thermidor, *named after a month in the French Revolutionary calendar. To make it, lobster meat is folded into a cream sauce spiked with brandy, mustard, and tarragon, spooned back into the shells, and broiled with shredded Gruyère cheese until golden. It's been on and off the menu at Le Cirque since the restaurant's early days. In Chef Craig Hopson's hands, the dish is delicate yet intensely flavored, airy yet creamy. (He whips the cream.) Like its namesake, this Thermidor is a regime-changer.*

4 ENTRÉE SERVINGS

Salt

4 live 1½-pound lobsters

5 tablespoons unsalted butter

6 ounces white mushrooms, halved or quartered if large, thinly sliced

2 large shallots, finely chopped

1 garlic clove, finely chopped

¼ cup all-purpose flour

¼ cup dry white wine

3 tablespoons Cognac or brandy

⅓ cup chicken stock or low-sodium broth

⅓ cup sauce américaine (see Lobster Risotto, step 1, page 153)

2 tablespoons Dijon mustard

Hungarian sweet paprika

Ground cayenne

3 large egg yolks

1 cup heavy cream, whipped (see Tips)

1 tablespoon chopped fresh tarragon, or 1 teaspoon dried tarragon

1 tablespoon chopped chervil or more tarragon

Shredded Gruyère cheese, for sprinkling

1 Bring a large pot of water to a boil over high heat. Season with salt. Add 2 of the lobsters (or all 4 if your pot is large enough) and cook over high heat until they're medium-rare, about 6 minutes. Fill a very large bowl with ice water. Using tongs, transfer the lobsters to the ice water and let them cool slightly; remove to a cutting board. Repeat with the remaining 2 lobsters.

2 Remove the rubber bands from the claws. Twist off the claws, crack them, and remove the meat. Using a large chef's knife, cut the lobsters lengthwise in half. Clean out the heads. Remove the tail meat and discard the dark intestinal veins. Slice the lobster meat ½ inch thick. Reserve the lobster halves.

3 In a large saucepan, melt 2 tablespoons of the butter. Add the mushrooms and cook over medium heat, stirring, about 5 minutes. Transfer to a small bowl.

4 In the same saucepan, melt the remaining 3 tablespoons butter over high heat. Add the shallots and garlic and cook over medium heat, stirring occasionally, until softened, about 2 minutes. Add the flour and cook, stirring, over low heat for 2 to 3 minutes. Add the wine and Cognac and bring to a simmer, scraping up any bits stuck to the bottom. Stir in the stock, sauce américaine, and mustard over low heat. Season with salt, paprika, and cayenne. Remove the pan from the heat and whisk in the egg yolks; let cool slightly.

5 Heat the broiler. Fold the lobster meat, mushrooms, whipped cream, tarragon, and chervil into the sauce. Arrange 4 of the reserved lobster halves on a baking sheet. Spoon half the lobster mixture into the lobster shells and sprinkle with cheese. Broil on the top rack of the oven until lightly browned, about 5 minutes. Transfer 2 lobster halves to each plate. Repeat with the remaining lobster halves, lobster mixture, and cheese and serve.

TIPS
The long list of ingredients makes this recipe look more complicated than it really is. In fact, it's surprisingly manageable if you have all your ingredients prepped and lined up before starting step 3. Little ramekins are helpful for holding the small quantities of flour, wine, herbs, and so on.

The sauce is quite thick until the whipped cream is added in step 5, lightening the mixture.

It's always best to whip cream using very clean beaters in a chilled metal bowl (which gets and stays cold) set in a larger bowl of ice water. Chilling helps keep the cream from turning into butter and makes it easier to whip.

SERVE WITH
Pass an herbed rice pilaf with the lobster for soaking up the rich sauce.

MAKE AHEAD
The recipe can be prepared through step 4 and refrigerated for up to 4 hours.

VARIATIONS
Try grilled salmon instead of pan-seared salmon, or substitute sea scallops.

SERVE WITH
Craig Hopson suggests steamed rice as a side dish.

To start, serve Spring Pea Soup with Parmesan Frico (page 210).

SALMON FILLET, BABY CARROTS, PARSLEY, AND ORANGE JUS

The idea of simmering orange and carrot juices together to make a sauce came from Craig Hopson's stint working at Lucas-Carton in Paris. Instead of thickening the sauce with a flour-and-butter roux, Hopson blends in a cornstarch slurry, and light grapeseed oil replaces the expected butter enrichment. With a speckling of chopped parsley, it's a gorgeous accompaniment to pan-seared salmon.

4 ENTRÉE SERVINGS

1 cup fresh orange juice

1 cup fresh carrot juice

½ tablespoon cornstarch mixed with ½ tablespoon water

¼ cup plus 1 tablespoon grapeseed oil

Salt

1 tablespoon fresh lemon juice

1 pound baby carrots, peeled, tops trimmed to ¼ inch, or regular carrots, peeled and sliced on the diagonal ¾ inch thick

4 (5- to 6-ounce) skin-on salmon fillets

Freshly ground pepper

½ cup finely chopped parsley

1 In a medium saucepan, combine the orange and carrot juices, bring to a simmer, and cook over medium heat until reduced to ½ cup, about 20 minutes. Using an immersion blender, blend in the cornstarch slurry until the sauce thickens slightly. Remove the pan from the heat and blend in ¼ cup of the oil in a thin stream. Season with salt and the lemon juice.

2 Meanwhile, in a large saucepan of boiling salted water, cook the carrots until tender, 8 to 10 minutes; drain.

3 In a large skillet, heat the remaining 1 tablespoon oil until shimmering. Pat the salmon dry and season with salt and pepper. Add the salmon skin side down to the skillet and cook over medium heat until crisp and golden, about 6 minutes. Turn and cook the fillets until not quite opaque, about 4 minutes.

4 Gently reheat the sauce and stir in the parsley. Arrange the carrots in the center of each plate. Set a salmon fillet on top and spoon the sauce around the plates. Serve, passing the remaining sauce at the table.

HALIBUT POACHED IN COCONUT MILK WITH CHANTERELLES AND DRIED TOMATOES

Thick halibut fillets have a great texture, but the fish itself is bland. In this Mediterranean twist on Thai shrimp soup, the meaty fillets are poached in coconut milk infused with kaffir lime leaves, lemongrass, and ginger. Oven-dried tomatoes and mushrooms lend an earthy flavor.

4 ENTRÉE SERVINGS

FISH AND ACCOMPANIMENTS

½ pint cherry tomatoes, halved

¼ teaspoon sugar

Salt and freshly ground white pepper

3 garlic cloves, 2 minced, 1 crushed

3 tablespoons unsalted butter

1 tablespoon extra-virgin olive oil

8 ounces small chanterelle mushrooms (about 2 cups)

4 (5- to 6-ounce) skinless halibut fillets

4 ounces baby spinach

COCONUT BROTH

2 kaffir lime leaves

2 shallots, sliced

2 garlic cloves, sliced

1 lemongrass stalk, pale core only, sliced

1-inch piece of ginger, sliced

1 tablespoon canola oil

¼ cup dry white wine

2 (13.5-ounce) cans unsweetened coconut milk (about 3 cups)

Pinch of crushed red pepper

Pinch of salt

1 Make the oven-dried tomatoes: Heat the oven to 225 degrees. Line a baking sheet with foil and spread the tomatoes, cut side up, on the sheet. Season with the sugar, ¼ teaspoon salt, and ⅛ teaspoon white pepper. Sprinkle the minced garlic on top and bake for 2 hours, until the tomatoes are semi-dry. Remove and let cool.

2 Make the coconut broth: In a medium saucepan, combine the lime leaves, shallots, garlic, lemongrass, ginger, and oil. Cover and cook over medium heat, stirring occasionally, until softened but not browned, about 5 minutes. Add the wine, bring to a simmer, and cook, stirring, until reduced by half, about 1 minute. Add the coconut milk, crushed red pepper, and salt. Cover, bring to a simmer, and cook over low heat for 30 minutes. Remove from the heat and let steep for 30 minutes.

3 Meanwhile, in a large skillet, melt 1 tablespoon of the butter in the oil over medium-high heat. Add the mushrooms and crushed garlic and season with salt and white pepper. Cook, stirring occasionally, until tender and lightly browned, 3 to 5 minutes; drain.

4 Add the halibut to another large deep skillet. Strain the coconut broth over the fish. Cover, bring to a simmer, and cook over low heat just until the fish flakes easily with a fork, 6 to 8 minutes.

5 In the skillet with the mushrooms, melt the remaining 2 tablespoons butter over medium-high heat. Add the dried tomatoes and spinach and cook, stirring, until the spinach wilts, 1 to 2 minutes.

6 Mound the mushroom mixture in shallow bowls and top with the halibut. Spoon some of the coconut broth around the fish and serve.

TIPS
Do not let the coconut broth boil when cooking the halibut in step 3. Poach it at a bare simmer.

The oven-dried tomatoes keep well, so you can easily double the recipe and save the extra to add to a variety of dishes, like soups, stews, and pasta.

VARIATIONS
Halved plum or medium tomatoes on the vine are also delicious oven-dried, and they're less fiddly (see Tomato Tatin, step 1, page 196).

For a stronger Mediterranean accent, sprinkle the tomatoes with herb sprigs like oregano, marjoram, rosemary, or thyme before oven-drying.

The rich coconut broth is a great poaching liquid for other types of seafood. Try striped bass, crab, or jumbo shrimp.

SERVE WITH
Accompany this fish with something plain like steamed basmati rice or warm naan bread.

MAKE AHEAD
The oven-dried tomatoes can be refrigerated for up to 1 week. The coconut broth can be refrigerated overnight.

PAN-ROASTED CHICKEN WITH RED PEPPER PUREE AND BROCCOLI RABE

When Craig Hopson makes a dish, he looks for elements that not only complement each other but also contrast. Chicken doesn't have a lot of character itself, so a sweet and tart red pepper puree is added to the plate. Broccoli rabe, sautéed with raisins, contributes sweetness and bitterness; frico makes a salty and crunchy foil.

4 ENTRÉE OR 8 APPETIZER SERVINGS

1 cup coarsely grated Parmesan cheese (about 4 ounces)

4 tablespoons extra-virgin olive oil

1 large red bell pepper, finely chopped

1 shallot, thinly sliced

1 tablespoon honey

1 tablespoon sherry vinegar

Salt

1 pound broccoli rabe, thick stems discarded, cut into 1-inch pieces

2 tablespoons golden raisins

Freshly ground pepper

4 boneless skin-on chicken breast halves

1 Warm a nonstick medium skillet over medium heat for 1 minute. Sprinkle ¼ cup of the cheese into the skillet in a 4-inch round. Cook the cheese until it melts and becomes a lightly browned disk, about 4 minutes. Using a thin metal spatula, loosen the frico from the skillet and drape it over a rolling pin to form a half-cylinder; it will crisp up as it cools. Transfer the frico to a wire cooling rack to cool completely. Repeat to make 3 more disks.

2 In a medium saucepan, heat 1 tablespoon of the oil until shimmering. Add the bell pepper and shallot, cover, and cook over medium-low heat, stirring occasionally, until very soft, about 25 minutes. Add the honey and cook for 5 minutes. Stir in the vinegar and season with salt. Using an immersion blender, puree the bell pepper until smooth.

3 Meanwhile, bring a large saucepan of salted water to a boil. Fill a medium bowl with ice water. Add the broccoli rabe to the boiling water and cook for 2 minutes. Drain, then add to the ice water to cool as quickly as possible, 1 to 2 minutes. Drain, shaking off the excess water.

4 In a medium skillet, heat 2 tablespoons of the oil until shimmering. Add the broccoli rabe and raisins and cook over medium-high heat, stirring occasionally, until tender, 2 to 3 minutes. Season with salt and pepper.

5 Heat the oven to 400 degrees. Season the chicken breasts with salt and pepper. In a large ovenproof skillet, heat the remaining 1 tablespoon oil until shimmering. Add the chicken breasts, skin side down, and cook over medium-high heat until they are richly browned, about 3 minutes. Turn the chicken breasts and transfer the skillet to the oven. Roast until just cooked through, about 10 minutes.

6 Spoon some of the red pepper puree on each plate and set a chicken breast on top. Mound the broccoli next to the chicken, add 1 frico to the plate, and serve.

RABBIT À LA MOUTARDE

Hopson's is a refined version of the typically homey rabbit in mustard sauce. The legs are in a rabbit stock made with Riesling wine from Alsace (that's the traditional part) but then the delicate loins are pan-seared along with house-made rabbit sausage. (Chicken or pork sausage is a good substitute.) He brings the dish back to its roots by pairing it with spaetzle, tiny dumplings served in eastern France, which he flavors with mustard and tarragon.

4 SERVINGS

4 tablespoons extra-virgin olive oil

1 (3-pound) rabbit (see Tips), cut into 2 boneless loins, bones reserved; 2 whole back legs, halved; and 2 forequarters

1 carrot, finely chopped

1 onion, finely chopped

2 shallots, finely chopped

1½ cups dry Riesling wine

4 cups chicken stock or low-sodium broth

5 thyme sprigs

2 rosemary sprigs

1 bay leaf

2 tablespoons Wondra flour

Salt and freshly ground pepper

3 tablespoons unsalted butter

1 (4-ounce) chicken or pork sausage

4 ounces small chanterelle mushrooms (about 1 cup), halved or quartered if large

Mustard-Tarragon Spaetzle (page 232)

4 ounces baby spinach (about 2 cups)

¼ cup grainy mustard

Splash of sherry vinegar

Finely chopped tarragon, for garnishing

1 In a large saucepan, heat 1 tablespoon of the oil until shimmering. Add the rabbit bones and forequarters and cook over medium heat until lightly browned all over, about 8 minutes. Transfer to a bowl. Add 1 tablespoon of the oil, the carrot, onion, and shallots to the pan and cook, stirring occasionally, until lightly browned, about 8 minutes. Return the rabbit to the pan, stir in the wine, and bring to a simmer over medium-high heat, scraping up the browned bits on the bottom. Add the stock, thyme, rosemary, and bay leaf, bring to a simmer, and cook until reduced by half, about 30 minutes. Strain into a large glass measuring cup.

2 Spread the flour in a baking pan. Season the rabbit legs generously with salt and pepper and dredge in the flour, patting off the excess. In a small enameled cast-iron casserole, heat 1 tablespoon of the oil until shimmering. Add the rabbit legs and cook over medium heat until lightly browned on both sides, about 8 minutes. Add the rabbit broth, cover, and cook over low heat until tender, about 1 hour.

3 Remove the legs from the pot and simmer the cooking liquid over medium-high heat until reduced by half, about 15 minutes.

4 Meanwhile, remove the bones from the legs, keeping the meat in large pieces, and return the meat to the pot.

5 In a large skillet, melt 1 tablespoon of the butter in the remaining 1 tablespoon oil over medium heat. Season the rabbit loins with salt and pepper. Add the loins and sausage to the skillet and cook until lightly browned all over and cooked through, 5 to 7 minutes.

6 Meanwhile, in another large skillet, melt the remaining 2 tablespoons butter. Add the mushrooms and cook over medium-high heat, stirring occasionally, for 2 minutes. Add the

spaetzle and cook, stirring occasionally, until lightly browned, about 5 minutes. Add the spinach and cook, stirring, until wilted, 1 to 2 minutes. Season with salt and pepper.

7 Bring the braising liquid to a simmer and whisk in the mustard and vinegar. Season with salt. Cut the rabbit loins crosswise into 4 pieces. Cut the sausage on the diagonal into 4 pieces. Mound some of the spaetzle on plates. Arrange the sausage, leg meat, and loin on top, and spoon some of the sauce around the plates. Garnish with the tarragon and serve, passing the remaining sauce and spaetzle separately.

MUSTARD-TARRAGON SPAETZLE

Instead of serving plain spaetzle (which is also excellent), Craig Hopson marries this accompaniment to the main dish of Rabbit à la Moutarde, flavoring it with two of the stew's main tastes: mustard and tarragon.

4 TO 6 SIDE SERVINGS

Salt

2 cups all-purpose flour

2 large eggs

¼ cup milk

1½ tablespoons dry mustard powder

1 tablespoon chopped tarragon

1 Bring a large pot of salted water to a boil. In a food processor, combine the flour with the eggs, ½ cup water, the milk, mustard, tarragon, and 1 teaspoon salt and process until smooth.

2 Fill a large bowl with ice water. Scrape the batter into a colander with ¼-inch holes. Set the colander over the boiling water and, using a rubber spatula, press the batter through the holes into the water. Stir the spaetzle once or twice to separate them. Using a slotted spoon, transfer the spaetzle as they rise to the surface to the ice water to cool as quickly as possible, about 1 minute; transfer to a clean colander to drain. Shake off the excess water, transfer to a bowl, and serve.

STEAK TARTARE

The creaminess in this classic chopped steak salad comes from mixing in mayonnaise instead of the traditional raw egg yolk.

4 ENTRÉE SERVINGS

1¼ pounds best-quality beef tenderloin, cut into ⅛- to ¼-inch dice

¼ cup extra-virgin olive oil

3 tablespoons finely chopped shallots

2 tablespoons finely chopped cornichons

2 tablespoons finely chopped drained capers

2 tablespoons fresh lemon juice

1 tablespoon mayonnaise

2 teaspoons Worcestershire sauce

1 teaspoon Dijon mustard

1 teaspoon hot sauce

Fleur de sel (see Lobster Salad Le Cirque, Tips, page 150) and freshly ground pepper

1 In a medium bowl, mix the meat with the oil, shallots, cornichons, capers, lemon juice, mayonnaise, Worcestershire sauce, mustard, and hot sauce. Season with fleur de sel and pepper.

2 Mound one fourth of the mixture on each plate, shaping it into a round cake, and serve.

TIPS

Hone a chef's knife for slicing the meat. Also, freezing the meat slightly, about 20 minutes, makes the dicing easier.

Lean flatiron steak, top round, and sirloin can also be used.

VARIATION

Add the condiments to individual bowls, mound the chopped meat on plates, and let each guest mix in as many and as much of the condiments as desired.

SERVE WITH

Hot, crisp French fries—such as Duck-Fat Fries (page 242)—are the best accompaniment. Or pass a basket of toasted, sliced country or whole-grain bread. At Paris cafés, where steak tartare is a summer staple, it's frequently paired with a green salad.

MAKE AHEAD

The mise en place can be prepared (meat chopped, condiments chopped and measured) up to 4 hours in advance. Keep the meat covered and refrigerated.

BRAISED SHORT RIBS WITH MASHED SUNCHOKES AND LACINATO KALE

To make a special winter dish, Craig Hopson teams up tender, braised short ribs with nutty sunchokes and earthy kale—both in season in the cold weather.

4 ENTRÉE SERVINGS

3 tablespoons canola oil

2 pounds boneless beef short ribs, cut into 1½- to 2-inch pieces

Salt and freshly ground pepper

1 medium onion, coarsely chopped

1 medium carrot, coarsely chopped

1 head of garlic, cut in half horizontally

4 thyme sprigs

2 bay leaves

1 teaspoon whole black peppercorns

2 cups full-bodied red wine

1 cup port

3 cups beef stock or low-sodium broth

Mashed Sunchokes (page 235)

Braised Lacinato Kale (page 235)

1   Heat the oven to 350 degrees. In a large enameled cast-iron casserole, heat 2 tablespoons of the oil until shimmering. Season the meat generously with salt and pepper. Working in two batches, add to the pot and cook over medium heat until browned on all sides, about 10 minutes per batch; transfer to a medium bowl. Discard the fat.

2   Add the onion, carrot, garlic, thyme, bay leaves, peppercorns, and the remaining 1 tablespoon oil to the pot. Cook over medium heat, stirring occasionally, until softened, about 5 minutes. Add the wine and port and bring to a simmer over medium-high heat, scraping up the browned bits on the bottom. Cook until reduced by half, about 10 minutes. Return the meat to the pot along with the stock, cover, and bring to a simmer. Transfer to the oven and cook until the meat is tender, about 3 hours.

3   Remove the pot from the oven and transfer the meat to a medium bowl. Strain the braising liquid into a large saucepan; discard the vegetables. Bring the braising liquid to a boil over medium-high heat and cook until slightly thickened and flavorful, about 10 minutes.

4   Spread some of the sunchokes on each plate. Arrange a few pieces of the meat on top and spoon some of the kale on the meat. Ladle some of the sauce around the meat, and serve. Pass the remaining sauce, kale, and sunchokes separately.

MASHED SUNCHOKES

Instead of the same old mashed potatoes, try these underappreciated tubers with a unique hazelnut flavor. They have one big advantage over potatoes: You don't have to peel them.

4 SIDE SERVINGS

1 pound sunchokes, cut into 1-inch pieces

1 cup whole milk

Salt

1 tablespoon extra-virgin olive oil

1 In a large saucepan, combine the sunchokes, milk, and enough water to cover. Season with salt and bring to a boil over medium-high heat; immediately lower the heat to a simmer and cook until the sunchokes are tender, about 30 minutes.

2 Drain, reserving the cooking liquid. Return the sunchokes to the saucepan and add the oil; using a potato masher, mash until mostly smooth. Stir in some of the reserved cooking liquid to moisten.

TIPS
The small, knobby tubers of a North American sunflower, sunchokes (also labeled Jerusalem artichokes) taste nutty and creamy when boiled or roasted.

VARIATIONS
Celery root can be prepared in the same way. Or experiment with a mix of new potatoes, sunchokes, and celery root.

SERVE WITH
Like mashed potatoes, mashed sunchokes make a delicious accompaniment to red meats, meatloaf, or roast chicken.

MAKE AHEAD
The recipe can be prepared through step 1 and refrigerated overnight.

BRAISED LACINATO KALE

Kale has a deep woodsy flavor and stands up well to braising. You can cook it for a long time and it still keeps its texture. This recipe may become your new favorite technique for cooking all kinds of hearty greens, like collards or mustard greens; it softens and lightly coats each leaf with a sheen of butter.

4 SIDE SERVINGS

4 tablespoons unsalted butter

½ medium onion, thinly sliced

5 garlic cloves, thinly sliced

2 bunches (about 1 pound) lacinato kale, stems and center ribs discarded (see Tips)

Salt

1 cup chicken stock or low-sodium broth

1 In a large skillet, melt the butter over medium heat. Add the onion and garlic and cook, stirring, until softened, about 5 minutes. Add the kale and season with salt. Cook, stirring, until soft, about 10 minutes. Add the stock and cover; lower the heat to low and cook until tender and dark green, about 25 minutes. Serve.

TIPS
Lacinato kale is also known as Tuscan kale, cavolo nero, or dinosaur kale.

To remove the kale stems and center ribs, fold the leaves in half with the rib side out, then pull up on the stems.

VARIATIONS
All kinds of winter greens, including turnip or mustard greens, or dandelions can replace the lacinato kale.

SERVE WITH
This buttery, tender kale would also be delicious with roast chicken or turkey, Côtes d'Agneau Champvallon (page 140), and Braised Veal Shank for Two (page 166).

MAKE AHEAD
The braised kale can be refrigerated overnight.

OLIVIER REGINENSI
2011 to present

Art by Tim Flynn.

SPAGHETTI WITH POUTARGUE FROM MARTIGUES

From the apartment where he grew up in Martigues, Olivier Reginensi could watch fishermen collecting roe-rich mullets from the nets (calins) that stretched between the banks of the canal connecting the Mediterranean to the freshwater Etang de Berre. The pressed, salted caviar of the mullet (poutargue) is often added to regional dishes, like this pasta, tossed in shellfish broth and dotted with shaved poutargue and crumbles of garlic confit. It's just what you want in a first course: a few forkfuls of bold flavor, setting you up nicely for the rest of your meal.

4 APPETIZER SERVINGS

1 small head of garlic, cloves separated but not peeled

⅓ cup canola oil

Salt

8 ounces dried spaghetti (see Tips, Spaghetti Primavera, page TKK)

2 cups mussel broth (see Moules Marinière, page TKK) or bottled clam juice

2 tablespoons unsalted butter

2 tablespoons extra-virgin olive oil

1½ ounces poutargue (see Tips), crumbled (about ½ cup), plus more for shaving

2 tablespoons chopped parsley

Freshly ground pepper

1 In a small saucepan, bring the garlic and canola oil to a simmer, then cook over medium-low heat, stirring occasionally, until golden, about 20 minutes. Transfer the garlic to a small bowl, let it cool slightly, then peel and finely chop. Transfer the oil to a jar, refrigerate, and reserve for another use.

2 Bring a large pot of salted water to a boil. Add the spaghetti and cook, stirring occasionally, until almost al dente; drain.

3 Meanwhile, in a large skillet, bring the broth to a boil. Add the butter, olive oil, and garlic confit and boil until emulsified, about 5 minutes.

4 Add the spaghetti and crumbled poutargue to the skillet. Cook over medium-high heat, stirring and tossing with tongs, until al dente. Add the parsley, season with pepper, and toss to coat. Transfer the spaghetti to shallow bowls or a serving dish, shave more poutargue over the top, and serve.

Branzino or black bass fillets can stand in for the sea bass. Béarnaise sauce with tomato is called *sauce choron* in French.

VARIATIONS

At Le Cirque, a server stirs the tomato and herbs into the béarnaise just before adding a dollop to your plate. At home, you can stir it up in front of your guests or beforehand in the kitchen, which is traditional.

Instead of tomato paste, you can add tomates concassées (stewed diced tomatoes) to the sauce, which is what a pro like Reginensi does.

A spoonful of tomato béarnaise on steak or eggs is also delightful.

SERVE WITH

For a first course, serve Lobster Salad Le Cirque (page 150) or Moules Marinière (page 117).

Try the Caramel-Walnut Soufflés (page 186) for dessert.

MAKE AHEAD

The fish in its pastry wrap can be assembled and refrigerated up to 4 hours before baking.

STUFFED SEA BASS IN PUFF PASTRY WITH TOMATO BÉARNAISE

Olivier Reginensi's fish baked in a golden pastry crust is a tribute to the great Paul Bocuse, who is as famous for his loup en croûte as for his black truffle soup (another Le Cirque favorite). Bocuse adds herb sprigs to the cavity of a whole fish. In this home-friendly version, Reginensi spreads spinach-fish mousse between fillets for easy serving.

4 ENTRÉE SERVINGS

SEA BASS

4 ounces baby spinach (about 2 packed cups)

2 ounces mixed coarsely chopped chives, tarragon, and chervil or parsley (about 1 packed cup)

4 ounces skinless white fish fillet

1 ice cube

1 large egg, separated, yolk beaten with 1 teaspoon water

Salt

Cayenne pepper

3 tablespoons heavy cream

2 (12-ounce) skinless sea bass fillets

All-purpose flour, for dusting

1 pound cold all-butter puff pastry dough, halved

TOMATO BÉARNAISE

¼ cup dry white wine

¼ cup white wine vinegar

¼ cup finely chopped shallots

1 tablespoon finely chopped tarragon

Freshly ground pepper

2 large egg yolks

½ cup clarified butter (see Caesar Salad Le Cirque, step 1, page 194)

Salt

1 Make the sea bass: Bring a large saucepan of water to a boil. Add the spinach and herbs and blanch for 1 minute. Drain in a sieve and rinse under cold water, then drain again well. Squeeze dry and chop.

2 In a food processor, grind the fish fillet with the ice cube, egg white, 1 teaspoon salt, and a pinch of cayenne until well chopped, about 30 seconds. Add the cream and process until smooth. Blend in the spinach and herbs. Refrigerate this fish mousse for at least 30 minutes, and up to 4 hours.

3 Heat the oven to 375 degrees. Line a baking sheet with a nonstick liner or parchment paper. Season the sea bass fillets with salt and cayenne. Set 1 fillet on a work surface. Spread with the fish mousse, cover with the second fillet, and refrigerate.

4 On a lightly floured work surface, roll out 1 puff pastry dough half to a rectangle ⅛ inch thick. Set the stuffed sea bass on the dough. Roll out the second dough half to a rectangle slightly larger than the first. Brush the dough around the fish with the egg wash. Lay the second dough rectangle on top and press around the fish to seal. Trim the dough around the fish, making a generous border and mimicking the shape of a fish. Brush the dough with egg wash. If desired, cut out an eye, mouth, or other decorations from the dough scraps and glue them on with egg wash; brush the decorations with egg wash too. Using the tip of a paring knife, make decorative scales and fins. Transfer to the prepared baking sheet and bake until golden brown, about 30 minutes. Transfer the fish to a platter and let rest for 5 minutes.

5 Meanwhile, make the tomato béarnaise: In a small saucepan, boil the wine, vinegar, shallots, tarragon, and ¼ teaspoon pepper until reduced to 2 tablespoons, about 3 minutes. Strain through a fine sieve into a small glass measuring cup, pressing on the vegetables; discard the solids.

GARNISHES

Thinly sliced lemon halves, pink peppercorns, and chervil leaves

1 tablespoon finely chopped chervil or parsley

1 tablespoon finely chopped tarragon

1 tablespoon tomato paste

6 In a medium saucepan, bring 2 inches of water to a simmer. In a medium heatproof bowl, whisk the egg yolks with the reduction. Set the bowl over the saucepan and whisk the yolks constantly until thickened slightly and bright yellow, about 1 minute. Remove from the heat.

7 Gently heat the butter; very gradually, whisk it into the yolks until a slightly thick sauce forms. Season lightly with salt and pepper. Keep warm over the hot water off the heat.

8 Surround the fish with the lemon slices and dot the lemons with pink peppercorns and chervil leaves. Transfer the béarnaise to a sauceboat, mound the chervil and tarragon in the center, and dollop the tomato paste on top. Slice the fish at the table. Pass the sauce separately.

TIPS

Foie gras, truffles, and duck fat are all available from dartagnan.com.

Fleur de sel, fine white sea salt from France, is available at specialty food stores.

VARIATION

For an even more luxurious bird, push black truffle slices instead of parsley leaves under the skin.

SERVE WITH

This roast chicken is rich, because of its pancetta-foie-gras stuffing, so serve a light appetizer to start, such as Nantucket Bay Scallops Crudo, Green Apple Gelée, Mustard Seeds (page 212) or Marinated Tuna with Clementines and Avocado Tapenade (page 214).

MAKE AHEAD

The chicken can be prepared through step 3 the day before, but refrigerate the chicken and stuffing separately.

PARSLEYED ROAST CHICKEN WITH FOIE-GRAS-AND-BLACK-TRUFFLE STUFFING

When Olivier Reginensi worked in the kitchen at Alain Ducasse's restaurant Louis XV in Monaco, executive chef Sylvain Portay had this stuffed roast chicken on the menu. The dressing, made with the bird's giblets, pancetta, and fried croutons is intense, more like a condiment than a side dish; a few tablespoons is all you want. It makes a great small holiday bird.

4 ENTRÉE SERVINGS

CHICKEN

1 teaspoon canola oil

2 ounces pancetta or bacon, cut into ½-inch dice

1 (3½-pound) pastured chicken, liver and heart trimmed and cut into ⅜-inch dice

Salt and freshly ground pepper

2½ ounces raw foie gras, cut into ⅜-inch dice (see Tips)

2 slices of firm white bread, crusts removed, cut into ⅜-inch cubes

1 large fresh black truffle (about 1½ ounces), cut into ¼-inch dice (see Tips)

10 flat-leaf parsley leaves

2 tablespoons unsalted butter, softened

½ cup veal or chicken stock or low-sodium broth

½ cup dry white wine

1 Make the chicken: Heat the oven to 400 degrees. In a medium skillet, heat the oil until shimmering. Add the pancetta and cook over medium heat, stirring occasionally, until lightly browned, about 5 minutes. Using a slotted spoon, transfer to a medium bowl. Add the liver and heart to the skillet, season with salt and pepper, and cook, stirring often, until lightly browned and pink in the center, about 30 seconds. Transfer to the bowl.

2 Add the foie gras to the skillet, season with salt and pepper, and cook over medium heat, stirring often, until lightly browned and pink in the center, about 30 seconds. Using a slotted spoon, transfer to the bowl. Add the bread cubes to the skillet and cook, stirring, until lightly browned on all sides, about 2 minutes total. Add to the bowl, fold in the truffle, and season with salt and pepper.

3 Season the chicken cavity with salt and pepper and spoon in the stuffing. Bend back the chicken wing tips and tuck them under their first joints. Using your fingertips, carefully loosen the chicken skin without tearing it, working your hand under the skin all the way up the breast. Distribute the parsley leaves evenly under the skin. Tie the legs together with kitchen string.

4 Set the chicken in a medium roasting pan. Rub it all over with the butter and season generously with salt and pepper. Transfer to the oven and roast until the chicken is browned and the juices run clear, about 1 hour; baste with the pan juices every 15 minutes and rotate the pan halfway through.

5 Meanwhile, make the duck-fat fries: In a large deep skillet, melt the duck fat over high heat. Working in batches, add

DUCK-FAT FRIES

8 ounces duck fat (see Tips)

4 large Idaho (baking) potatoes (about 14 ounces each), peeled and cut lengthwise into 8 wedges

2 garlic cloves, unpeeled

Fleur de sel (see Tips)

1 tablespoon chopped parsley

the potatoes and garlic in an even layer and cook over medium heat until lightly browned on the bottom, about 10 minutes. Turn the potatoes and continue cooking until the potatoes are crisp and tender, about 5 minutes. Using a slotted spoon, transfer the potatoes to a platter, season with fleur de sel, and keep warm; repeat with the remaining potatoes. Sprinkle with the parsley.

6 Tilt the chicken to drain the juices from the cavity into the pan; transfer the chicken to a carving board and let rest for 10 minutes. Spoon all but 1 tablespoon fat from the juices in the pan. Add the stock and wine and boil until slightly thickened, about 3 minutes. Season with salt and pepper. Strain the sauce through a fine sieve and pour it into a sauceboat. Carve the chicken and serve with the stuffing. Pass the pan sauce and fries separately.

PORCHETTA-STYLE STUFFED RABBIT

This whole rabbit, boned out, then stuffed and rolled into a thick log, recalls Italian porchetta (boned, stuffed, and rolled pork). But compared to its rustic namesake, this recipe is refined and painterly; each slice is filled with a colorful jumble of bright green peas and bits of red bell pepper, Swiss chard, and herbs.

4 ENTRÉE SERVINGS

TIPS

Rabbit is available at butcher's shops, farmers' markets, and from dartagnan.com.

To make a bouquet garni, tie 3 thyme sprigs, 6 parsley stems, 1 bay leaf, and 3 leek or scallion greens in a bundle with kitchen string.

If using frozen peas, defrost them but do not blanch in step 2.

VARIATION

Reginensi sometimes adds cubes of pancetta to the stuffing: Cook diced pancetta in a little olive oil over medium heat, stirring occasionally, until lightly browned, about 5 minutes, before beating it into the stuffing in step 4.

SERVE WITH

At the restaurant, the serving platter is covered with a bed of blanched Swiss chard leaves, and the stuffed rabbit is surrounded with glazed pearl onions and wide strips of oven-dried tomatoes. For a recipe describing the oven-drying technique, see Tomato Tatin, step 1 (page 196).

As a side dish, Reginensi tosses house-made fettuccine noodles with butter, chopped parsley, and chervil for soaking up the rabbit's braising liquid. You can buy fresh or dried fettuccine. To make the pasta from scratch, see Fettuccine with White Truffles (page 136).

MAKE AHEAD

The rabbit can be prepared through step 5 and refrigerated overnight.

2 ounces Swiss chard leaves (about 1 packed cup)

1½ ounces Swiss chard stems, peeled if thick and cut into ¼-inch dice (about ½ cup)

2 tablespoons shelled peas

1 (3-pound) rabbit (see Tips), boned in one piece, liver, kidneys, and bones reserved

1 teaspoon plus 2 tablespoons extra-virgin olive oil

Salt and freshly ground pepper

1 tablespoon sherry vinegar

2½ ounces pork fat, diced

2 ounces peeled roasted red bell pepper, cut into thin strips (about ⅓ cup)

¼ cup chopped chervil

2 tablespoons chopped parsley

2 large eggs

½ cup chopped onion

½ cup chopped leek (white and light green parts)

½ cup chopped carrot

½ cup chopped celery

1 head of garlic, cut in half horizontally

1 cup dry white wine

1½ cups chicken stock or low-sodium broth

1½ cups veal stock

1 bouquet garni (see Tips)

1. Bring a medium saucepan of water to a boil. Add the chard leaves and blanch for 1 minute. Using a slotted spoon, transfer the leaves to a colander and rinse under cold water, then drain well. Squeeze dry and finely chop.

2. Add the chard stems and peas to the boiling water and cook until tender, about 2 minutes. Drain in a colander and rinse under cold water, then drain again well.

3. Trim the liver and kidneys and cut into ¼-inch dice. In a small skillet, heat 1 teaspoon of the oil until shimmering. Add the liver and kidneys, season with salt and pepper, and cook over medium heat, stirring often, until lightly browned and pink in the center, about 30 seconds. Remove from the heat and add the vinegar, scraping up the browned bits on the bottom.

4. In a food processor, finely chop the leg meat with the pork fat. Transfer to a medium bowl and beat in the liver, kidneys, chard leaves, stems, peas, bell pepper, chervil, parsley, and eggs. Season with 1 teaspoon salt and ¼ teaspoon pepper.

5. Spread the rabbit boned side up on a work surface and season with salt and pepper. Spoon the stuffing in a mound down the center. Wrap the rabbit around the stuffing, shape into a neat log, and tie with kitchen string. Wrap well in foil and refrigerate.

6. Heat the oven to 325 degrees. In a large enameled cast-iron casserole, heat 1 tablespoon of the oil until shimmering. Add the bones and cook over medium-high heat, stirring occasionally, until lightly browned, about 5 minutes. Transfer to a bowl.

7. Discard the fat in the pot. Add the onion, leek, carrot, celery, garlic, and remaining 1 tablespoon oil and season with salt. Cook over medium heat, stirring occasionally, until softened, about 5 minutes. Add the wine, bring to a boil, and simmer until nearly evaporated.

8. Add the stuffed rabbit, bones, chicken stock, veal stock, and bouquet garni, cover, and bring to a simmer. Transfer to the oven and cook, turning the rabbit every 15 minutes, until the stuffing is cooked, 45 minutes to 1 hour.

9 Remove the pot from the oven and transfer the rabbit to a cutting board. Strain the braising liquid into a medium saucepan; discard the solids. Bring the braising liquid to a boil over medium-high heat and cook until slightly thickened and flavorful, about 10 minutes. Season with salt and pepper.

10 Discard the foil and string from the rabbit. Cut the rabbit into thick slices, arrange on plates or a platter, and season with salt and pepper. Spoon some of the sauce over the rabbit and serve. Pass the remaining sauce separately.

BEEF TRIPE À LA PROVENÇALE

In Olivier Reginensi's childhood home, the dough used to seal the casserole in which the stew cooks was leavened with yeast, making a light crust good enough to eat. The crust never burns because it bakes at such a low temperature. Reginensi does it the same way at Le Cirque.

4 ENTRÉE SERVINGS

TRIPE

2 pounds beef honeycomb tripe

1 calf's foot, split lengthwise

3 tablespoons extra-virgin olive oil

Salt and freshly ground pepper

¼ cup Cognac or brandy

2 carrots, peeled and sliced 2 inches thick on the diagonal

2 celery ribs, peeled and sliced ½ inch thick

1 large onion, coarsely chopped

4 garlic cloves, crushed and peeled

4 plum tomatoes, peeled and quartered lengthwise

1 tablespoon tomato paste

2 cups dry white wine

2 cups veal or chicken stock or low-sodium broth

1 bouquet garni (see Tips, page 244)

CRUST

1 teaspoon active dry yeast

1¼ cups all-purpose flour, plus more for dusting

1 teaspoon extra-virgin olive oil

½ teaspoon salt

1 Make the tripe: Trim any fat from the tripe and rinse under cold water. Cut it into 1- by 3-inch strips. In a large enameled cast-iron casserole, cover the tripe and calf's foot generously with water and bring to a boil. Reduce the heat to medium and simmer for 20 minutes; drain in a colander.

2 Meanwhile, make the crust: In a medium bowl, combine the yeast and ½ cup warm water. Let stand until foamy, about 5 minutes. Using a wooden spoon, stir in the flour, then the oil, and finally the salt. Knead until smooth, 3 to 4 minutes. Cover the bowl with plastic and refrigerate.

3 Rinse out the pot and in it heat 2 tablespoons of the oil until shimmering. Add the tripe, season generously with salt and pepper, and cook over medium-high heat, stirring often, until lightly browned, about 5 minutes. Add the Cognac and bring to a boil, then tilt the pot and, using a long match, carefully ignite it. When the flames subside, drain the tripe in a colander.

4 Heat the oven to 275 degrees. Add the carrots, celery, onion, garlic, and remaining 1 tablespoon oil to the pot. Season with salt and cook over medium heat, stirring occasionally, until softened, about 5 minutes. Add the tripe, calf's foot, tomatoes, tomato paste, and wine, bring to a simmer over medium-high heat, and cook until the liquid reduces by half, about 10 minutes. Add the stock and bouquet garni and bring to a simmer.

5 On a lightly floured work surface, roll the dough into a rope long enough to fit around the rim of the pot. Transfer the dough to the rim and press the lid on top to seal. Transfer to the oven and cook until the meat is tender, about 6 hours.

6 Serve the tripe in the pot, breaking the seal at the table. Spoon the stew into shallow bowls and garnish each with a piece of the crust.

TIP

Olivier Reginensi serves the stew still in the sealed casserole at the table for a dramatic presentation. But it's easier to do some preparations in the kitchen. After displaying the pot, whisk it away and break the seal (the servers at Le Cirque use a flat sauce spoon, but you can use a knife), reserving the crust. Discard the bouquet garni; remove the bones and gristle from the calf's foot and return the meat to the pot before serving.

VARIATION

Reginensi sometimes adds peeled pearl onions to the other vegetables in step 4.

SERVE WITH

As an accompaniment to the saucy stew, pass a dish of boiled, peeled Yukon Gold potatoes.

MAKE AHEAD

The tripe cooks for 6 hours, so plan ahead. If the crust is omitted, the stew can be refrigerated for up to 2 days.

STRAWBERRY SHORTCAKE

Pastry chef Romina Peixoto thinks its fun to pick apart a familiar dessert and recombine the components into something new. Here she plays with the flavors in strawberry shortcake. "I didn't think the traditional biscuit was elegant enough," she says. Her inventive take is a light lemon-and-vanilla-scented cake, accompanied by fresh strawberries, but also strawberry sorbet, strawberry syrup, and gorgeous ruby-red strawberry meringue. It's an exquisite dessert.

8 SERVINGS

LEMON CAKE

Unsalted butter, softened, for brushing

All-purpose flour, for dusting

1½ cups cake flour, sifted

2 teaspoons baking powder

½ teaspoon salt

1 cup heavy cream

2 teaspoons pure vanilla extract

Finely grated zest of ½ lemon

¾ cup sugar

2 large eggs

SYRUP, MERINGUES, AND SERVING

2 pounds strawberries, quartered, plus ½ pint halved

½ cup sugar

Juice of 1 lemon

1 teaspoon meringue powder (see Tips)

1 pint strawberry sorbet

Small basil sprigs, for garnishing

1 Make the lemon cake: Heat the oven to 350 degrees. Brush the bottom and sides of an 8-inch square baking pan with butter and dust with flour, tapping out the excess. Line the bottom of the pan with parchment paper. Brush the paper with butter and dust with flour.

2 In a medium bowl, sift the cake flour with the baking powder and salt. In another medium bowl, combine the cream, vanilla, and lemon zest. Put the sugar and eggs in a third bowl and, using an electric mixer, beat at high speed until light and fluffy, 3 to 4 minutes. Beat in the cream mixture until smooth. Working in two batches, fold in the flour mixture. Scrape the batter into the prepared pan and smooth the top. Bake until the cake is light brown, 25 to 30 minutes. Run a knife around the pan, invert the cake onto a rack, and let cool completely. Remove the paper.

3 Make the syrup: In a large stainless-steel bowl, stir the quartered strawberries, sugar, and lemon juice. Cover with plastic wrap and set over a large saucepan of barely simmering water. Cook, stirring occasionally, until the strawberries have given off their juice, about 20 minutes. Strain into a large glass measuring cup without pressing on the berries to keep the syrup clear. Let cool completely. Reserve the cooked strawberries for another use.

4 Pour ¼ cup of the syrup into a medium bowl. Add the meringue powder and whip at medium speed until firm peaks form.

5 Cut the cake into 2-inch squares. Set 2 pieces in each shallow bowl. Pour some of the syrup around the cake. Arrange the halved strawberries and dollops of the strawberry meringue around the plate. Set a scoop of sorbet and meringue on top, garnish with basil, and serve.

CONVERSION CHARTS

All conversions are approximate.

LIQUID CONVERSIONS

U.S.	METRIC
1 tsp	5 ml
1 tbs	15 ml
2 tbs	30 ml
3 tbs	45 ml
¼ cup	60 ml
⅓ cup	75 ml
⅓ cup + 1 tbs	90 ml
⅓ cup + 2 tbs	100 ml
½ cup	120 ml
⅔ cup	150 ml
¾ cup	180 ml
¾ cup + 2 tbs	200 ml
1 cup	240 ml
1 cup + 2tbs	275 ml
1¼ cups	300 ml
1⅓ cups	325 ml
1½ cups	350 ml
1⅔ cups	375 ml
1¾ cups	400 ml
1¾ cups + 2 tbs	450 ml
2 cups (1 pint)	475 ml
2½ cups	600 ml
3 cups	720 ml
4 cups (1 quart)	945 ml
	(1,000 ml is 1 liter)

WEIGHT CONVERSIONS

U.S. / U.K.	METRIC
½ oz	14 g
1 oz	28 g
1½ oz	43 g
2 oz	57 g
2½ oz	71 g
3 oz	85 g
3½ oz	100 g
4 oz	113 g
5 oz	142 g
6 oz	170 g
7 oz	200 g
8 oz	227 g
9 oz	255 g
10 oz	284 g
11 oz	312 g
12 oz	340 g
13 oz	368 g
14 oz	400 g
15 oz	425 g
1 lb	454 g

OVEN TEMPERATURES

°F	GAS MARK	°C
250	½	120
275	1	140
300	2	150
325	3	165
350	4	180
375	5	190
400	6	200
425	7	220
450	8	230
475	9	240
500	10	260
550	Broil	290

INDEX

IMAGE CREDITS